STEPPING WESTWARD

Bright moon in a cold sky.
Bird cries skree! skree!
Now

STEPPING WESTWARD

THE LONG SEARCH FOR HOME IN THE PACIFIC NORTHWEST

Sallie Tisdale

HarperPerennial

A Division of HarperCollins*Publishers*

A hardcover edition of this book was published in 1991 by Henry Holt and Company, Inc. It is here reprinted by arrangement with Henry Holt and Company, Inc.

HarperCollins books may be purchased for educational, business, or sales promotional use. For information, please write: Special Markets Department, HarperCollins Publishers, Inc., 10 East 53rd Street, New York, NY 10022.

First HarperPerennial edition published 1992.

Designed by Claire Vaccaro
Map by Kathy Reid

Library of Congress Cataloging-in-Publication Data

Tisdale, Sallie.
   Stepping westward : the long search for home in the Pacific Northwest / Sallie Tisdale.—1st HarperPerennial ed.
      p.   cm.
   "A hardcover edition of this book was originally published in 1991 by Henry Holt and Company, Inc."—Copr. p.
   ISBN 0-06-097510-5 (pbk.)
   1. Northwest, Pacific—Description and travel. 2. Natural history—Northwest, Pacific. 3. Tisdale, Sallie. 4. Northwest, Pacific—Biography. I. Title.
[F851.T59   1992]
917.9504—dc20   92-52618

92 93 94 95 96 MB 10 9 8 7 6 5 4 3 2 1

TO BOB, FOR ALL HE'S DONE AND BEEN

ACKNOWLEDGMENTS

This book had its source in a conversation with Sara Lippincott, who first gave me reason to think my entanglement with the Pacific Northwest held interest for anyone but myself. I owe much, and hope to owe more, to Channa Taub, a merciless editor and good friend. I am also grateful for the long and loyal support of my agent, Katinka Matson.

In the course of my work, I was more than ably supported by Amy Boothe, who worked as my research assistant with dogged energy and unflagging good cheer. Without her help much would be missing from this book. Pamela Mombell provided me with considerable assistance in the early stages of research. I would like to thank Allen Hunter for his clerical patience and conversation and Kathy Kremer Reid for directions. Because she knows what I mean, and picks up the phone even when she's busy, a curtsy to Karen Karbo.

A number of people cheerfully provided interviews, expert reading, and suggestions, often at a moment's notice. I would like to name all of them, and can't, but a number of employees of the National Park Service, the Forest Service, and both federal and state branches of Fish and Wildlife Services were of help. I am particularly grateful to the serene staff of the Oregon Historical Society; Ellen Morris Bishop of Eastern Oregon State College; Bob Hofstedter of the Western Forestry Center; Daniel Mathews and Tom Edwards of Whitman College; John Hart, Linda Keene, Bill Robbins of Oregon State University; Gordon Dodds of Portland State University; and Jeff LaLande. Any mistakes that remain are my own.

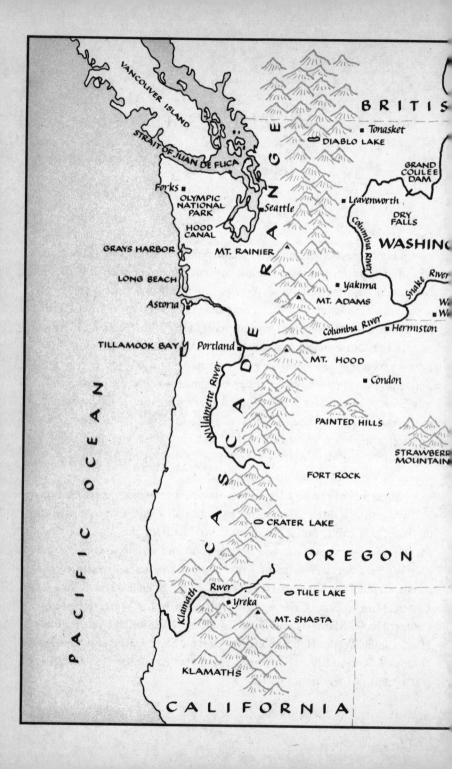

STEPPING WESTWARD

'What, you are stepping westward?'—'Yea,'
—'Twould be a *wildish* destiny,
If we, who thus together roam
In a strange Land, and far from home,
Were in this place the guests of Chance:
Yet who would stop, or fear to advance,
Though home or shelter he had none,
With such a sky to lead him on?

The dewy ground was dark and cold;
Behind, all gloomy to behold;
And stepping westward seemed to be
A kind of *heavenly* destiny;
I liked the greeting; 'twas a sound
Of something without place or bound;
And seemed to give me spiritual right
To travel through that region bright.

The voice was soft, and she who spake
Was walking by her native lake:
The salutation had to me
The very sound of courtesy:
Its power was felt; and while my eye
Was fixed upon the glowing Sky,
The echo of the voice enwrought
A human sweetness with the thought
Of travelling through the world that lay
Before me in my endless way.

—William Wordsworth

PROLOGUE

The history of the West can be read in maps—in the faded Latin and fanciful coastlines of European cartography. Mapmakers sketched a changing planet, and added ships, their sails full of wind, mermaids with cunningly concealed breasts, and giant serpents. In time, mapmakers added the Northwest Passage. Claims of its discovery were frequent; for a time every explorer who came across a big lake or found a new bay assumed he'd found the Passage. One man even produced a map showing the Passage in support of his thesis that the Passage was there to be found, as though a pattern of the idea could make it come true. Beliefs, theories, cherished hopes were copied down on linen in rare inks, and whole lives bent to their power.

The Western Hemisphere took on a fattened, oval shape as time passed, speckled with interior seas, its westernmost coast sliding cheerfully to the east. On some later maps the barrier between the early colonies on the Atlantic and the waters of the Pacific was little more than a spit of land. In another the northern continent was divided cleanly in two by a strait from the St. Lawrence River to the Gulf of California. For details, the artists added the mythical lands of Zeno, the veiled island of St. Brandan, more mermaids, more monsters.

The dream of the Northwest Passage was a potent one. It was more than opinion: It was creed. We have forgotten, now, that the dream was real, that the Passage had to be there—certain, unattainable, drifting just out of reach.

Columbus struck land, with perhaps a little surprise and relief after all, and for a long time people thought the North American continent must be some strange, untamed part of Asia. When Vasco Núñez de Balboa crossed Panama in 1513 and saw the Pacific, it was just like striking land again. Not only was he suddenly standing on a new continent, he was looking at a new, unimagined ocean. The wild land was truly an obstacle, a great wall between Europe and Cathay. Such a thing would not do.

The admirals of empire set out with all the confidence of their kings, to find what had to be there. The Northwest Passage meant the trade of Asia; the trade of Asia meant a great deal. The search for the Passage was driven with such power that enormous difficulties were overcome in its pursuit; the coincidental discoveries made along the way seem hardly to have been noted. On the earliest trip overland across the North American continent, in 1789, Alexander Mackenzie traveled through what is now Canada, thinking he would reach the Pacific. He found the Arctic Ocean instead, and great forests. No rejoicing. He named the rough water he'd followed much of the way the River Disappointment. But he stayed for a time and nursed his wounded hope. They all stayed, straying away and returning again and again, in memory if not in body—restless, powerful men stung by dreams. Juan Francisco de la Bodega y Quadra, one of the most dauntless explorers of the Northwest coast, wrote, "I pressed on, taking fresh trouble for granted." In pursuit of the Passage and the setting sun, the Europeans traveled hundreds of thousands of miles over open seas, and circled the globe.

The search for the Passage began along the Atlantic, as a series of forays into colder and colder waters. Found almost as afterthoughts were waters that proved nearly as valuable as a true Passage might have been: Chesapeake and the great Hudson Bay, the waters of the Arctic around Baffin Island, the Narrows of New York Harbor. The explorers passed into ice and death, they sank, drowned, froze, and disappeared, and there was no Passage. But the repeated failures simply made it all the more enticing; so many of our dreams do that to us. The Passage would naturally be hidden in proportion to its worth. If it wasn't easily found, it must be more valuable than anyone had imagined it could be.

Centuries passed. The wall of land that was America took on its own intrinsic worth. The Spanish moved into Mexico and were probably the first Europeans on the northern Pacific coast. They had found and raped the fantastic cities of the Incas and Aztecs, and heard various tales about other cities and other temples of gold at the end of a long waterway to the north. The rough water and inhospitable coastline made for few landings, and all that could be seen by sailors—and then only when the fogs cleared—was a thick, dark forest extending to distant mountains.

And still the Northwest Passage kept getting found, and lost, and sought again. The records are full of stories, of bays leading into rivers, rivers crossing the land to far seas, streams passing the villages of undiscovered peoples, paradisiacal and forbidding lands. On the optimistic maps the northern edges of the new continent faded gently into obscurity, unfinished, its boundaries open for the asking. The Northwest Passage was a wish made real for the strength of the wishing. It was a passage into a new way of life.

A Greek man named Apostolos Valerianos, who called himself Juan de Fuca, claimed to have sailed up the Northwest coast in 1592, and found there a Passage crossing the continent from sea to sea. De Fuca was a braggart, and chose for his own reasons to embellish his story with details of treasure and hidden cities. He might not have found anything; he may not even have made it as far north as he claimed, but some people believed him. He described latitudes and landmarks with a certain veracity. "We saw nothing like it," wrote James Cook in his diary, regarding the Greek's claim, "nor is there the least probability that ever any such thing existed." Cook had set the standard, though on one of his maps of the far north he described an area only as "Nobody Knows What." Perhaps Juan de Fuca was telling tales out of school. But then again, perhaps he found the wide, deep, singular channel that now bears his name. In 1787 Charles Barkley, twenty-six, and his wife

Frances Hornby Trevor, only seventeen, sailed on an English ship along the north coast. They found a strait to an inland sea and named it the Strait of Juan de Fuca. It was left to George Vancouver to send men exploring there; one, Lt. Peter Puget, had the waters named after him. His companion, Joseph Whidbey, got an island.

To understand the magnitude of this very real find you have to know something of Puget Sound. The inland shoreline, protected and bound, runs for twenty-one hundred miles. Two dozen rivers and uncountable streams empty into a glacial furrow several hundred feet deep, thick with fertile silts, broken by a multitude of rocky, wild islands. Through the long, wide Strait of Juan de Fuca, the Sound runs in and out of the sea, winding its twisted, hidden heart into endless salty canals pulsing with tides, full of cold, oxygenated promise. This is how big and deep Puget Sound is, how hard to miss: Paul Bunyan is said to have dug it when Babe, his blue ox, was dying. He'd brought her here to the West, in the faint hope that whale's milk would cure her. And in his grief at her illness, he dug her grave, a big man bent to a big task, scrabbling out dirt. He finished, she got well, he left behind the Sound, the islands, and the Cascades, the neat mounds of soil all in a row up and down the spine of the land. Puget Sound and its neighborhood hold the tallest trees, the largest octopus, whales as long as sailing ships, and clams the size of cantaloupes, and no one could find it. No one could find it because it wasn't what they were seeking; it wasn't the Passage of Dream.

So empire rolled on westward. What seems in hindsight to have been a smooth, even graceful journey was in fact a lurching series of fits and starts. The torchbearers of Europe took steps forward and steps back, and moved toward the horizon in the voyages of a few and the stumbling steps of the many—the least, the worst, the needy, and the lost. Traveling westward eventually had a name all its own: *westering*, and it was no passing trend. Westering became, in all senses, a verb: movement in one direction, without return.

By the latter part of the 1700s, the myth of the Northwest Passage had shrunk a little, become somewhat less fabulous—less perfect. It became the lesser dream of the Great River, a channel running, if not from sea to sea, at least from the heart of the new continent to its farther shores. It was thought to rise perhaps somewhere in the Great Lakes, or from the Missouri River. It was called variously the Long River, the *R. de l'Ouest*, or River of the West, or the River Buonaventura, or the River Oregon. And like the Northwest Passage, it was real.

Both James Cook and John Meares, another Englishman, missed the mouth of the Columbia River when they sailed up the northern Pacific coast. They traveled at night as well as during the day, and the days were often stormy and foggy in the extreme. All the clues of a river were there: floating logs, muddy water, complex currents and waves. Meares even named it Deception Bay because he believed that in spite of all appearances, there was no river there.

Bruno Heceta was the first European to discover that the Columbia was a river—at least, his journal entries indicate he knew he'd found a large river or bay. But Heceta's men were weak from scurvy and Heceta himself was in a hurry—he was looking for the Northwest Passage. He either couldn't or wouldn't cross the river's bar. Then George Vancouver passed it, too, this nearest thing to a Great River the West holds, dismissing it with a few words in his journal. Robert Gray passed the mouth in May 1792 in his ship, the *Columbia Rediviva*. He passed but something made him turn around; perhaps he thought a new source of fur might lie up that rough water. He brought his ship back and waited for hours until the right combination of waves and current and wind came, and then he entered. Near what is now Chinook, Washington, a crowd of Indians watched, curious, eager to trade, empty of the future's dread, as Gray's great sailing ship crossed the bar.

The Columbia River is more than twelve hundred miles long, often more than a mile wide, and its waters drain an area almost as big as the state of Texas. More than any other landmark, this river ties the region together; it drains the three states of Idaho, Washington, and Oregon, crosses desert and high plains, flows through wheat land and cattle land and grassland, from aridity to dampness, through the remnants of the glaciers and the volcanic age, between buttes and forests into the sea. The Columbia is the largest river in the Western Hemisphere to empty into the Pacific Ocean, hitting the sea with such force that fresh water pours from its mouth miles out to sea. To the first European explorers, the Columbia River seemed virtually impassable. It was crisscrossed with rapids and sandbars that boats could not traverse. It was nothing like a passage at all.

When I was little, the electric company had a history program on the radio called "Pacific Powerland." I went home from lunch every school day and settled at the kitchen table, with a melted Velveeta cheese sandwich and a bowl of Campbell's soup, and listened. I was far too young to understand the irony at work, listening only for the sonorous tones in the voice of Nelson Olmsted. I cherished the corny jokes, the drama in his stories of the old Northwest, which seemed so far away and gone. I lived in a different Northwest, a place with towns such as Electron, Voltage, and Electric City. The "Pacific Powerland" tales were tales of a lost place where there had been no dams, and no hydroelectric conglomerates to pay for reminiscence.

Today there are eleven dams on the Columbia, eleven dead backwaters, and no rapids. Only about fifty of its thousand-some miles are free-flowing. Dredges gouge the river all year round to clear a channel deep enough for oceangoing ships. When I drive up and down beside the Columbia River now, I might be driving along a different river altogether. Down past Wallula just north of the Oregon border, where the placid Snake River empties into the Columbia, the water spreads wide and deep as a lake, lapping up against the dry talus hills. The river fills the whole low land, broad and untempered and raw. On either side are tan hills, with sagebrush blooming dark golden, the color of copper and saffron. I count heaps of low buttes piled first with rocks and then, following the river down into the gorge, with trees, a row of pale blue and grey walls in the afternoon haze. Across the gorge long trains go by, and on the water, grain barges and sawdust barges. Almost seventy trucks a day travel up the narrow road of the gorge, hauling garbage from Portland and Seattle clear out to Arlington.

As I work my way out of the dry wheat land into the moisture of the west side, toward the sea, the river narrows, the buttes straighten and rise into cliffs. The water is gleaming and steady and calm; at Hood River windsurfers bounce across the tiny whitecaps. One tall trailing waterfall after another shoots out and down, hundreds of feet, the surprised leap of a stream with its bed cut off by ancient floods. Emblems of basalt leap from the banks, tall eroded rocks as big as skyscrapers—called Beacon and Rooster now instead of the pioneers' more proper obscenities.

At Celilo Falls, the wide terraced cataracts in the northern end of the gorge, the big river had to pass through such a sudden narrow canyon it was often described as a river set on its edge. Celilo with its spray and tumble was the Indians' best fishing ground. But Lewis and Clark, passing through in 1805, were downright critical: "This agitated gut," wrote Clark, "this bad whorl & Suck . . . swelling, boiling & whorling in every direction." They marched the portage and tossed in the canoes to the entertainment of Indians they considered "badly clad and illy made," but who nevertheless were long used to the lethal rapids. "The whorls and swills arriseing from the Compression of the water," Clark wrote, "water passing with great velocity forming & boiling in a most horriable manner." Celilo Falls, once a layered white cascade of foam and salmon, is drowned today in the backwash of a dam. It is a quick tourist hop off the road, a mild ache of wishing in the sepia photographs and neat scripted explanation.

Toward Portland the jetskis start, and boats of every kind: catamarans and sailors tacking across the wakes of the grain barges and merchant ships filled with Japanese cars. Portland is 110 inland miles from the Pacific, but still the tide drops noticeably, the Columbia sinks as though it were holding its breath farther west, shrinks back from its mudflats, and leaves a rippled beach behind until the tide returns. Near Portland the planes begin to dart like fish, Lear jets and 747s, National Guard fighters swinging in an arc above the water. A tinge of blue fume hangs in a cloud over the boat ramps here, a smell of oil and gas.

There was no river. No passage. No vast, inland sea, no easy road from there to here (though Walt Whitman could write of "the circle almost circled," and mean it). And yet there was—the best measure of the fever is that the Columbia River and Puget Sound were disappointments. Such dreams as the dream of the Passage are only very slowly and reluctantly released. They never really die, fading instead into a melancholic wonder, a wonder that lingers, driving the dreams of generations, rolling down time.

ONE

As much as we live in a place, we live in *place*; we inhabit a condition of the soul. The geographer Yi-fu Tuan calls *place* "a special kind of object," something too big and broad made close and dear. When we join ourselves to a place, we join air and land as though they were clothes to wear. We live where we have made definitions, and in the process of making definitions we create a place in which to live. Another writer, Eugene Victor Walter, coined the word *chorophiliac*, "place-lover," to explain his own appetite—he loves the sense of place wherever he goes. He feels at home not only at home, but in places which *are* homes, the homes of others.

I have made my own definitions here, large and small, and they belong to no one else. In a way I live here alone, because I live within my interpretations as much as my environment—within my own local cosmology. What is the Pacific Northwest? Where does it begin, end; where does it blend? I'm not too concerned with the random straight lines between states and countries, though the lines play with my interpretations. Oregon and Washington, separated by the wavering trough of a river, are my center. Because it was settled in much the same way, because the forests and geological landmarks crisscross, because the native tribes crisscrossed as well, I take in western Idaho. For the same reasons, I embrace the far northern reach of California, where the great conifer forests begin, where the spine of the Cascades begins. I ignore Canada. My prejudice, my choice, my appetite. How early such appetites begin, how momentary and specific the sources can be: for one person, trickling water, for another, a narrow street, a kind of cloud, the scent of corn near harvest. The Pacific Northwest is my place, and consequently it is a kind of bound. I live here sometimes as though it fenced me in, and I can't leave even when I long for leaving. I am a chorophiliac, of this *choro*, here, outside my room: this spherical universe wrapped layer around layer with the cunning of nesting dolls.

Aristotle called *place* "the innermost motionless boundary of what contains." He named it *topos*, a pure, immutable object—an object of being. One man or one thing occupied a position in the world and in relation to other men, other things. This was fundamental to Aristotle's *Physics*. Without boundary, where was law? But admitting the existence of place wasn't enough. He wanted to put his hands on it. Without movement, said Aristotle, we would never notice space at all; without space, we would be unable to move. Space had to be a thing, because when you take water away, air fills in where the water had been. But the air in an empty jar fills what? When wine is poured in the jar, what is the wine in? When the wine is poured out, what remains?

There he is, kneeling by a stone wall, pouring wine in, out, in again, brushing away the droplets that spill on his hands. Drawing shapes in the dust by his knees. Standing in a doorway, considering the nature of the olive tree in his yard: that tree which takes up more space every spring. If only he'd seen a wet stand of fir and hemlock, marching to the sea, instead of a little olive tree. Would he have produced more, or less, inside that concentric and irregular ring of time? "What then shall we say about growing things?" he mused. "It follows from these premisses that their place must grow with them, if their place is neither less nor greater than they are. . . . the potency of place must be a marvellous thing. . . ." Place, he concluded, was a tautology of experience: It was only "this place which contains no more than you."

We use all our senses to create a definition of space. Yi-fu Tuan writes of the "experiential perspective" of space and place, in which we expand and extrapolate the seen and the felt into a larger place beyond what we could possibly touch or see. This is mythic space—mythical space—where we become attached to places with which we have little or no direct experience, like nations, regions, lands of idea, but also the summits of mountains we've never climbed, views we've imagined but never seen, weather we've heard of and never felt. "Distance," writes Tuan, "is distance from self." (And intimacy is nearness to self; the most outlandish surroundings can be home if they fit our expectations.) From the top of a mountain we see a distance that is far from our own selves, and expand into it, so that everything we see is nearby; imagining the heights and the far reaches, we invent a comfortable nearness. We turn the whole wilderness into our home.

The Pacific Northwest as a place has the quality of bouncing back—a kind of durability, both visual and psychological. It is resilient, exuberant. Some of that, I'm sure, comes from its polymorphic landscape. Rain forest and desert, grasslands and sand dunes, coastline and wheat fields, volcanoes and glaciers, sometimes all in the same view. Labyrinthine caves and churning ocean, barren buttes, inaccessible canyons split by wild rivers, a profusion of spring blossoms and golden, sweet-breathed falls. People—perhaps all people—harbor a dream of the land. And because the land here is peculiarly comfortable and near in certain ways, the dream is, too. The land is uncovered, bare beneath your feet. People talk for long spells about the land, about building on it, how it would be; they talk about doing it even if they know they never will. Sometimes that's enough. The land is the source of safety here.

The early explorers bent over their journals by candlelight, and over their drawing pads by day, trying to convey the scenery—the promiscuous, wild, indifferent lands by turns hard and soft, calm and terrifying. The wild view, the raw shores and mountains, were exotic and stirring, but their preference was for the cultivated view: the occasional meadow; the overgrown, burned-out valley of the Willamette River; the rolling hills of the upper Columbia. The botanist David Douglas thought that grand vista looked in spring "like English lawns." The explorers—and later, the settlers—relished the scenes most like home. The rolling, velvet

"English" lawns promised that this rough, unfinished place, a place so often inhospitable and unwelcoming, might someday be the Eden they were seeking.

Seemingly endless volumes about the Northwest were published in the middle and latter nineteenth century, florid tales by civilized travelers in a strange land. The title of one book by Gustavas Hines reads: *Wild Life in Oregon: Being a Stirring Recital of Actual Scenes of Daring and Peril Among the Gigantic Forests and Terrific Rapids of the Columbia River (the Mississippi of the Pacific Slope) and Giving Life-Like Pictures of Terrific Encounters with Savages as Fierce and Relentless as its Mighty Tides, Including a Full, Fair and Reliable History of the State of Oregon, its Crops, Minerals, Timber Lands, Soil, Fisheries; its Present Greatness, and Future Vast Capabilities, and Paramount Position.* The author calls himself "Gustavas Hines, the Fearless Explorer of the Northern Pacific Coast." But guides like this—tales of "wild life," deprivation, savages, the rapturous anarchy of the untamed West—followed by decades the actual settling of the frontier, even if some of the reported events took place earlier. It was as though one could not comfortably read about the disorder of the wilderness until it was done. Halfway through, in the midst of it, the Oregon Trail pioneers wrote no poetry at all. They kept diaries of flat prose, little more than catalogues of the journey. Poetry—and romance—had to wait.

The Oregon Trail pioneers floated down the Columbia River still covered with the dust of southern Idaho, climbing out every few miles to portage the rapids, wondering at the moisture in the air. The story goes that at one of the crossroads on the Trail, a sign marked the way to Oregon and a pile of rocks the road to California—a guarantee that the literate would take the northern route. They came off the Plains and over the mountains tired and dry, crossed the spine of the Cascade Mountains, and stopped in what seemed like heaven. In their relief, their grief and joy, they started towns. These are the tiny Oregon hamlets called Donnybrook and Wonder, Amity, Friend, Nonpareil; Rest, Wise, Startup, and Horse Heaven. This is Lookingglass, so named because the green grass reflected sunlight. Everyone had big plans: When a few hungry worn-out settlers gathered up close on the skirt of Puget Sound at the mouth of the Duwamish River, they shivered in the fog and the isolation. They named their smoky village New York–Alki—Alki from a local Indian word that means "by and by."

I have an old cherry tree in my backyard, ill-shapen, ugly, prolific. It is a full two stories tall and every spring splashes a great mass of white blooms against my bedroom window, a cloud of perfume and color that lasts less than a week before the flowers start to fall. That's when I like to take my chair outside; the petals fall steadily night and day and coat the grass like light snow. I sit beneath it, reading a diary of the Trail—a litany of disaster—while the flowers fall.

People raised in the Pacific Northwest rely more on the pathos of past adversity than is quite seemly. Our stories are pioneer stories, courage stories. Oregon sells a special birth certificate, suitable for framing, for people born in the state—for native Oregonians, as though such a wild accident not in one's own control had status of any kind. But of such status is this place made. It comes from the stories, and it comes from the land. William Kittredge, born and raised into adulthood in a remote part of southeastern Oregon, retains a resonant belief from those years. It is, he writes, "the notion that my people live in a separate kingdom where they own it all, secure from the world...."

I remember Walt Whitman's swelling self-description:

> We must bear the brunt of danger,
> We the youthful sinewy races, all the rest on us depend....

So our stories are full of disdain for all things East and South, full of complaints about the weather, the crop, the interloping transplants. I read, and the petals fall in my small heaven.

One, two, three at a time, they drift down around me and I keep sifting through the stories, the varieties of loss possible in a single season's journey. The blossoms will all be gone in a few days, swept to the side. I pick them off my lap and my hair, and off the pages of this book, the steady mourning of a young woman who lost one child to disease, another to the crushing of a wagon wheel, who dragged herself through heat and mud and over mountains to get halfway to where I sit now. And then a tiny, plump milk-green cherry worm falls plop onto the book's binding and lies there, stunned, all at once newborn into the world's spring.

The historian Malcolm Clark calls the hunger for an Eden in the West the "major apparition of the American Dream." Why should we go at all? And why, going, do we go west? Toward the sun, the light, the golden dome of sky? West in search of the fruits of imperialism. West for John Locke's definition of riches: "having more in proportion" to someone else. West for an embarrassment of riches. West to make something to fall back on when the East didn't work out. West to flee failure and seek success, west to escape from complex troubles and difficult decisions, west for the possibility of perfection, for the new and unknown, for the raw, simple, solid life free of the workaday harness. West into anarchy and violence, degradation and labor lethal in its demands. West to heaven, or hell.

A journalist named John L. Sullivan spoke of it as destiny, in 1845 after the first wave of migrants crossed the Plains: He called it "our manifest destiny to overspread the continent allotted by Providence for the free development of our yearly multiplying millions." (This from the man who earlier had written, "All government is evil. . . . The best government is that which governs least.") Thomas Jefferson, who wasn't entirely comfortable with imperialism at first, came to terms with it at last in such a way, somewhere around the time of the Louisiana Purchase. He came to see expansion as a tool in the radical American experiment of self-government. It was partly Thomas Jefferson himself who began this; Jefferson the philosopher-king, as optimistic as a demigod. Jefferson leaned toward the new. He came to see westward imperialism as a way to spread democracy. And, coincidentally, to drive the British and French out of the Western Hemisphere.

And who hasn't leaned west, at least once? Caught in the longing for something far off, over a hill, around a bend—something just glimpsed in the falling sunlight of evening and tinted gold. We are each caught that way once or twice, struck dumb by the possibility of a life altogether new. And some of us are struck for good. William Wordsworth said it best, describing a simple walk at twilight. He is asked: "What, you are stepping westward?" And answers with a pilgrim's excess: "Yea. 'Twould be a wildish destiny."

The real place in which I live has descended from that bigger world, that darker, more pregnant place my ancestors called the West. My home now is not so much a shadow of the larger world as a map of it—geometrically accurate, but lacking a piquant visual truth. I grew up surrounded by people who hungered for a past more noble and more true than the present, and far more noble than the real history of our own flesh, than the facts. They didn't know this is what they hungered for, but they invented it when such a kind past could not be found. No better place for it than the imagined West of the first explorers, the world where I still live in my heart of hearts.

It is in my heart that I can find the Northwest Passage, where I know the Great River runs: the world of New Caledonia and New Albion; the many-bordered country of the last, lost virgin place; the unsettled, undiscovered far corner of the great Northwest. It is huge, this place, and full of secrets. Here the mountains are sixteen and twenty-five thousand feet high. Here the mountains used to be people—not people turned into mountains, but walking, talking mountains, rough-skinned and heavy, shaking the ground with their steps, prone to backache. The sweat runs down their faces in trickling streams. It is a place of elysian valleys and unlimited forests and giant beaver as big as grizzlies with teeth like scythes to cut the giant trees. Here live savages brilliant with the grip of the wild, and streams dark with salmon, fields thick with elk, white-draped peaks and huge, quiet harbors. This is Albert Bierstadt's Northwest. Bierstadt drew with a more emotional light than that cast by the sun, drew a natural world of power and travail. The light! With one dot of ivory, a tiny stroke of a paler blue, his sun breaks out and highlights every stone in the still lake, every pine needle on the trees, radiant in the wet air.

My great-great-great-grandfather Elijah Waters made it all the way west before he died. His son William died in Jacksonville, Oregon. And so on down, Mary Hunter and William Tisdale, Charles Gentry and Amanda Gresham, German and English and Scots born in Washington and Oregon and in the Trinity Forest of northern California, and dying there, of typhoid and tuberculosis and an endless amount of hard work. And ever since, my family has been getting born and dying here at the end of the line, shoved up against the ocean with no place else to go.

My great-grandfather, Andrew Calkins, was the Siskiyou County sheriff for sixteen years, and his polished gold badge, outsize and ornate, is a kind of totem for my father. He gave the badge to a museum, but he keeps a photograph of it in a dresser drawer. There is a kind of hold at work on my family, all these generations, aunts and cousins and shirttail relatives growing up in the same houses in which they were born, living and dying on the same block, within hailing distance of the same people. I'm the lost sheep, the only one gone, the only one moved, or moving. In all the desultory stories I was told when I was young, parceled out with stingy quiet and missing facts—stories about babies incubating in woodstoves and children lost in snowstorms, and Indian women taken in long enough to have a few children of their own—in all the stories I've pieced together there's an element of amnesia. Only the heroic and tragic events are remembered—never the ugly ones. It is as though we share a cultural, unconscious memory—as though all these wonderful, terrible things happened to *us*, long ago, and we've forgotten from the shock of them. I've wondered what I would discover if I knew why my otherwise-lugubrious relatives have such patchy memories and so few details. And it doesn't seem to matter which of the stories are true, or whether the woman down the street I knew as a neighbor was really a cousin twice removed. These ruddy pioneers I call my forebears started keeping records before they left, caught in the myth they were making, a long fable about hunger and hope. They were assiduous historians, intent on recording the world into which they thrust themselves—a world and a history they invented by the day, edited, revised. They held with a faint hope and an almost genetic weariness to the possibility of the River, somewhere, of Eden, of the West: a River, a Sea, the Passage: the Great Roadway, the Oregon.

What matters, what came to matter a century ago, was not the facts of what happened but the chance to imagine what might have happened, what could, what—in the real paradise—would happen. The road west was paved first with ships, then men in pairs and trios, then the martyred missionaries. Those earnest missionaries, belabored and high-collared, literally plowed the virgin fields for the settlers to come, for the losses and terrors that would come. They shot Indian dogs and handed over hoes and shell combs and long skirts. Then, in the cold nights and in the poor, fragrant light of the oil lamps, they worked at translating the Book of Job into the fluid and guiltless language of the Nez Percé and Chinook and Yakima. This was the first lapping of the growing wave. This was the first inkling of what would come, like scudding clouds before a changing wind. The missionaries were God's locusts, a warning before the first-born died.

With what must have seemed an extraordinary abruptness, the wagons crossed the Continental Divide, the oxen haggard and huffing in the first cold mornings of fall, the men and women dirty and scared and less than patient by the time they arrived. Altogether, 300,000 people covered the Trail to the West in a few years, and many thousand more died trying. They came to join a dream world, to start fresh, to build. They joined genocidal farmers, unprincipled miners and gamblers, anti-papists and pro-slavery newspapermen, loggers tugging at the saw, politicos, pimps, and entrepreneurs—all having come to share a beautiful, world-shaking dream of something completely different from what they made.

It took less than fifty years to invent a different past. One belonged, in my hometown, to the historical society, the Daughters of the American Revolution, the 4-H, or the Drum and Bugle Corps. If you found Great-Grandma's wedding dress or her pearl-handled pistol in the attic, you gave it to the museum, and they put it in a glass case with a label and a thank-you note. Once or twice a year, you took the kids to the museum, which changed less than most places, and showed them the case, read them the label. Nothing moved there, one rarely spoke, gazing with half-focused eyes at the heavy iron blacksmith tools, the single mammoth tusk, the delicate baskets filled with dried roots dug by dead Indians. So I went to the museum, and gazed at the tools and the baskets. Later I wore the long, layered skirts of the hippie girl pining away for a hand-built cabin and a kerosene lamp. We held to the myth with all our hearts, without the imagination needed to make another one: What would replace it? What else could there be? A hundred years after they came, when I was born, all the dust and nobility was swept away and in its place was nothing but asphalt, mine tailings, and a story.

I believed—a little guilty in my soft bed, in my warm house—that my great-grandparents and their grandparents before them belonged to a special breed. We had only the pride of descending from those who had borne "the brunt of danger." "Have you your pistols?" Whitman asked. "Have you your sharp-edged axes?" They were the last willingly uprooted souls, and so of course I thought the life they'd led had to be a fundamentally more significant one than I seemed to be leading. From dream and disappointment we acted it out, from guilt and wishes, child and adult alike: We had Forty-Niner Days and Gold Rush Days and Pioneer Days, we had rodeos and parades and the county fair, and we always had the Fourth of July, to witness and remember our own imagined, uplifting heritage.

At the age of seven, I was taken to see a show, a young Karuk Indian's demonstration of native dances. The Karuk tribe believed the center of the world was their village on the lower Klamath River, and they called it *sivsinenachip*; from out of that place where the trees and salmon and people were born, the rings of time traveled in growing concentric waves, spreading all the way to the mountains beyond.

The show was at the fairgrounds south of town, an expanse of packed dry ground where I learned to drive at fifteen, in my mother's lumbering Chevrolet Impala. On sunny days, clouds cross the hills nearby, sliding over the scrubby land like the shadows of huge coasting birds. The dry, mahogany-colored hills are broken by ravines and coated with pale thistle and golden poppies and blue bachelor's buttons. I have never had any boundaries here, any sensation of forbidden or private land; we only stayed out of the hills and woods when deer season opened. Then the shots would ring out with the smack of a steel bell before dawn on the first day and continue, gradually less frequent and farther away, throughout the weeks.

I was used to the fairgrounds for pitch-dark fireworks on the Fourth of July, and the twinkling, noisy, perfumed county fair. Instead I saw one big group of people in a single corner of the empty acreage, all facing in one direction. The crowd was close in the hot sunlight; I was short and jostled damp, bare skin for room. I could see the Indian in the distance, his bare brown feet pounding the stage at the height of smiling faces, his floor-length headdress of eagle feathers waving back and forth, back and forth as he nodded and shuffled to a drum.

Sometime in the sweating cheer, my name was called—a mysterious, never-explained gift—and I was pushed forward through the people and made to climb the stage. I had lived near, grown up beside, Indians all my life. They were the descendants of the Karuks in the mountains behind my home, big families, still bearing the names given their ancestors by the gold miners more than a century before. The miners invented diminutives and declined surnames, so a grown man became Tall Henry, or Little Jim Joe. When nothing else persisted, when *sivsinenachip* cracked and the rings of the world broke apart, the names persisted. My playmates and neighbors were the Oscars, the Toms, the Jerrys, and the Crows. I never thought of them as "Indians," as anything special or apart, better or worse, than myself. They weren't Indians, but neighbors.

So that day, at seven, I climbed the steps to meet my first Real Indian, astonished at my good fortune and hypnotized by his beauty. He was tall, bare-chested, shiny with sweat, and he smiled down at me from a great distance, holding a microphone. The long eagle feathers were silky and radiant in the sunshine and he was my Real Indian, my longed-for brave. He asked me to dance for the crowd. Without a moment's thought, without a hint of self-consciousness, I danced the Twist, my own native dance, and felt glad that when the time had come, I had known what to do.

I grew up in a place once described as a "choice of bar, den and dive," a gold-mining camp turned into a mill town called Yreka, stuck between canyons in rough land just south of the Oregon–California border. Yreka—pronounced *why-reé-ka*—is eternally confused with Eureka, a mill town on the northern California coast often wreathed in fog and, to my mind, a considerably gloomier place. (Yreka is famous in the strangest places for a palindrome, the name of a shop a few blocks from where I lived: Yreka Bakery). For a long time, Yreka had both a bar and a liquor store for every general merchant. "There are more drunkards here than any place I ever was before," wrote one young miner. Joaquin Miller, an incautious writer, wrote of Yreka and parts north: "In most parts of America the morning salutation is, 'How d'ye do? How's the folks?' But on the Pacific it is, 'How-dy-do? Take a drink?' "

A man named Fred Stockslager came to Yreka when he gave up on the gold-mining life in the hills. What he found was almost enough to drive him back to Illinois, as he complained to a relative in a letter: "I will also state I never led an intemperate life or gambled or other vises that are so common in California. I seen enough of that stile to disgust me at once when I first come to Yreka. I come here on foot in the night. I come to a house had music in it. the Best fiddlers to be found, tables the whole length of building stacked full of money. each table was stacked with money. the house was cramed with people. a great number was gambling. each table had a female sitting along side the gambler after taking a look all around I went out. up street I soon come to music again. I soon found plenty of them kind of houses. in them days there was no society here."

The whole history of the West, that grand subject, can be approached in smaller, more comfortable ways: One is seeing it as a fight between temperance and dissolution, a fight won by the drinkers. Phoebe Goodell Judson, a young mother and old-fashioned Christian, came over the Oregon Trail in 1853, into the fray of the fight. Phoebe was a literal Bible reader, a kind woman, nevertheless full of righteous condemnation in the face of sin. She singled out for particular censure savages, gamblers, those who didn't keep the Sabbath, and Mormons. Phoebe's adult life was, she wrote, "a pioneer's search for the ideal home," and it drew her across to the West and then north into unsettled Washington, and finally almost to the Canadian border, where she and her husband and several other settlers started a town called Lynden. It was, at last, her dream. "Alas, for fair Lynden!" she wrote. "The saloon, with its woeful influence, was planted in our midst. I have lived long enough to realize that unless the government prohibits the manufacture of that curse of the world—that fell destroyer of mankind, 'rum,' it will be utterly impossible to rear on this mundane sphere an 'ideal home.'"

My great-grandfather ran a saloon in Yreka called the Dew Drop Inn. He was a Methodist, a common religious choice in the West, but he didn't consider it something to hamper him at work. But at last the sober congregation suggested he find another business, considering that the Methodists were teetotalers. He refused. The suggestion turned to a demand. Not only did he keep serving liquor, he had his four daughters baptized Roman Catholic. My grandmother Estelle, who was seven years old at the time, added Mary to her name and started going to Mass.

As a child, I knew none of this. All I knew was that my elderly grandmother and her equally elderly sisters were Catholics, a religion that brooked no dissent and admitted no possibility of error. I watched them drive to Mass, in formal dress, every Wednesday evening, every Saturday evening, every Sunday morning. They do so to this day; their schedule of worship has always had a relentless quality, as though the town Methodists were still watching. But my father married outside the church, and my siblings and I were raised Lutheran. I disliked the lukewarm flavors of Protestantism. I yearned for the solemn discipline of the Catholics, the big, dark church with its flavors of confession and sacrifice, and it was denied me. My father's apostasy—a mere whisper among my brother and sister and me—seemed a brave, if mortal, sin. I believed him to believe himself headed for hell, to believe himself beyond redemption. For many years I credited his melancholy silences to the knowledge of impending doom. And, like his grandfather, he took a drink now and then.

Drinking was what we did—hard not to do in a place described shortly before I was born as "the deadest town, these forty years, in all the world." Starting about the age of thirteen, we drank from big, cheap jugs of wine hidden ever so discreetly in paper bags. My older friends bought it—boys out of high school with nothing to do and nowhere to go, happy to provide. We drank from flasks of sharp whiskey, choking it down straight under the bleachers during football games, gasping and laughing and jeering at the cheerleaders before we wandered off to walk the length of town and back again, sometimes twice in a night, stopping at Sambo's for fries and a Coke. And later, in basement apartments and little rooms on the third floors of faded old houses, salt and tequila and lemon lined up on old chipped coffee tables, a record spinning in the background, talking about nothing, nothing at all. Small town. Small forms of small joys.

Sometimes I had to retrieve my father at the Elks Club a few blocks from home, or hand him a message from my mother. He was often there, in the pine-sided, windowless building kitty-corner from the firemen's hall. There was no sign, nothing to identify the place to outsiders: only a small plaque, a flush, silent door, and a small red button embedded in the door frame. I would stand on the sidewalk in the bright, dry sun and push the button, which made no sound I could hear; after a few moments, the door would partly open, and I could see into a dark, glittering room, to a bar and the mirror behind it reflecting the plush red wallpaper. My father would be there, belly to the bar, with other nice men I knew—teachers, truck drivers, mill men. My brief business done, the bartender closed the door, and I would turn and face into the daylight, blinking from the dark I had just seen.

Oh, but there are many kinds of intoxication here, not all found in bottles. I knew that from the start, slipping on the creek rocks chasing water skippers, hopping after rabbits in the meadow behind the school.

I knew it leaping off the Kelsey Creek Bridge and falling akimbo thirty feet to the cold, dark water of the Scott River. I know it now.

A few years ago, I worked for the summer at a children's camp in the Santiam River valley of Oregon, near Mount Jefferson. There was a low-roofed shed in the middle of a meadow there, near the river, and no one ever disturbed it. I would stand in front of the shed at twilight, waiting. Bats lived in its roof and emerged from a tiny hole at the roof peak, just under the eaves, at a certain undeniable moment when all the yellow had gone and left the sky the dead-white color of a moth's papery wings. One, then two, then dozens of bats fell from the hole right at my head, veering away at the last inch. Each was far smaller than my hand, as soft as a mouse and with a mouse's nose, a monkey's mouth, a child's eyes. They held their leathery wings folded up beside their bodies, like origami waiting to be opened, until they left the shelter of the eave for the sky and opened their wings. One, two, then suddenly a mass of bats poured out all at once, a river of bats, splitting to each side the way a river is split by an unseen rock—left, right, left. Just before the last light was gone, we tricked them, tossing tiny bits of gravel five or six feet above our heads so that the hungry animals, thinking the rocks were mosquitoes, would swoop in close to our heads and upstretched arms.

When I was sixteen, I went into the redwoods near my home with three friends. It was a lark, without a plan; we bought an incongruous collection of groceries, packed inadequate clothes into the nearest packs, and drove down the Smith River Highway into the Siskiyou Mountains, through the rain. The narrow road was a wet, black ribbon, a cooper's slat; the endless cone-shaped trees massed together like the crowd on a subway, pressed up chest to back, pocket to button. We found a wide spot in the road, parked, shouldered packs and food, and walked away from the car straight into the forest.

After a while we found a leaf-coated trail meandering inward, rising slightly, and followed it. The hanging ceiling of boughs and moss gave way only now and then to a tiny corner of sky. The rain fell lightly, endlessly, as it would for days, and as we walked deeper in, we spoke less and less. I felt like an ondine, a water spirit, all soft edges. The ondines love the rain, especially this drifting, silky rain that never stops but only takes a breath now and again before it lets a sigh of moisture go. Ondines pull the sap up tree trunks, make the leaves widen and grow, encourage the tiny tides of the woods: not tides like the Columbia's great heave, but miniature ones, the plump sponge of the woody floor, the gasp of the foliage when you cross through. These dancers are drugged with the rain, curled up in it like a twisted sheet in the morning, drifting.

In what seemed the very center of the wood, the *sivsinenachip*, there was a short, flat, very solid log bridge across a deep stream. The bridge was marked with a plaque dedicating it to a certain Boy Scout troop, an idea so strange among the occult trees that we laughed out loud, a sudden noise.

By evening we were completely wet: tent and clothes, sleeping bags, shoes. The forest was dim and growing dimmer, the floor boggy with rain and long-dropped leaves. I found a slight opening between the close and hugging trees, and someone else found a little dry wood sheltered from the rain by a downed tree. We made a fire, a task that seems slightly miraculous to me now, and set tents, spacy and lost under a canopy of trees.

There were four of us, and the night leaned in, strong; the firelight was hot and yellow and close. Outside the flickering dome of light was a sooty, soft dark. The night was like water to wade through. The furry trees were flung against the sky in black relief. We cooked egg noodles in Campbell's tomato soup and passed around a bottle of brandy. I remember this now as though I stood outside the light alone and watched, and wished I were there, too, by the fire. The sweet tomato sauce on the buttery noodles was our feast, the cheap brandy was hot and sharp, and we sang softly whatever came to mind. We huddled under our hoods in the rain, not bothering to crawl into our moist tents, and water fell off the lids of our hoods and dropped hissing into the fire. My friends' faces were dark and shadowed, and their words rose from under the shelf of coats.

I find it hard now to imagine ever being happier than that, or being more willing or able to be happy than I was that night. I was a very small thing in a very large place, at the mercy of great forces. And there was tremendous relief in that, because it was a small immortality that I felt. My significance had to do with fit, not size, and I had no greater duty than to be troubled about nothing. How many of the people who stumbled down the Continental Divide into this most lovely place found its beauty too big and inhuman to take? How many others watched its beauty slowly transformed into the muddy streets of small towns, and reached for another drink? Aristotle said that *place* was "this place which contains no more than you." The world contains so much more than me, and happiness—ecstasy—often seems a matter of being put in my proper place. And being there, knowing that's where I am.

Oregon Country was an enormous, ill-defined tract of wilderness, stretching south from Russian Alaska to what was Spanish California, and east from the Pacific coast to the Rocky Mountains. By 1818, England and the United States held joint occupancy, challenged on several sides by the Spanish and the Russians. The first true settlers of the territory were French-Canadians—retired Hudson's Bay trappers who took homesteads near the Willamette River in 1829. The geography and climate, the location of mountain passes and the number of natural resources in this huge region were seen in almost reflexively military terms, by those who traveled the area and by their distant governments both. It was almost a given that another nation would be built in Oregon, another country, or kingdom, braced by ocean and mountain, bounteous and self-sufficient. Whoever got Oregon, all agreed, would get the entire Pacific. The names of the mountains changed to accommodate the disharmonious past and the foreseen future: Tahoma became Rainier, and Klickitat became (eventually) Adams, Wyeast turned to Hood, and Loowit to St. Helens. Each honored man was a man of war or negotiation. The names of our mountains are the names of long-forgotten foreign seamen and bureaucrats, men who never came to the Northwest and never saw the mountains.

It was too big, and something had to give. Chunk by chunk, the "country" split in three. First, the northern border. The English (in the body of the Hudson's Bay Company) wanted all the land north of the Columbia River for their Canadian holdings. It was a barely charted wilderness far from the central government, unthinkably distant, large, and empty. "Oregon" stretched far and wide into what is now Canada, Montana, Utah, Nevada. The idea of sanctioning such a foreign and untamed place as "Territory" brought powerful resistance in the East, centering on the almost unimaginable size, the isolation, the difficulty of travel and settlement. Better that "Oregon" be another country than a part of the United States so self-reliant and distant it could foment revolution. (A long time later, complaints were heard in government about "the abnormal and foolish radicalism of the Northwest, particularly Oregon.") As Frederick Jackson Turner warned, "The frontier is productive of individualism . . . , pressing individual liberty beyond its proper bounds."

The Oregonians, for their part, mostly entrenched south of that line in the Willamette Valley, demanded "54–40 or Fight"—that the United States keep all the land to the fifty-fourth parallel, plus forty minutes—a region stretching far into what is Canada today. James K. Polk, elected in 1844 on a platform aimed at Texas and the fifty-fourth parallel, got only Texas. He compromised on the Northwest and took the forty-ninth parallel instead, what is now Washington's northern border. But that was enough, given the distance. A necessary self-sufficiency of mind was built into the Oregon Territory. The settlers wanted government, but a plain and immediate government in their own image. It was like the dime-novel frontier fantasies, in which a man could lead a life of such simple raw necessity that all acts were anarchy and were excused by the nature of their context.

Our increasing expansion westward, inexorably and without ceasing over the course of two hundred years, gave us impetus to keep the Territory. Americans gradually opened and settled more new land than the British ever did, reaping reward time and again. In 1854, one of the newspapers that sprung up near Puget Sound burst with the exhortation "that we shall have the boundless Pacific for a market in manifest destiny. We were born to command it."

When the explorer Ewing Young died in 1841, he left behind a large estate and considerable property. But he died without leaving a will. A committee appointed itself to dispose of his goods. In the sparsely populated, wild land of Oregon Territory, the meeting of a committee of any kind was a rare thing. It was the first bare beginning of government, and included the rather skittish election of a judge, a "court of clerks," and a "high sheriff." But the ragged group of a few dozen was shy of too much law-making, and no rush of legislation appeared. In February and March of 1843, many of the same settlers held what has since been called the "wolf meetings," to discuss the varmint predators: wolves, lynx, bear, panthers. A subscription was raised, officers were appointed and a set of plans proposed. It was one of the first truly administrative acts in the Territory, and the beginning of the end of fur-company depotism—an end long in the coming. A provisional government was soon to appear, and in 1844, the foundation of all governments was added: tax laws. As marshal, Joseph Meek set to finding an equitable way to determine taxes for the settlers; at various times he taxed the number of horses each owned, the amount of acreage, the number of mature trees, even the number of windows in a house.

Washington became a territory in 1853, the year Phoebe Judson began her search for the ideal home: "When we left home the point of our destination was Puget Sound, 'Oregon.' We started the first day of March, and later in the same month Washington was created, by severing from Oregon all the country north of the Columbia. There was a slight sense of disappointment at the change of name, for the word 'Oregon' had grown very dear to me as the name of the country wherein lay my 'ideal home.'" Oregon was made a state on Valentine's Day, 1859: Its leftover parts—now Idaho—were added to Washington Territory, which remained an ungovernably large place until Idaho Territory was created in 1863. The separation of Idaho Territory from Washington Territory was precipitated more by Washingtonians than Idahoans: The former were largely Republican; the latter, gold and silver miners, were

Democrats or perceived that way, and the Washington pols wanted them out of voting range.

At the end of the nineteenth century, a few short decades after statehood, Frederick Jackson Turner wrote, "The free lands are gone, the continent is crossed, and all this push and energy is turning into channels of agitation." A man could no longer flee from his mistakes to the frontier, or hope for a new beginning in a new land; there was no more *newness*. This is the real amalgam of the frontier character on the ocean shores: nowhere to go but settlement, or back.

My great-aunt Lois, a plump woman old when I was a child, owned a cabin on the Klamath River. That stretch of the Klamath, just into California from Oregon and heading west to the sea, is rarely bridged for cars. It is crossed now and then by narrow swing bridges, sometimes nothing more than a few short planks strung between two pairs of parallel ropes; the most modern of the bridges is bare wood wide enough for a single car. The banks are coated with boulders and thorny shrubs and heaps of gravel thrown up by dredging, mining, and roadwork, lined with wild purple lupine and yellow daisies in the spring. The road itself is speckled with stones. Below the road is the river—cold, fast, bone-breaking water, serious water, deceptively quiet from the road unless you stop a moment and watch its hard, dark-green surface swirl by and count the seconds it takes for a log to float past.

Every few miles the road widens into a gravel parking space marked by a NO TRESPASSING sign; a few feet down the bank is a winch and cable strung across the water, with a square box hanging from it large enough to carry a person or a few boxes of groceries. NO TRESPASSING, NO HUNTING, NO FISHING, NO PARKING, PRIVATE PROPERTY, KEEP OUT.

Redwoods still grow deep in this wood—the ones not yet cut for planters and picnic tables—in among the Douglas fir and hemlock and rare Port Orford cedar. (The Port Orford doesn't grow anywhere else. It is dying of a rare fungus, and even if the constant exportation of seedlings to Japan, where it is treasured as an ornamental, is stopped, the fungus will kill it. Not everyone would agree, but to the naturalist Daniel Mathews, Port Orford cedar has a smell "so exquisite that I would wear it for perfume if I could.")

Up the Klamath Highway and north into the wilderness grow darlingtonia, the rare carnivorous pitcher plants, rhododendrons taller than houses, strange flowers such as the phantom orchid. There are foxes here, martens, the disappearing fisher, bobcats, and bears. John Hart, who has hiked the Klamaths quite thoroughly over a period of years, told me: "One thing I loved and still love about that region is that it doesn't come at you with big obvious landscapes. It doesn't grab you by the scruff of the neck and say, 'Look at me.' I value that. It's deep, it keeps on offering things." Hart talks of rumored ancient bonsai yew trees, and a Douglas fir fifteen hundred years old. This last, I suspect, is chimera, like the reports from several people who have seen giant salamanders a little south of here—salamanders longer than a man is tall. Both have the scent of truth; left alone, the forest grows some wondrous things. I know there is much here we've never seen, that for every big tree we find, the possibility exists for a bigger tree no one has seen. The trees we've found—the trees we've long ago cut down and turned to planks and shingles—were beyond dreaming, beyond the grasp of fantasy. Why not a tree seeded the year King Arthur died, in the decades when Wu Ti was emperor of China?

Aunt Lois' cabin is built of logs, whole coppery tree trunks full of piny knots and oiled to a shine. The rooms are big, dim, spacious—every room an addition to the big parlor and its giant fireplace made from river stone. It is always cold in that cabin, always shaded, but it has the luxury of electricity and running water. Most marvelous of all in that dry, deckled canyon, it is surrounded by a thick green lawn cool and fragrant in the constant breeze.

On summer visits, my brother and sister and I stayed out, away from the adults drinking scotch and smoking in old Adirondack chairs on the grass. We chased ground squirrels through the fir trees and turned over rocks on the edge of the bank, never straying too near the rough water. Late in the day, my father called us to him for a summer ritual. He stood in khaki slacks and a white T-shirt straining against his stomach, a cigarette dangling from his lips, and required us to lift our shirts and drop our shorts for inspection. He ran his hand over our pink skin, lifting arms, peering behind knees, and then rubbed my dog's fur backward, searching for the ticks that dropped from shrubs and clambered aboard as we swished through the vines.

But it was not our Real Place, not real like our other cabin, on the Scott River, a minor tributary of the Klamath emptying from the south. Aunt Lois cultivated a gentle home in a rough land; I craved a rougher, harder road. The cabin wasn't ours; it was owned by my father's step-father and had been built in turn by his father. But children own the world—at least I did, those summers on the Scott.

My father drove the pickup, the back crowded with boxes of food, duffel bags of clothes and towels, sweaters, books, beer. We three chil-dren rode in back, too, with the dog, hitched up against the truck's cab, scuffing our bare knees on the splintery wood of the truck bed. We watched the acres of alfalfa and timothy hay give way to tall pines and the asphalt give way to gravel and dirt. When the wheels began to spit up clouds of dust, we crawled under Daddy's tarp, a greasy curtain smelling of sawdust and motor oil. Our dog, Star, leaned against the wheel well, straining for the woods in a kind of bliss we each recognized, his chin propped on the lip of the truck. He let his eyes drift closed and his jaw loosen until his tongue wagged in the force of a perfumed gale of the country, until a child grabbed him by the collar and dragged him back, beneath the tarp, forced to lie near our feet in the warm and fragrant dark.

If anyone wanted attention, we had to lean against the cold metal cab and rap on the window. My mother covered her hair with scarves whenever she had to ride in the pickup; when I looked through the glass, my own hair tossing in the wind, I could see her, magically changed. She was a woman with a scarf, riding high above the road, eyeglasses jaunty above her smile, and she turned to Daddy and talked and laughed silently. All I could hear was the clatter of tires on a pebbled road and the rush of air; I kneeled and hung on the windowsill, looking into that small place and the backs of their heads, and through, to the world ahead, beyond the glass.

Daddy turned the truck down the dirt driveway, bumping through its ruts, and while we unloaded boxes, he climbed the hill across the road to turn on the sewer pump. My mother slid her hand along the dusty door frame till she found the key and unlocked the door. We carried in Fritos corn chips, beer, Orange Crush, soft loaves of round white bread, hard green apples, cornflakes, enough food to last for weeks.

The Scott River, like the Klamath, runs through a forested canyon, but the Scott had softer sides for most of its route, long slopes of trees and brush leading down from tall hills to the water. The road cuts across one banked hill, and for long spells the slope from road to water is just gentle enough to allow zigzagging paths. The floor of the forest is soft from generations of yellowed pine needles and bits of dropped lichen, lumpy with flood-tossed river stones, crackling from the tan layer of dry oak leaves.

The cabin was a small, boxy, two-story building with a deck; the dirt drive was nothing more than a tractor cut straight to the door. What we called the porch was a deck perched on stilts outside the front door, a room-size wooden platform with a rail on three sides and a dusty porch swing in constant shade.

The whole of it was little more than two large rooms. On the first floor was a long and narrow kitchen that was lined floor, wall, and ceiling with a wood so old it was black with the years of wood and lamp-oil smoke. Oilcloth curtains hung by the windows but were never shut, even on the blackest night. On the east wall by the front door was a long wooden counter with a chipped white sink, and on top of the counter there always stood a bright silver pail with a ladle. One of us would grab the pail and run out the back door on the opposite side of the room, down three steps and off the path, to a spring that trickled from the ground beneath the house. The ground there was always boggy and the plants wet with dew condensing in the shadows, and I held in my fist the knowledge that we were here for a time, a long time, an infinite time. With every arrival at the cabin, the most recent departure was finally undone. These remain the hardest departures of my life, and I held on to them quite tightly, refusing to relinquish the grief of leaving until we arrived again. I would hold the pail under the trickle and wait happily while it filled, inhaling the exuberant perfume of the woods, my bare feet cold in the spreading edge of the clear water.

The trail ran away from the spring on a winding course to the water, zigging and zagging in hairpin turns, edged on every side by a deep, viny tangle of shrubs and poison oak. Under ponderosa pine and oaks, sugar pine and madrone, grew a mass of blackberries, daisies, and tiny wildflowers; they grew in pell-mell glory around the bare trunks of the tall trees. The bank was dim and cool, but through the trees I could always see the river below, sparkling like tinsel in the hot morning sun.

I dragged the heavy pail up the steps and into the kitchen, splattering black spots of water on the gritty floor, and then drank. The bowl of the ladle banged on the silver pail and tingled against my teeth; the water was cold as ice, and clear and clean as the high note of a trumpet, and then I could be excused, and go.

The miracle of the Scott River in this wild place is that it has beaches, pale beaches—light, camel-colored sand hot on the surface and cool and moist below. Dozens of short, soft beaches along the south side of the river are broken by tough little bushes, lined with the minute swinging tracks of racing lizards and snakes, and the deep grooves of deer hooves.

In the early spring of 1908, two young white women, Mary Ellicott Arnold and her best friend, Mabel Reed, came to "the Rivers" as field matrons in the United States Indian Service. They were among the first white women to appear in Karuk country, then still a wild region reeling from the corruption and disturbance of the moribund gold rush. Mary Arnold and Mabel Reed were from New Jersey and had come west looking for adventure of some undefined kind, knowing only that settling down into marriage and motherhood had to wait until more of the huge world had been seen.

In the course of their search for some risky undertaking, the two women had an interview with a Mr. Kelsey in the Sacramento Valley:

We learned he was Special Agent for all Indians in California, and we told him we should like to see what a really rough country was like. Mr. Kelsey looked at our pleated skirts, seven yards around the bottom, and his eye hardened.

"Shall I send you to the roughest field in the United States?" he asked.

I think he expected us to refuse. But of course we did not refuse. It was the chance we had been hoping for.

So Ms. Arnold and Ms. Reed received their commissions, and a promised salary of thirty dollars a month each and traveling expenses, to go into "the Rivers country" of far northern California and carry the benevolence of the Indian Service to the disadvantaged Karuks. They had never before lived in rural circumstances, and neither had ever ridden a horse before they crossed the narrow trail over the Trinity Alps by mule. They stayed, in varying degrees of primitive discomfort but with a kind of overwhelming joy, for two years.

When Arnold and Reed first arrived, they learned to speak of their life "on the Rivers" as though the cascades and the banks and the rushing water dictated the landscape that rose around them. The Father Klamath was never a neutrality, never a mere mark on the land, especially when it ran high. "You do not think of the Klamath as a river when it is in flood," wrote Arnold. "It is a great evil force. It is alive, and it means you ill." Their first winter, in 1908–09, the river ran eighty feet higher than in summer. The Indians who lived here had a complex set of laws surrounding obligation and debt, but no degree of enmity allowed you to refuse passage across the river. A person stood on one bank and called across for ferrying, and those who heard had to come; to refuse was worse than incurring a debt; it was to incur a dishonor, to be *tanapâsirip*, and no good. Passage across the river was the law, a natural law of a kind.

I thought of the floods as an ancient phenomenon, something finished and done. But they weren't. Grandpa used to say the flood made his beach. I rarely saw the cabin in rain and never in the winter, and year by year by year, nothing changed. The rocks and sand and river channel were carved of a kind of stone, a childish, fantastic stone, harder than the granite of the hills.

Down the road from our cabin about a quarter of a mile was a modest summer estate, a great white house with a wrought-iron fence and green lawns and its own power plant. It stood all the way across the road from the river beyond a bridge, along the banks of a creek. I have only the most dreamy memory of the place, standing in the shade of tall pines surrounded by emerald grass in a dry canyon that didn't grow grass. There had been logging up the creek that summer, the kind of rough-and-tumble logging that takes every sizable tree from a given site, leaving an opening called a clear-cut.

Clear-cutting—the word can be a noun, an adjective, and a verb—is almost always the best way to make money on trees. This kind of logging leaves nothing of the woods behind except its trash. (Timber economics dictates that trash may mean whole trees, too small or young to be worth milling, or of a species considered poor for lumber. Such trees are often just cut and tossed aside.) Clear-cuts are full of a peculiar kind of garbage called slash—torn trunks, broken branches, uprooted stumps, an almost impassable surface of organic waste strewn across the ground. On this particular clear-cut up the river, the slash remained when winter came, and with it the heaviest rains in recent memory. The slash tore down the creek bed and piled up near the house, blocking the water. A huge lake appeared across the lawn, spreading up the hillside behind a dam of branches and logs, bigger and bigger, until it finally tore through. And when the dam broke and the lake burst out, it took the house, the fence, the lawn, the power plant and its concrete foundation, and it took the bridge, too, as an afterthought, as a reminder.

That same flood must have dictated the tumbled boulders and uprooted trees I remember, in the dreamy haze of childhood, as eternal. We spent our days on the river, my brother and I, as braves and warriors; our sister was more timid and slow. We woke wild in the mornings to face long days with full hearts; we read by yellow lantern light in the evening, spent, and brushed moths away from the pools of brightness. There were grownups nearby, but never close; they never seemed to say anything more to me than the calm exhortations I'd always heard:

Stay out of the poison oak. Don't bother the snakes. Be back for dinner. We stood impatiently, nodded with exceptional vigor, and were gone. The winding back trail of the cabin led straight to our private beach, and we reached it each morning as fast as we dared, brushing the poison oak carelessly as we ran, kicking up sand onto the last few feet of trail.

The first and largest of the rocks was a granite boulder shaped like an egg. It was perhaps twelve feet high and half as wide at its middle, and it had been thrown by a forgotten flood down the river and up against a pile of lesser boulders on the edge of the water. All the rocks around were curvaceous and hard, smoothed by rough winter water, and they hunched up against each other with narrow, dark places in between, shaded holes holding spiders, blue-belly lizards, and the occasional snake. One side of the big boulder leaned in the sand at such an angle that a nimble child could scramble up the pile to its top; the top, in turn, leaned out over the clear, deep river as though placed there for no other purpose than our pleasure. I ran to the rock's height and flew off into water clear and cold and deep, and sliced through its green-black skin, feet first, to the sandy bottom lost in froth.

Along the west wall of the cabin ran a square, open stair, marching up the stretch of the hill, leading to a single upper room twice as large as the kitchen. At the top of the stairs on the right was the bathroom, a sink and toilet and shower, the floor of the shower gritty with sand and the cold water trickling slowly.

The upstairs room was cluttered and piled with trunks and furniture, a huge array of things my grandmother had no use for in her home, dusty couches and an elaborate Japanese folding screen behind which my sister and mother and I changed clothes. There were boxes and crates of books and magazines—*Look* and *Life* and *The Saturday Evening Post*—and clothes, coats, pots and pans, folded curtains, and photographs.

Off the front of the cabin, over the kitchen, was a sleeping porch, a narrow screened room facing the river, lined with several iron beds, each bed piled with two or three musty, lumpy mattresses atop each other. I slept on them in perfect peace. Sometimes, weary of sun, I rummaged for a magazine in midafternoon and curled up there, shivering with pleasure in the cool air filled with pine, and read about Marilyn Monroe and Queen Elizabeth, Elvis Presley and the young Jack Kennedy.

Some of the cabins built in the 1930s had ninety-nine-year leases with the Forest Service; our nearest neighbor had one. Stockmen and packers and guides could get special forest use permits to build cabins on federal land. My Uncle Gus—Gustav—was a packer for deer and elk hunters and had a permit like that. He was my Grandpa Doc's brother, and he spent all his adult life in a small cabin in a meadow high above the river. Our cabin was on a patent, a private rectangle of land running from the road to the river, in the midst of a national forest, forever.

My father's family name is Meek. I found it a dreary name, and was dogged all my days by jokes and aphorisms both obvious and sly. Knowing that mountain men like Joseph and his brother Stephen had carried the name cheered me; they were surely men worth descending from, and able to elevate even so trivial a sound to something transcendent. So I assumed with carefree confidence that Joseph and Stephen Meek were my relatives, my uncles, my cousins.

When I asked questions about family, about ancestry, I heard only vague, ephemeral answers. Loquacious and gossipy, voluble—sometimes insistently so—my relatives weren't given to anecdotes about the past. A few hours into an evening, a few sheets into the wind, an aunt or grandparent would tell a tale, giving a memory or two; they concerned people down the block, or living relatives never met, and were of little use or interest to me in my own selective search. I asked a few times about Joseph and Stephen and no one seemed to care, though one uncle liked to wink about it. The lack of a solid denial encouraged me. It smacked of mild scandal, secrets.

My father's father, Leonidas Virgil Meek, died at the age of forty-three, died when my own father was only sixteen. My father was an only child, though he had five aunts and two uncles. No one talked about Leonidas Virgil, who had married into my grandmother's extended set of siblings, or of his father, Oscar Leonidas. I didn't know until adulthood that he was buried in the cemetery nearby, a dry place of oak trees and grass where I hiked as a child and necked as a teenager. I thought of family as my parents, my grandmother and her endless siblings, my mother's taciturn mother. There had to be some good reason why that particular family line ended so abruptly a few decades earlier.

Joseph Meek was born in Virginia in 1810. He became a mountain guide and fur trapper, joined the Hudson's Bay Company as a beaver man at the age of seventeen, and drove the first wagon to Oregon, to prove it could be done. He was "a droll creature," Joseph, who liked to paint himself the fool in his stories, instead of the hero. He was both the first sheriff west of the Mississippi and the first U.S. marshal in the Oregon Territory. When speed was essential and nothing moved quickly, he took the territorial petition from Oregon to Washington, D.C., by horse in less than a month. His best friend was a man named Bob Newell, called Doc by everyone, and the two of them, Doc and Joe, became brothers-in-law when they married Nez Percé sisters. Well, fuel for the fire: My mother's maiden name was Newell and my grandfather was called Doc—the last, admittedly, a stretch, but when you're looking for happy coincidence, anything will do.

Joseph spent his time in the Oregon Territory, but Stephen came to northern California, lived near where I was raised, is buried a few miles away. Whenever we went to the museum, I spent time in front of the huge sepia photograph of Stephen, a picture almost life-size. He was long-bearded, unkempt, and wore a fringed leather coat. In the picture he is down on one knee, balancing a gun against his thigh. He wears a belt of beaver skins, a hat of fur. There was no doubt in my mind that he was a relative. He was mine, this fearless man, he and his brother Joseph and the Indian blood they'd married.

Stephen Meek wasn't half the mountain man his brother became; he had, in the polite words of one historian, "never distinguished himself." But for one event, and that the kind of distinction no one invites. He knew the trail from the Missouri River and its landings through the Plains all the way to the Willamette, and at one point he decided he also knew a shortcut through the dangerous and wearing

Blue Mountains. Somewhere in Idaho he gathered together two hundred wagons, filled with almost a thousand people, more than two thousand cattle, a thousand goats, and eight hundred oxen. The pioneers paid Meek five dollars a wagon for guidance. He led them out into the northeastern Oregon desert and promptly got lost.

The Oregon desert is not quite the fertile land of wheat farms found in the rich Palouse country of eastern Washington. While wheat is grown there by the ton, it is as much a rocky, windy, wild land for cattle, sheep, bands of wild horses, enormous vistas reminiscent of the widest views of the Dakotas or the Rockies. It has winter lakes that dry up in the first wave of sun, tiny towns of one store and a few houses, oceans of spring green color passing across the hills like a kind of shadow. Few people settled long, especially in the southern reaches, and few people live there now. You have to be willing to live a certain way, to be prepared for the snow all winter long and to sweat through the haying in the summer and fall. People who live there consider it a more than fair trade. But the Oregon desert is no place to get lost. Stephen Meek got his wagon train to the Deschutes River, which probably kept the party alive, and then went on ahead. He was in fact afraid to return, afraid for his own life at the hands of his employers. Forty people eventually died. The rest were rescued by a black trapper from Kentucky, Moses "Black" Harris, and headed down the Columbia with all the worn-out parties of pioneers who stayed on the main trail in the first place.

There was one high note in what is now called "Meek's Cut-off": While looking for waters, or waiting for help—the stories are many and various—the lost settlers found big rocks full of gold flakes, which made good fishing sinkers for the few patches of water. In several versions, children gathered up the rocks in a blue bucket and then discarded them along the trail, creating the legend of the Blue Bucket Mine, a gold claim to outshine all the others, lost in the dry desert and never mapped.

On the Fourth of July, I attended the Joseph Meek Picnic, a private affair held every year several miles west of Portland, near land Joseph once owned. Dozens of people came to the shady grove of oak and cottonwood trees facing a sunny field of wheat—dozens of branches and twigs on a family tree hundreds of years old, stretching throughout the West. By twos and threes, people arrived, bearing platters of deviled eggs and coolers of beer, aluminum chairs and paper plates and pots of baked beans. A man with long jowls bustled about in the growing crowd, carrying a register and checking to be sure each guest signed. An elderly, white-haired man stood guard over a box of the leather-bound family genealogy—a long, long list of names, dates, birthplaces, anniversaries, deaths down the generations. They were all Meeks, or married to Meeks, great-granddaughters and great-great-nephews of Joseph L. A tall man gently placed a neat black binder on one of the redwood picnic tables and turned the plastic leaves for a group of women to see, one page at a time: newspaper clippings and photographs of tombstones and homesteads, steps on a journey.

I met people from California and Arizona and Utah, and scoured lists of cousins and nephews a century dead, looking for the names on my own thin genealogy. We ate barbecued chicken and someone's aunt's famous spaghetti; the children squabbled over the swings and got their good clothes dirty; and a dour, silent man threw horseshoes by himself. Babies gurgled and crawled off their blankets into the long, flattened grass; a tan young man leaned over and kissed his grandmother on her powdery cheek. It was a hot day, and we stayed under the enormous, fragrant trees, and in the distance I could see the faded white farmhouse where Joseph had lived for a time in the middle of his restless, lucky life.

I riffled through the books and it was quickly, too quickly, clear we weren't relatives at all, these ordinary, friendly people and me. The fat, distracted woman handing me a plate of Jell-O salad, the handsome state representative glad-handing his cousins with campaign literature—they were no more my family than you are. I felt a brief regret, but brief.

What is the attraction of descent, the cachet? Why did it seem to matter so much in younger years? We think the pioneers did a tran-scendent thing, and somehow think those of us descended from them shine with a certain light—even that those of us who live where they once lived gain a little glory. How else to explain the Miss Oregon Pioneer contest? It is a strange kind of pride, the pride in someone dead before you were born. It is pride at a particular mix of chromosomes, a circumstance of relation that, after all, might have been more than regretted at the time. In the end, in the tender shadows of the trees, I thought about ownership, and all that possession expressed: our land, our farms, our people. Joseph had strength and courage, he had the character I once believed was inherent in the settler, inevitable on the frontier. But now I think character is less certain, more mutable, than that, and not always heritage. I promised to call, and I folded up my family tree so its sideways digressions to Iowa and Kentucky didn't show. I didn't mention it; I think it would have mattered more to them than to me.

TWO

In the winter of 1836, "during the great conflagration," a New York physician named Elijah White came home from a night call "shivering with cold, seated himself by the fire; and while warming his benumbed fingers, took up the *Christian Advocate* for a few moments' perusal, and, glancing over its contents, suddenly, in his usual jocular manner, observed to Mrs. W., that there was a call for them from Oregon; that the board of missions advertised for a clergyman, physician, &c., &c., and as he could act in the capacity of pill-pedler, he thought it might be well to respond thereto. She did not immediately answer; and looking up, he was surprised to find her weeping."

Some of us who have lived through more than one winter in the western slope of the Cascades might understand her inexplicable tears; there have been weeks when I would have preferred "a great conflagration," to another day of rain. But Mrs. W. had a secret. Unbeknownst to her beloved mate, she had always had "a deep and abiding interest" in the region of the great Columbia, and she had harbored a desire to see it that she thought would be most unseemly in a wife and mother. She had presumed the whole fantasy impossible. But a few months later, Dr. and Mrs. White were appointed to the Oregon Territory by the board of missions. With their one-year-old son and an adopted teenager named George, they joined an odd party: maiden schoolteachers, a carpenter, a blacksmith, and the self-announced betrothed of the missionary Jason Lee who was already in the Territory. In those days before the Oregon Trail, the route to the Pacific Northwest was a long sea trip in close quarters, around the Horn to the Sandwich Islands—now Hawaii—before reaching the mouth of the Columbia River.

Dr. White and his Mrs. W. found a new world when they arrived on the misty Columbia—a savage garden flowering with trees. Mrs. W. remembered a tree lying on the ground with a circumference fifty-seven feet nine inches and three hundred feet in height, "perfectly sound." Canadian loggers had cut it down because they believed it to be the largest tree in the world. (It would be something to have done—to have cut down the world's biggest tree, sinew and spit and a saw. But there were bigger ones.)

The trees, the magnificent trees, were too big, too dark, too cool for the brave new man. The trees were "indecently large," unheard of, improper. Visitors complained of a "peculiar melancholy," of trees "startling and strange." Wrote one climber of the huge woods on the slopes of Mount Rainier, "We were not the least happy." The dark, damp rings of the center of the world leaned in hard on the easterners, who were so long used to plants of a more conventional, manageable size.

These were trees tall enough to stand shoulder-high to the Washington Monument. These were trees taller than the Statue of Liberty, base and all. Trees so big—if you could still find one—that you could park a Cadillac on a single stump. The trees were so big the loggers couldn't pull a saw back and forth in a straight cut. They had to go at each tree by angles, cutting inward piece by piece; with the biggest, they would sometimes cut out a chunk and plant dynamite just to get started. The trees were so tall it took "two men and a boy to look to the top," according to Stewart Holbrook. Even now, the tallest trees in the Northwest contain microclimates, different miniature weather patterns at root, trunk, and crown; back then, they must have contained microstorms, miniature lightning bolts flashing through tiny clouds stuck in the limbs. No one knows how big the biggest trees got: There are photographs of trees with diameters that appear to be nearly twenty feet, bigger than ordinary houses (and stories, of course, of trees considerably bigger than that). The Mineral Tree near Mount Rainier—long ago cut down, yes—is the largest known Douglas fir on record, fifteen and a half feet in diameter and four hundred feet tall.

The Northwest held the biggest then, and holds the biggest now, of the false firs and the true firs, of the hemlocks, the spruces, the cedars, and the pines. The trees were so big that whole families lived in the stumps. A photographer kept his studio in one near Clallam Bay in Washington. The post office in Elwha, in the Olympic National Forest, was a stump—which says something about Elwha, but more, perhaps, about the trees. It was roomier than a lot of local cabins and there was plenty of headroom. In 1895, a United States postal inspector dropped by and demanded improvements, so they added a roof. Children were raised in these gnomish caves, reared up in the must and spores of the upright, dying foot of a tree, with a little stovepipe sticking out at a jaunty angle, the small double-sash window cut through the foot-thick bark and Father in a chair on the "porch," leaning back into the whorled roots.

They were mostly troublesome, these big weeds, this "green desert." One of the first parties to climb Mount Rainier wanted to gather black-berries but found the growing dark hampered their progress. So they set a large standing dead tree on fire for light. "Speedily the flames were climbing to the top of the withered branches, and casting a cheerful light for a hundred yards around," wrote the party's leader in his mem-oir. "But what we found very convenient for gathering berries proved to be a great annoyance when we wanted to sleep."

Big, old trees. A four-hundred-year-old Douglas fir was young, an eight-hundred-year-old tree a fine, comfortable Douglas fir. (A young Douglas fir was called a "bastard fir": no use to anyone.) The redwoods weren't grown until they had at least eight hundred rings. When a logger, wrote Stewart Holbrook, "said these trees were older than Jesus H. Mackinaw, it meant something more than a logger's pleasantry."

They're all gone—all except a few stolid individuals off the track, locked away in wilderness, guarded by borders and laws. The Mineral Tree and many more are gone. In 1850, the Mark Twain Tree, a sequoia, was cut down for a traveling exhibition. When it finally fell, after days of breathless work, fifty men stood side by side around the edge of its stump. Cut into sections and put on display by P. T. Barnum, the tree was dismissed as a fake. The stump of another giant, the Discovery Tree, was turned into a dance floor where dozens of couples could waltz. And—and—so many stories, so many frozen photographs of an act brazen in the extreme, committed with absolute deliberation.

"On your right is Oregon," wrote a travel writer named Charles Nordhoff of his trip up the Columbia, "its hill-sides a forest so dense that jungle would be as fit a word for it as timber; on the left is Washington Territory, and its hill-sides as densely covered as those of the nearer shore. This interminable, apparently impenetrable, thicket of firs exercised upon my mind, I confess, a gloomy, depressing influence." Nordhoff arrived in Astoria and the wild Washington woods in the early 1870s, to add to the long series of cautionary guides for the growing number of casual tourists interested in the Pacific Northwest and its curiosities. Decades after logging began, he was oppressed by what remained, melancholy in the trees growing hither and thither wherever he looked, seeming to lean down upon him in his passage with a kind of malevolence. He described "a saw-mill, which is sawing away for dear life, because if it stopped the forest would doubtless push it into the river, on whose brink it has courageously effected a lodgement," and yet making "scarcely an appreciable impression upon the belt of timber which so shuts in Astoria that I thought I had scarcely room in it to draw a full breath."

He went into the logging woods and watched a tree fall—a tree six feet across and a few hundred feet high, a middling-size tree—and he called it "one of the grandest and most majestic incidents of forest life . . . a very great sight, not soon forgotten." Like his peers, Nordhoff didn't see the hand of God in the trees themselves. He saw God in the strength of the small hand that could bring the giant trees down.

It wasn't only the trees that were big: They filled the land in unimaginable forests, covering the land "like hair on a dog's back," wrote a man who grew up in a logging camp. Squirrels could travel from California to Canada without touching the ground. From the ground, much of the world was a three-dimensional box of trees. These forests, in fact, seemed more than even the white man could use. They stretched from far north into Canada, a thousand miles south, broken only now and then by the natural savanna grasslands of a few fertile valleys. Trees grew to the very edge of every mile of coast and along almost every river and stream bank, climbed the mountain slopes to the very limit of the snow line, and marched up and down hills too steep for a horse to walk. The forests were unsurveyed, unclaimed, free for the taking if a man could only figure out how. The forests were so huge that the fires in them were beyond belief; even a hundred years later, fires might last for months, explosive balls of flame leaping from tree to tree without a break for miles.

Three times in twelve years, the same section of forest burned. The Tillamook Fire burned more than 355,000 acres, a total of 13.1 *billion* board feet of timber, and left a mark on the land now known as the Tillamook Burn. All the fires were caused by logging operations. The first, and largest, of the fires exploded with a force rivaling that of Mount St. Helens, burning 220,000 acres in twenty hours and sending smoke almost eight miles high. A fire front almost a hundred miles long crossed the woods. Enough timber burned in that fire to match the nation's annual output that year, and it covered only a portion of a small part of the forest.

Looking east and south off the slope of Mount Hood near my home, holding my hands near my face to block the towns, roads, and clear-cuts, I can still sense the unlimited forests: In places the land still falls away from the mountain in a clotted, blanketing evergreen. It is a march of sameness, like water, rolling, rolling. There is something creepy in these woods, if you're inclined that way: so little variation on the surface, such endless variation inside. The traveler through is bound to be lost.

In the 1840s, when the Oregon Trail was first being crossed, there was little open land. But for a few hard-won forts and some grassland, the only clearings were those burned by the Indians to run game and make small meadows for grass and honey flowers. The early settlers were a little discouraged, gnawing like beaver against the edge, pushing back from the scarce flat ground near the water, burning the stumps in fires lasting weeks, the grey smoke hovering like smudge over the shaded clearing. "The land on which these large trees grow is good," wrote one, "but the labor of clearing it would be such as to prevent any one from undertaking the task." Phoebe Judson described how tree after tree was removed by slow fires. Two holes were drilled in a tree, at angles to pull a draft. Burning coals were put in the holes, and several days later the trees were burned to hollow shells and could be cut down more easily. One by one by one: The fallen trees had to be burned in the same way, in many sections, over a whole season. In its early, muddy days, Portland was nicknamed Stumptown, because there were giant stumps in the middle of all the streets. (Some of the stumps were whitewashed so they could be seen at night.) Said Samuel Bowles, "It is impossible to calculate the time when, cut and saw as we may, all these forests shall be used up, and the supply become exhausted."

No one, Indian or white man alike, could imagine it gone. I have the benefit of hindsight, buckled on every side by clear-cuts and parking lots and the skeletons of malls. I look at such steady loss now and review the losses past: the decimation of the once-populous sea otter down to a few hundred single animals, the near-extirpation of the beaver from the Northwest, the steady disappearance of one thing after the other. Elk, salmon, wolves and the wolverine, even the native people dying and retreating in vast numbers. And no lessons learned. No one expected the trees to disappear. The forests were beyond such a reckoning; otters and salmon and even Indians could at least be held face to face, one at a time. A Douglas fir or western hemlock in full-grown glory turned a man into a child, into a eunuch. It turned him into prey, running for his life in the dark woods.

The Northwest is composed of forest zones, each zone dominated by a particular species of trees. Even the bare plains east of the Cascades are a zone of western juniper; what looks bare from the road hides woodland in the draws and valleys. But it is always and everywhere the conifers that crowd the eye. The wet winters and dry summers make a strange climate for trees; the result is a mirror reflection of rain forest, where great quantities of water fall and moisten the woods, but at the wrong time of year. Big deciduous trees with their broad, seasonal leaves are at a distinct disadvantage in the hot, even droughty summers. The conifers keep their needles and suck up moisture all winter long, holding it tight in their enormous trunks and wide-ranging roots.

We call these never-logged forests *virgin* with a soft and harmless ring, as though it bore its purity by our largess. And so it does. (Pretty big virgins: strapping, thick-thighed trees.) These days we talk about *old growth*, a specific kind of forest, and not necessarily the oldest. The Douglas fir is a very long-lived tree. Old growth, a dull term, means a forest with every element of the forest occurring at once: an ur-forest. Old growth has mature trees more than two hundred years of age, standing dead spars, large fallen logs on the ground and in the streams, a varied canopy of shade and broken sun. The pattern of an old-growth forest seems chaotic up close, orderly from a distance, because trees this old take on powerfully individual shapes: individual natures, each with a unique outline, an unduplicated silhouette. It has the beauty of function, and of age. An old forest, a forest undisturbed, reaches a state called *climax*. It is a proper word, erotic and unfinished, this place quiet and ripe and hanging eternally at the cusp, the peak, the zenith of its reach. Relatively few forests go so long untouched by fire or people; most old-growth Douglas firs in the Northwest are around four hundred to five hundred years of age. Such a stand is filled with huge trees, a thick understory, all the elements of the old forest, but it isn't yet a climax forest. The places where the trees are left alone, in the stands hidden away by luck or topography or the law, the forest will grow, age, and change for century upon century. It won't reach the most stable stage, the sustained stage of climax, until the largest trees in the stand are twelve hundred years old. And there are such stands here, hidden away.

An old-growth forest is so complex, so layered, that biologists sometimes shrink from trying to describe their forms—twelve hundred invertebrate species can be found in a single tree. Consider that the forest is not only area, but depth, space, dimension: The red tree vole often spends its whole life in the canopy of interwoven branches, never touching earth. Why should it? There is a whole world up there. In the old growth, in the untouched woods, is a cluster of time, old trees mingling with newborns, and kinds of birds and mammals and insects and fungi found nowhere else.

The bald eagle, Roosevelt elk, clouded salamander, the silver-haired bat, Vaux's swift, roughskin newt, shrew-mole, red-breasted sapsucker, the tailed frog, the marbled murrelet: Haven't heard of them? They all depend to one essential degree or another on the untouched mature forest. Now might be a good time to learn their names; most forest ecologists figure hundreds, thousands, perhaps many thousands of species will disappear or decline sharply when the forests are gone. Several dozen vertebrates can live nowhere else, and virtually all of the old-growth forests have been cut down. What a starker, harder planet this will be when the last acres have disappeared—for good. I wanted to slip that in; see, all along I've been trying to figure a way to slip neatly into a hearty discussion of forests the fact that almost all the old forest is gone. I want the reader to keep reading seamlessly on, learning about trees—and yet I have to point. I have to say, Look! Where forests once ranged for hundreds of miles, there are no trees. Where giant firs and pines used to grow in great variety, there are only unbroken tree farms as even and ordinary as golf courses. A cup half full or almost empty? This region—Oregon, Washington, Idaho, and far northern California—still holds 104 of the record largest trees of their species. Conifers, deciduous, doesn't matter: but they are smaller than they used to be. Time goes by, and the biggest trees get smaller. A brochure for the Oregon Caves brags of the surrounding forest being filled with "huge Douglas firs" between three and six feet thick. Babies! Baby trees. (More than big enough to log.)

All things being equal, a western hemlock would always dominate the Douglas fir, because the hemlock is a fecund seeder and loves its own shade: A hemlock births one new hemlock after another in its own shadow. Douglas fir likes sun and grows slowly in the hemlock's selfish dark, but it has a few advantages, given time. In this environmental jungle filled with endless variations in soil and temperature, torn by microclimates and high peaks, and uncountable species jostling each other for a niche, the Douglas fir is evolution's prodigy. It is the only tree equally abundant on both sides of the Cascade chain, common from low to moderately high elevations, the only tree found throughout the forests of the Northwest. Once a Douglas fir reaches the partial sun in the canopy, it grows taller and straighter than anything else around, outskirting the hemlock, the grand and noble firs, the western red cedar around it, eventually forming stands composed almost purely of itself. It grows to be, all things considered, "the strongest, straightest, fastest-growing tree" in the world, says Daniel Mathews. "If you see a big evergreen tree," he adds, "it's probably a Douglas-fir." In its youth, the Douglas is knotty and wide-grained, second-class timber. As it matures, it grows more slowly, piling on rings with close, fine grain, free of knots, adding bark inches thick. An old Douglas fir is so big that the grooves of its corrugated bark are deep enough for a child to sit inside.

And the Douglas fir digs adventure: It thrives on fire and storms and various catastrophes, including human beings. It thrives, I mean, *with time*, with a fair amount of given time. A fire or a windstorm or natural erosion clears out a sunny space for the fire-resistant trees and blows the seeds and cones around. (On the east side of the Cascades, where the drier, colder weather gives rise to the giant parks of lodgepole and ponderosa pines, fire has another result. The ponderosa is the most fire-resistant conifer around, and usually survives. The cones of the lodgepole have a special resin that seals at high temperatures; after the fire, when the trees have burned away, the fallen cones open up and spread seeds across an empty, beckoning land.) The newly opened spaces chase out certain species, invite in others, and it's that dynamic change a Douglas fir seems to need. Given time, in increments of centuries, all these western forests strive to the crest called climax, like a wave on the frequency of planets. Imagine this, a climax more stable than the state that led to it, a diverse and potent system functioning as a single, dominant thing. A climax forest reproduces itself, maintains itself, is so thick with biomass and diversity that it can hardly be defined in ecological terms. Left alone, it will pulse its own slow pulse, exhale its own slow breath, forever. There is little on this earth more immortal.

South of the Strait of Juan de Fuca, west of the long fingers of Puget Sound, is a great plot of land known as the Olympic Peninsula. The peninsula can be defined easily as a set of concentric circles. In the middle is pure wilderness—untrailed, not entirely surveyed, peaks, wet valleys, and enormous, unparalleled trees. This circle of wilderness goes out and out in rings, all about the same, but as the rings expand from the center, one finds trails, campsites, bits of litter, signs, and finally roads. About halfway out is a ring of mobile homes and resorts and sportboats—the edge of the Olympic National Park. The effort to create the Olympic National Park was long and hard—too many logs locked up in there. It started with President Grover Cleveland, was made a national monument by Theodore Roosevelt—who, on an official visit, saw what was ever after called the Roosevelt elk—and was finally sealed as a national park by Franklin Roosevelt. The next ring is clear-cuts, and small logging towns, and the Quinault Indian Nation. This ring spreads out and out, broken only by highways and other towns. The Olympic Peninsula has water on three sides—the Strait, a part of Puget Sound called Hood Canal, and the Pacific Ocean. The fourth side, the south side, is land—clear-cuts, highways, replanted timberland, towns and harbors full of log rafts, a nuclear power plant, the world.

I was camping in the summer of 1990 in the forest near Soleduck Falls, in what was once the country of the Quileutes in the northern boundaries of the Olympic National Park. I left Highway 101 from the north side, into the park, where the barren logged acres slouch against the park border like thugs. Each parcel holds a sign reading MANAGED FOREST, listing the dates of cut, burn, and sometimes replanting. I could see infant cones of Douglas firs hidden among the stumps. One such sign has been altered; above MANAGED FOREST, a visitor has painted POORLY. I drove in, up the Elwha Valley past crests of bright and shadowed fir, the trees shoulder to shoulder running up near-vertical slopes, and from a distance as unvaried as the skin of a sponge. The forest seen this way has the texture of needlework, the nubbed knotting of yarn carefully wound. Closer, each tree takes on a silhouette and detail unique to its age, its position, its happenstance of soil and neighbor.

There are hot springs at Soleduck, and long ago they were co-opted by a resort of faux-alpine cabins, swimming pools, gift shops. Children ride bicycles up and down the paths, past groves of slim alders thick as grass and scattering light, and trees glorious and indifferent in their height.

My friend and I hiked up to Soleduck Falls early in the morning, along a path cobbled with small stones and hard, webby roots. All along the open edges of the forest, near the roads that end in trailheads, were blooming carpets of foxglove, tall pipes with hanging purple and white bells full of digitalis. The stream beside the path was clear as gin. Everywhere, a plethora of elk tracks, big and small, overran each other in the mud at the center of the narrow trail.

Soleduck, Queets on the southwestern corner of the Olympic Park, the forest right off the road into Mount Rainier National Park, and other places best kept to word of mouth—this is true old growth, as emblematic as the idealized forests of the textbooks. This forest has an interior, silent logic. It is easy to imagine, I think, reading the dismayed descriptions of the early settlers, that an old forest is so thick one can hardly pass between the trunks. There is a thick canopy, thick enough that little snow hits the ground, and the rain that condenses into new drops on the needles is called *throughfall*. (The elk gather here in winter, where it stays dry and the food is never hidden under a drift.) The light is green, the trunks rusty red, and I see colonnades near and far—neat rows of tall, indifferent trees. The air seems filtered through a curtain, and it flickers as though the curtain moved in the breeze. What seems like a rolling landscape of miniature hills and ravines is really the topography of decay: gentle streambeds rolling underneath the melting death of fallen logs, the disguised hump of root balls, piles of needles and leaf, middens and dens. It is dark, in the sense of shadows: it is dark enough that I need a flash on my camera. The unlit photographs are blurred and undescriptive, like those pictures people take of ghosts and flying saucers on the wing. There is something in the picture, something vague that could be interpreted in many ways: it could be real, barely seen, a flicker in the corner of the eye. In these big trees hung with lichen and moss there is always something falling: twigs, spores, seeds, a small drop of excrement or a leaf, chewed needles, bits of bark, a lost feather, a tuft of fur. It is called *litterfall*, this drifting haze in the air; between it and the light filtered from the green plants and the brown wood, the trees rise up as though from smoke.

The biggest trees, the giant Douglas firs and western hemlocks, are spaced in gentle patterns, just so, each with room enough and no more. They are immensely tall and at once relaxed: tall without effort. They make tall look easy, and I, looking up, feel vertigo at the spin and weave of their crowns. There are no branches on their lower trunks, and the biggest trees began to branch only a hundred feet in the air, in the forest heights where sunshine filters in. A young Douglas fir is a perfect Christmas tree, a little cone of green sharpening to a point, branches brushing the ground like brooms. But the big ones are shaped more like bottle brushes. When towns decide to have a great big municipal Christmas tree, they often cut a tall Douglas fir, and then someone spends a week or so on a scissor lift, fitting extra branches into holes drilled into its trunk, all the way around and all the way down, so that it looks like a Christmas tree after all.

There are only so many templates of design in the world, repeating in infinite variation—in pleasing, familiar profusion. Each template is here: crescent, disk, fan, chevron, the curl of wire and the shape of the heart, the cloud. Every texture, too: skin, bone, and fur; trees furry like animals to touch, like the velvet of an elk's rack. Each shape, each texture is pleasing in and of itself, and still the whole has the greatest power: the placement of variety together, similar, unique. I can think of nothing with quite the same flavor of animate perfection. The small templates blend into one large template called *forest*, a fundamental pattern. It is forest archetype, forest blueprint. The perfectly evolved organism.

A few miles in, at the falls themselves, the trees and shrubs and rocks are sparkling and wet. The river shoots down a cataract, all white foam and white noise and sun-shot droplets. Across the impossible, slippery log bridge I could see a small tent perched neatly above the rushing stream, dripping with spray.

From the ground, from my puny place, the trees are trunks, straight and true, whorled and gnarled and unmoving. The reason travel through this country is hard is not the standing trees but the fallen ones. Everything grows not only near everything else, but over, under, and through everything else. The ground is chaotic at first glance and orderly ever after, a mass of vine maples, oxalis, rhododendrons, and salal. Here is the ghostly trillium. Here are sword ferns five feet tall and devil's club, hidden in a bog with burning spines. There is the vanillaleaf—sometimes called sweet-after-death because its faint perfume isn't released until the leaves are dried—and berries and plate fungus and toadstools, mosses and lichens and ivy. All this fungus has work: decomposition, yes, but also food (truffles grow here) and the protection of healthy trees with distasteful toxins, the breakdown of trees by invasion, to make more, the fixing of nitrogen for the trees and flowers of the next generation. I look across the bumpy ground and see a topography of vegetation, a rolling, hilly horizon of entwined plant life. The northern forests, in fact, have more biomass—more dead and live weight, more organic material—than the tropical rain forests. They are oxygen machines. A single mature Douglas fir can have sixty million needles: A half-dozen of the hundreds of trees I can see in one glimpse here at Soleduck have more needles than this country has people.

In a mature forest, much of the bumpy ground is composed of logs. These fallen trees, which may take many decades to drop, last almost as long down as they did standing upright. They are called nurse logs, and they pass through distinct stages of decomposition and decay. New trees grow out of and over nurse logs, and centuries later, when the log has slouched into the ground under a blanket of moss and the roots of the now-mature standing trees embrace it, they form what is called a colonnade—a straight row of trees. (When the same kind of growth happens on a stump, the new trees form a circle.) But even the oldest log has integrity in this cool, wet climate. A fallen cedar was found with three mature firs, thought to be at least a thousand years old, growing completely around and over it. When a fire burned the healthy firs, the downed cedar was salvaged, too, and its heartwood was still solid. Perfect for violin stock.

An undisturbed forest is quite different east of the Cascades. There, in the cliffs and canyons and across the rocky hills grow thick stands of ponderosa pine, lodgepole pine, and Engelmann spruce. High on the east-side slopes of the mountains grow incense-cedar trees, the aromatic source for number-two pencils. The lodgepole is ubiquitous, a scaly, grey tree majestic in its arid height. The forest floor wet or dry is made of duff, organic matter decomposing into soil, but it's only east of the Cascades that the dry, dusty word sounds right. The ground beneath is packed and almost powdery with needles, bark, lichens, moss, and layers of twigs. The middens made by squirrels are easily found here, where moss and ferns don't cover the ground: heaps of red pine cone scales and neat, chewed cores at the bases of trees.

I was camping with my friend Carol in the Strawberry Mountains in eastern Oregon, up from the jewel of Strawberry Lake to the ridge above. We had a steep and wearing climb through thick pine forest, past a stream that diminishes from a waterfall to a trickle. When we left the trees for the meadows, the lake was a pan of blue among the trees far below; at the trail's edge, the land fell away and the air was a bubble around us. A falcon swooped below me, a sight so unexpected I almost lost my balance. I see a lot of hawks here, mostly the red-tails that sit on fence posts and electrical transformers by the freeway, dignified and taciturn. And I see a fair number of falcons, outside the city above the country roads. But I had never seen a falcon or hawk below me, rusty in the light with its wings and tail spread for a deadly glide.

At this height the forest breaks apart, fragments into clumps split by trickling snowmelt streams and moist meadows, steep dropoffs and snowbanks that linger into August. The trees turn to krummholz, a form called more sweetly elfinwood: The snow, winds, and cold of the timberline turn the conifers to stunted dwarves, about as high as the average snowfall. We camped in a huge subalpine meadow, at nearly eight thousand feet. We were in an intersection. On one side of our camp was a mushy puddle of moss thick with mosquitoes and flies, near the noisy, freezing stream. Falling slowly away below us was a wet meadow marked with clouds of early wildflowers and the recent tracks of black bear, which my dog sniffed with a kind of reverent terror. We pitched our tents just under the shadow of the ragged, low-growing old pines and their crumbling dead fellows. North, where the trail disappeared under a thick rippled bank of snow, was rough rock, where the last sun touched. All the ground I could see was covered with gopher cores, seemingly miles of the wormy trails. The pocket gophers here rarely leave the underground, coming out only to mate and when tossed out by the mother; a lucky hiker can watch an entire plant pulled down by its roots. But in late winter, when the snow is soft and the ground hard, they tunnel through the drifts, and as soon as the snow begins to melt and the ground starts to soften, they retreat back under, filling the tunnels of snow left behind with the dirt detritus of their new digging. When the snow finally melts, the core of dirt is dropped to the ground. They look like loops of yarn fallen from heaven, scattered across the land. When I finally reached down and disturbed one, the fine dirt crumbled at a touch.

It was hot in the sun, hot enough to strip and lie batting at the droning bugs, stinking of Cutter's and pockmarked with the rough sticks and pebbles of the ground. Carol, who is fearless, camps alone throughout the Northwest, hiking off trail and across miniature glaciers, sliding down hills and clambering up ledges to find a new, unbroken view. As we steamed in the nearby sun, she told me camping stories. A few years ago, she camped alone in a meadow like this one, somewhere on the slopes of the Three Sisters in the central Cascade Mountains. She had seen no other hiker all day, so after she made camp, she stripped and went swimming, washed her hair in the stream, and then lay down to sunbathe herself dry. When she went back to her tent, all was as it had been, except for a freshly picked bouquet of flowers at her door.

Every day had been hot and clear, and the drifts of dirty snow were pouring off the mountains in chilly, spreading brooks; night fell hard and sudden and black. I awoke in the middle of the night to stretch and look at the stars, which populate these skies so much more thickly than in Portland, where I live. (I think sometimes that the stars live in inverse proportion to people; wherever there are many people, you see few stars. Here, where there are few people, the sky glitters with light.) I climbed out of my tent in the cold and stood for a moment, completely disoriented. I couldn't see any stars; I couldn't see anything resembling the sky. In the few hours since I'd gone to sleep, a cloud bank had dropped upon us and pushed the temperature down by thirty degrees or more.

Carol decided to climb higher and swing around the ridge past two more small lakes. I left the ridge for Strawberry Lake below. A few stalwart campers remained, huddled around smoky campfires, dozing in the small domes of brightly colored camps around the dark lake shore. One man in a yellow slicker bent over a fishing pole. The only sun was a ruby glint on a peak higher than where I had been. A cold rain came right after I made a new camp, and turned all at once to wild hail pounding in the trees and bouncing off the glassy water, and then rain again, changing to snow. Snow falling on the Fourth of July. The boot prints of departed fishermen walked into the water, into the drenched shallows, and out again. The lake grew choppy and splattered with drops as the fog rolled past in torn shreds, crawling over the lake; the dogs began yapping, running back and forth on the shore, snapping at the wavelets as though they were mice. Above the ridge, the big, shadowed clouds moved so fast it was like watching time-lapse photography.

On the far side of Strawberry Lake—trout leaping for mosquitoes in the drizzle and landing, plop, nearby—I could see huge fallen trees, hundreds of years old by their rings. Their tangled root systems jutted out all around them like rays, awry in the air as though the tree had exploded from inside out. When they fell from the ridge, they had knocked down lesser trees and pulled them along, so the trail around the lake passed like a bridge through a battlefield, the jumble of past violence, and new growth. Several times I heard the rumble of invisible landslides, dull grumbling muffled by the trees.

I stayed on the flat, sandy bank, in the shelter of pines, and counted the flowers I'd found: shooting stars and dwarf lupine, windflower and elephant's head. There is always a lot of easy firewood to be found in such woods even in the rain, cones like tinder and tiny sticks ready to light. It was there for the taking, among the crisscrossing lines of crumbling logs, under the furry branches of saplings, fallen from dead trees landed haphazardly in the arms and crotches of living trees. I was gathering wood off a hillside and my dog sat down and began to scratch vigorously. His rear leg beat the packed, dry soil like a drum, rat-tat-tat. When I touched a match to the small sticks, they shot out flame as though they'd been soaked in kerosene, and then shriveled to coal in a few moments.

All day and all night I could hear the sounds of the trees, a voice separate from the plop of fish, the call of a crow, or the swishing sound of a snowy wind. It was mixed with creaks and snaps and pops like a woodpecker's rhythmic beat, thunks like the dull sound of an axe hitting a small log. Tock-tock, tock-tick-tock: the sound of standing dead trees bumping against the living, the stretch of a branch an inch closer to falling. After a few hours of walking around, I could identify the specific sounds of individual trees and spars, gauge the distance between that tree and my tent. It was never far enough. Alone by the lake, under a sky dim with thunderclouds, I sat by a hot fire, snowflakes hissing as they fell. I could see logs and platters of broken slate tumbled right to the water's edge, and could hear that constant, irregular talk, a most lonesome and familiar sound.

"Now the valley grows narrow, the mountains east and west chassez across and in among each other." So wrote a passenger in the late 1800s, riding north on a stage into the land where I was born. I'm fond of the phrase that the mountains move with gliding steps like dancing partners, intertwined. Scott Mountain in northern California has a road that does the same, twisting on hairpin turns without rails up and through a series of cutaway hills, coated with evergreen and early blooming redbud shrubs, wild mustard, and balsam root. In 1903, William Randolph Hearst built an estate here called Wyntoon, an opulent, many-gabled, garish home of stone blocks and a steep, sloping, wood-shingled roof. It remains a strange place in this athletic forest, a gloomy English castle in the Wild West, with hung tapestries and iron hooks and heavy oaken sideboards, cold stone floors and long tapers flickering in the shadows. There are times when I drive this road and meet no cars at all; once I met a single vehicle in fifty miles, and that was a hay truck swooning under its lopsided load and climbing at five miles an hour. A way farther on, I passed the summit, 5,401 feet, passed out of the Klamath National Forest and into the Shasta–Trinity, and passed the Pacific Crest Trail where it crosses on its journey from Mexico to Canada.

There is a broad turnout here at the peak, one of the only places in nearly a hundred miles of road where it is safe to park, and you can read a plaque about the old stage road, stretch your legs and shake off the vague nausea of the curves, and look back at where you've been. Wherever I turn I see Douglas fir, ponderosa pine, alder, cedar and spruce and dogwood and more in a single glance, the pastiche of trees that leaves silviculturists feeling a little prim. This is one of my most favored views, a prospect in the most old-fashioned sense of the word.

Among certain tribes, when a person moves, it is he who has changed, not the land; directions are derived from his orientation to a permanent landscape. The landscape before the white man's arrival changed very slowly, and the Indian lived in it in such a way that he or she could chart those ponderous changes generation by generation. They told time by floods and the movement of a stream course, the gradual giving way of a stand of sun-loving Douglas fir to the shady western hemlock, or the cycles of fish spawning or deer runs.

I was driven along this road a great many times as a child, sleepy from Dramamine; I watched the turns repeatedly unfold from the back seat of a big car winding up, then down a poorly graded track. The road was only partly paved, and then, as now, the road climbed and sank and crossed over creeks jumbled with logs and rocks. The sun drifted through the massed trees into scattered shade and shone on the grimy snow still there in May, and back by September. The bark of the huge ponderosa pines looked like skin, random ragged ovals stitched together with black lines. When a logging truck appeared, there would be a complicated, polite series of maneuvers, the car backing up and sliding aside to let the truck scrape by. Small rocks scattered on the road, to be thumbed wildly away like marbles by the car's wheels, tink-tink, clack. My father sometimes went this way at night in the middle of winter with his friend, the undertaker, to retrieve a body in the fat black hearse. Once, when we were off the mountain and nearly to my great-grandmother's house in Weaverville, he turned to my mother and said, "Well, the brakes got a little spongy there toward the bottom, but we're here."

A miner who lived here in 1852 spoke of "the pleasantest climate I ever was in," with long summers and bright falls and cascades of flowers and blooming trees. When I came down to Scott Mountain last April, I drove from Portland straight down the Interstate through the strong, muscular spring. All through Oregon, north to south, the color was so extravagant and generous it was almost embarrassing to see; it was like watching a particularly intimate kiss. There were flat-topped cherry trees blooming like pink palms, Scotch broom in thick masses as yellow as evening sun, and new wisteria hanging heavily like coral. The road was crisscrossed with the swooping shadows of red-tailed hawks, catching the drafts.

North of Salem are iris fields that bloom all spring; the dark, healthy swords march in stately mobs for acres, splitting around poles and barns and trees like water to meet and continue on the other side, crowding right up against the fence next to the freeway.

The Pacific dogwood has a floating display, abandoned sprays of cream-white leaves around a dark central flower. The blooms are radiant as though lit from underneath—bright, like fireflies swarming. I passed a stand of tall, knobby firs a half-mile away across a long flat field of early ryegrass, and in among the black-green shadows was a lone wild dogwood. Even at that distance, I could see distinct and single blossoms, the tree lit by sun against the shadowy firs.

On a clear day, around the New Year, the sun blossoms in a great glare. At least one day like this a year, with feathered, happy light, like elf light, lightweight, light light. All the fat is trimmed away: all the leaves and green, the growth, the aromas and moisture and heat. The bare framework is revealed: the bones of the world. I can see the architecture of the trees, every branch and twig, and every bud dormant until spring, haloed by floating light. I see the direction and currents of the wind, I see through the trees to the trees beyond, the house peaks, the hills. Nothing is shadowed; nothing makes a shadow. Everything is springy, porous, hard, like pumice.

A few months later, another day that comes every year, like a holiday: unexpected summer heat in March. And a few weeks later, a week, a week that comes every year—this one week when everything relaxes and the tension of winter slips from the twigs and dirt and the anxious infant leaves in a kind of ecstasy. Everything grows madly night and day, hurtling toward summer like a racehorse given its lead to run. This week, already, is the most wealthy week, a slightly drunken week, sexy and full of promise. Clouds are the bare dreams of clouds, enough to define the sky, the merest suggested possibility of clouds, and every morning lights up with the same soaring light.

This multilobed landscape, gentle and harsh by turns, has hold of me; here I stay, a free woman, unable to move. I feel the land with my eyes, with my sense of balance, with all the details of how a breeze picks up perfumes off a hillside, the way a cloud is caught on the needles of a pine tree and torn into mist, how wheat is grown in crescents along the slope of an ancient ash mound. I pass from granite to meadow to soggy bottom, out into latitude and back into a corner, and in the end I've traced a circle. I wonder sometimes at the *me* that never grew because I grew here and not somewhere else, the *me* that would have grown elsewhere in place of the self I became. A given landscape permits and prohibits how one perceives, what one is literally able to experience. I live here, in the middle of a city that is itself in the middle of a tamed land in the middle of a long-sought, long-lost wilderness, and I live here beyond the senses.

In spite of the prepossessing hills and the precipitous climbs and falls, the Klamath region of northern California and southern Oregon is defined primarily by the Klamath River and its tributaries. The dry land is directed by water. The Klamath, like the Rogue River in Oregon, runs in an unusual, almost defiant pattern. A river typically falls out of a high mountain across a plateau; the Klamath and other major rivers in these mountains leave the flat plateaus and interior valleys of southern Oregon and cross down—up—into mountain canyons before reaching the ocean. On the western side of the mountains, south of the thick, wet forests of the Umpqua Valley and the steep Siskiyou Pass in its cleft of rock is the Hornbrook Valley, the bowl where the little town of Hilt once sat.

A few years ago I passed what was left of Hilt, a small logging-company town just south of the Oregon border. I turned sharply off the freeway to the west, past the café and gas station at the exit, and descended all at once into a deep, wide valley below the Siskiyou range. The road wandered across a strange and empty lake of dirt, with scattered domestic trees near old house foundations, past a schoolyard with bleachers and a baseball diamond, but no school. When the logging company left, they took everything from houses to street signs to fire hydrants. I followed the bumpy road very slowly north, past the last rubble, past cattle and sheep massed against barbed-wire fences. I was in the basin of the mountains under curtains of fir and pine, under a sky blowing cold and grey. Not long after the road gave way to gravel, I turned a curve toward another herd of sheep, driving a few feet at a time. Just on the other side of a fence sat a mature golden eagle, its legs thick columns of muscle and feather. The eagle was perched on the skinned pink carcass of a lamb, talons hidden in the flesh. It gazed at me, the only car and the only person in the apparent world, from one eye, and then spread seven-foot wings and lifted away, rising without effort off the still corpse. The huge wings beat into the bleak sky and were gone.

The dry, spare slopes here fall like plumb lines to the blunt hollow below, kinked and folded and bare. The rough, dry Hornbrook is fossil-bearing country, shallow-water sandstone that once was under ocean. I drive up and down steep curving canyons, peering down the cliffs at the distant frothy water. One winter, I passed this way on one of the perfect frozen winter days of the Klamaths, common and exquisite. The entire seen world was bright, clear, and cold as ice. It was a bleak, lonesome, extraordinarily beautiful place—beautiful the way the moon is beautiful, or a comet come to ground, or the splatter of stones across an empty beach. The ground was stone-hard and the autumn's dead leaves were glued by frost to the earth; there was no green, and the repeated steep chasms coated with manzanita and thistle and rocks were as grey and blue as the sky. Highway 199, from Happy Camp over the Siskiyous, into Cave Junction in Oregon, isn't open in the winter. Snowfall in the valley is light and brief, but early in the fall and late into spring, the passes of the Siskiyous sink with snow. The cold comes in and strange things happen; blizzards in full sun, fogs so thick, a logger would say, you'd have to cut blocks and set them aside to get through. A while back, I drove south on a hot, sunny day, far too warm and late in the year for snow and ice. At the summit I hit a fog bank like hitting a pillow, and for about five hundred yards, every branch and twig on every flower, shrub, and tree was frosted silver-white. No snow, no ice, no frost on the rocks, just a ghostly painting of the plants as though a wind of glitter had blown through. On the other side of the fog, the valley was warm and moist and green.

Before the freeway crossed the Oregon–California border in 1964, there was only one reasonable road to Medford in the north. That was Highway 99, a narrow, two-lane ribbon winding out of Yreka through the precipitous canyons of the Shasta and Klamath rivers. My father sometimes drove me there in his blue Chevy pickup. The rattly truck gave nothing for comfort; it smelled of oil and cigarettes, and I bounced unbelted high above the grey road, leaning on the cool, bare metal of the door. He would point out the solitary miners' cabins, perched with what seemed incredible luck on little shelves of rock above the road. I traced the dusty line of mule tracks leading up, and up, and the leaning broken frames falling into the manzanita and rubble. Below, very near, shot the rocky canyon wall, littered here and there with the wreckage of cars that slid each year nearer and nearer the bottom. The river—the only water around—was a curled white lip of shallow rapids, running through a little flat of land.

Now most of the cars and log-stacked trucks crossing this way take the freeway, and they wind up and down the curves, too fast and too slow, wavering halfway out of control on the rapid descents. The miners' camps are almost impossible to spot, and you have to know where to look, what tiny, unnatural scabs in the empty cliffs to seek. On the freeway you never leave the canyon walls at all until the canyons come to a stop on the eastern edge of the Klamaths. And suddenly there are no more curves, and, like a viewpoint at the end of a long, long corridor, the freeway straightens for a stretch of several miles. There is Shasta. She is skirted by an alluvial plain, green with runoff and wavering streams bordered by cottonwood. I've seen the view that way all my life, countless times, traveling south down Interstate 5 through the Klamaths to Yreka and the rivers. After the canyons, there is suddenly nothing hard left in the world, only a vast green land lying soft and damp in Shasta's creamy lap. The bosomy mounds of Shasta's debris hover in the low gold light of afternoon, and around them cattle graze and crops grow.

THREE

In the air, anywhere in the Cascade chain, a clear day reveals a line of peaks like the plates on the back of a Triceratops. All the ridges are shadow and light, and one after the other after the other of the sharp, white peaks disappears into the distance. They are volcanoes, and by no means dead ones. All the early explorers noted everything from lava flows, explosions, and earthquakes to boiling smoke and ash falls. I can look at the string of white cones in the Cascades and see a hidden river of heat and animation underneath, thrusting up where the cones now lie, here, and here, and there. Most of them are still active, a fact we conveniently forget in order to live in their shadow, scramble their sides: Lassen, Shasta, Bachelor, Hood, St. Helens, Rainier, Baker. All have had recent eruptions, all steam and shake and vent their heat. The earth opens like a fist bursting out of a box. A small blink of an eye in geologic time, but we persist—even when St. Helens rips itself apart and Hood rocks and rolls—in believing that these mountains are benign.

The least mountainous of the Cascades is Crater Lake, reached on narrow, steep roads, behind other huffing, staggering cars. As soon as Crater Lake was officially discovered, the tourists began to show up and haven't stopped since. (The first white men to find the lake asked the local Indians about it, but none would admit to its existence; powerful spirits inhabited its waters, and the tribes avoided the site.) Sometimes parties camped near the lake itself, down a thousand-foot trail, and amused themselves rolling boulders off the paths, through the trees, to splash into the water. Others discussed pulling the water off for irrigation, before the national park surrounding the lake was created. Cars have replaced the earlier struggle up the steep and wooded mountainside on horseback, on foot, in wagons, in snowshoes and lace-up boots, but the lake seems to change not at all. People were said to cry at the sight. Frances Fuller Victor wrote that when she first saw Crater Lake, she felt it had been made by God for His own private view.

After the long, slow climb, the parking lot is a surprise—at first an anticlimax. Where's the lake? The lake is just beyond the rim, right there over a low rock wall scattered with begging chipmunks, right there and down: to the blue, a blue velvet and crystal at once, flat, unrippled, cradled, still, and huge. To the blue, round and jeweled, with a scalloped rim and a staid, unruffled surface. In the summer it looks like nothing has ever touched the water—not the wind, not a bird, not a single flake of snow. In the winter the water is as smooth as polished stone. The poet Walt Curtis points out that the water, of course, is utterly transparent, not blue; the blue comes from the water's absolute clarity: "When you look up, that same evanescence reflects back into your eyes from the azure sky. Water mirrors blue sky.... Lonesome blue planet earth. Fie on energy drillers and economic speculators!"

Crater Lake is 1,932 feet deep and nearly six miles across. It is the deepest lake in the United States. What we call Crater Lake is the seven-thousand-year-old caldera in Mount Mazama, a tall, many-peaked mountain thought to be twice the elevation of the lake rim. Standing on the rim is like staring into the middle of a mountain; it is as though I stood halfway up Mount Hood and pushed the top off, and could see to the other side along a flat cut. And not just because the circumference and diameters are similar—but because it would be such a fine thing if the inside of every mountain were a lake of velvet water. Mazama blew so big and far that its ash reached British Columbia, Alberta, Nevada, across Montana, Puget Sound, into a corner of Utah.

Crater Lake has had several names, none of them good enough, because it was discovered several times. Around the turn of the century, a man named J. W. Hillman wrote a reflective letter to the editor of a local paper, commenting on the recent discovery of a so-called Crater Lake:

"I can only imagine one lake in Oregon worthy of that name, and that lake I had the pleasure of discovering, away back early in the '50s—say about 1854, but I am not positive about the year—it might have been a year later, as I took no particular note of time while living in the excitement consequent upon a frontier life . . . after ascending a long, gentle ascent, we came upon the banks of a precipice and far below us was the bluest lake I ever saw. . . . Each one suggested a name, and it finally narrowed down to the selection of one of two names. Mysterious lake or Deep Blue lake, and I think the latter was what it was named. We wrote our names in pencil on a slip of paper, stuck a cleft stick in the ground and left it in its solitude."

Mysterious Lake. Deep Blue Lake. Lake Majesty. And now Crater Lake. What unimaginative souls we all must have. Why not Lake Sidereal, or Hallucination Lake? Here is a region with an Opie Dilldock Pass and a Donner und Blitzen River—towns called Twisp, Topsy, Sappho, and ZigZag—other lakes called Hawksy Walksy and Fifteencent. But no one could think of a better name than Crater Lake for such serendipity of rock and water. Why not Lake Implausible?

The Cascades are considered to stop one peak farther south, with Mount Lassen, a sputtering, rumbling pile of rock and fumarole and steam. Between Lassen and Shasta, the forests have given out, and everything is flat and dormant, waiting, and rising very slowly in green and brown hues toward Shasta as though the earth had to get a running start to climb that high. Castle Crags, a giant intrusion of rock nearby, is a bare, grey fairy tower in the green trees. Now and then in the lowlands might be seen a flock of dirty sheep or a cluster of white bee boxes, or a few cattle, heads down, browsing the short, thin grass. The empty, quiet land is dotted with hundreds of old ash mounds long covered with short grasses and settled into the earth. In the moonlight they turn a soft, wrinkled grey; they glow when they catch the light and they cast big, sooty shadows. The undulant stone walls scribbled along the hills seem to be coded messages; one expects them to form giant pictures or words, like the images made by the Nazca lines a continent below. There are no people, no movement, no lights, few cars passing through. Everything seems to lean toward Shasta, from the horizons on every side, working its way up—as though building up speed, getting ready. And then Shasta, white and robed, flies up from the blanket of earth.

Shasta is a monumental peak—two peaks, really, one larger and higher than the other—always snow-covered, heavy and broad-shouldered, without delicacy. Its silhouette is visible for hundreds of miles. The tallest reach, a softened curve on the north side, is 14,162 feet high, a few hundred arguable feet shorter than Rainier and Whitney. Beside it and below is a rough, toothed crater pointing at an angle to the southern sky, jagged like a bottle with its neck broken off. The winds are too hard, the blizzards too extreme, for reliable skiing. The biggest single snowstorm in United States history fell on Mount Shasta. From February 13 to 19, 1959, snow fell unceasingly, to a depth of almost sixteen feet. The first ski lodge built on Shasta collapsed from the weight of wet and logy snow.

"As lone as God, and white as a winter moon, Mount Shasta starts up sudden and solitary from the heart of the great black forests of Northern California," wrote Joaquin Miller. "The immigrant coming from the east beholds the snowy, solitary pillar from afar out on the arid sage-brush plains, and lifts his hands in silence as in answer to a sign. . . ." Mount Hood, he added, is a fine mountain—"a magnificent idol; is sufficient, if you do not see Shasta."

I'm tempted to define Shasta by other comparisons, by pointing out that Shasta is four times higher than the highest point in New York state, but it doesn't do. A reader familiar with Mount Marcy in New York would only think Shasta a very big Mount Marcy. That Shasta is not. It stands in isolation, and that is part of its charm and terror: You can see it from almost a hundred miles away, from Sacramento and Nevada, said the first settlers, from so many places and so many angles that it embeds itself upon every view. Where Mount Hood is almost airily pyramidal, and the Three Sisters sharp and thin, Shasta is inelegantly massive.

Shasta's debris still litters the fields around its base. Portions of the mountain were turned into the hundreds of miles of stone fences that wander the country here, most of them built by itinerant Portuguese sheepherders in the 1860s. The soil was hard to put a posthole into, and posts were hard to get at all in those days of mule trains; the fences, which seemed to be such romantic constructs to me as a child, were nothing more than an obvious way to clear the fields. A clump of grass to feed a cow could grow where there had been a rock, and so, a fence. The sinuous lines rarely mark fields or property lines; for the most part, the fences simply wander through the areas most laden with rock, unchanged in 130 years. No matter how many rocks were moved to walls, the fields grow more rocks—sharp-edged, hard, dark stones that rise endlessly from the ground every season. It is as though the fields themselves grow walls, and they have spread over time along courses logical to walls.

Shasta is the centerpiece of religions and cults ranging from the Lemurians who escaped the sinking Pacific continent of Mu to tall, one-eyed gods. All the flimflam about green snow and wandering white-robed women is easy enough to believe if you've lived near Shasta, if you've ever seen her topped with lenticular clouds. They ride the sky like dinner plates, clean around the edges and piled haphazardly on top of each other, perfectly parallel to the ground. Stacked up in an open sky, lenticular clouds are lovely, sharp-edged things, white with darker underbellies, sliding, bottom to top, through the mound. But when they stack up on Shasta, it is like nothing I've ever seen. It happened not long ago, on an otherwise clear, warm day. I could see one edge of Shasta's southern slope behind a hill as I drove south—white and bright with glare in the sun. But when I came around the curve, I could see she was capped with clouds from her waist up: not just flat saucers of cloud in a column, but saucers geometrically diminishing by levels to a point like a witch's hat. The effect was one of an almost mathematical precision.

Mount Hood is a symmetrical, steep white cone, and its eastern valley is carpeted in orchards so thick you can't tell row from row. The orchards are corridors of white and rosy head-high flower. They climb every surface of the valley bowl, up the slope of the mountain, and each tree is as pretty and perfect up close as the whole of it is from a distance. When the blossoms fall in spring, the carpet is a hovering cloud of pink and white, hanging in the slight breeze like fog. Everything is hydrated, sponged up and full of water, as though every leaf and blade of grass were saturated, shiny and wet. The bottoms are impenetrable vine maple and lupine, dogwood and alder.

The mountain, so fine above the drifting blossoms, is a dangerous place, partly because it is so invitingly easy to climb when all conditions ripen. Hood has year-round skiing, and year-round blizzards. Early in the 1900s, an almost frantic need to set records centered on Mount Hood. On July 9, 1936, a single group of 401 people climbed to the summit. A few guides climbed to the peak hundreds of times. Fireworks were set off on the peak on the Fourth of July, year after year, and one man carried a violin to the top in order to play "The Star-Spangled Banner." (Then he slipped and smashed his instrument.) A woman reached the peak wearing high heels. Five-year-old children and at least one gibbon, imported from Thailand, have climbed to Mount Hood's summit. A small group of climbers carried a bicycle up in pieces, put it together, rode back and forth on the highest ridges, and then took it apart and climbed down again. A couple who met on the summit were married there a year later, on July 9, 1928. The groom was waiting at the top when his bride arrived; they stayed on the peak for the rest of the summer. A man named Gary Leech made the 7,200-foot climb to the peak of the mountain from the village of Government Camp in just two and a half hours. Two people sleeping on the summit woke up in the morning and found the day's newspaper and a fresh bottle of milk waiting outside.

Mark Weygandt, one of the original turn-of-the-century climbing guides on Mount Hood, was struck by lightning on its summit. For decades no one tried to climb Hood in the winter; by the 1930s, people left for the summit on New Year's Eve, jostling to see who could get there first. And in long slides, down crevasses, under the weight of falling rocks, people died. A mule fell into a crevasse in 1922 and is thought to be buried in the Eliot Glacier, which may, very slowly, release it. Nineteen high school students roped together slid a long way down the south side to a moat filled with boulders; one thirteen-year-old died and the rest were badly hurt.

The contests are disappearing, the frolicky, record-setting fashion finished. The climbing club Mazamas now limits the size of groups and recommends that even climbers intending to hike only a few hours carry survival equipment for overnight stays, as well as remote radio locators.

I see Mount Hood day after day. It is visible in clear weather from almost every bridge and hillock in Portland, from the east-facing windows of every third-story room. Snatches of the white peak appear in the distance when I turn a corner; the whole mountain floats above clouds on the grey horizon. It's like a ghost out there, plain, stark, untouchable.

In May of 1986, a group of three adults and ten teenagers left Timberline Lodge in the middle of the night, for a day-long climb to the summit. The group included students at the Oregon Episcopal School of Portland, a teacher, the dean of students, and a guide. The Mount Hood climb was part of the school's curriculum, and was required for almost all students, with whom the program was popular. A day hike, a tough day's clamber up the mountain we all see out of the corner of our eyes, a climb so common around here as to be almost a ritual of local life. One of the OES students was a neighbor of ours, a cheerful, thoughtful fifteen-year-old named Tasha, the daughter of friends. She had recently begun babysitting for our own children.

Even now, after the exhaustive, ugly analyses required of insurance settlements and a protracted lawsuit, the events on the mountain are confused. They've turned vague, impossible to define. The fine blue May sky changed and then everything changed, and took away the world.

The spring weather had been less than ideal. Other climbers had canceled their summit trips based on weather reports that weekend. But it was May, after all, and the school year was almost over, and group after group had ascended the mountain all spring, day after day. So they left, carrying a few basic supplies, hoping to make the effort as much as the peak. And as the tired group descended, the weather shifted into storm, as it will do anywhere in the Cascades, any time of the year. Suddenly no one could see more than a few feet; suddenly everyone was cold, a few were hypothermic. One of the adults was acting irrationally, the students were shivering, directions—even up and down—disappeared.

The climbers weren't equipped for snow camping; they were too high, too cold, and couldn't descend. In the sudden wild winds and blinding snow, the group lost some of what equipment they carried. They dug a small snow cave, so small they had to lie in rows atop each other. The remaining backpacks and skis were left outside, and disappeared in the blizzard which blew all night.

All we knew was that the group hadn't returned—"hadn't come down," one would say here. But rescues are far more common than deaths on these mountains, so we watched the news, and our neighbors drove up to the ski lodge with the other parents, and everyone waited. The next morning, the guide, Ralph Summers, and a student, Molly Schula, summoned their strength and hiked down to the lodge in the fading storm, almost losing their way again. The snow had changed the shape of things.

Summers and Schula described the cave; parents, friends, dozens of rescuers, reporters, and medical help crammed into the lodge. They stood in knots, stamping frozen feet, watching the white slope rising into high clouds. Searchers went out, came back, flew over, flew back, tramped the land, and came back.

For three days, various rescue groups searched, using helicopters, dogs, heat probes. Late on the second day, three students were found dead, lying in the open in the snow as though napping in the afternoon's weak sun. Summers and Schula crossed the grossly transformed terrain, looking, looking, and could find only the general area where the cave had been. Searchers began to dig into the fresh snow with long poles, moving a few feet apart up and down the fresh snow drifts, moving with a maddeningly slow pace, step by step. I watched the news, I watched the mountain, I watched my children. Finally someone hit the tarpaulin that covered the entrance to the sealed cave, buried under four feet of fresh snow. And false, happy word came down from the mountain, to the crowd in the lodge: They were found. They were alive. A man fell to his knees in the snow outside and cried aloud.

Great confusion; great grief. Bodies chilled to stillness. Amazing, in the end, that two of the eight who'd stayed in the cave lived, that one of them lost only his legs. Tasha drifted away in that dark womb below the snow, inside the storm, sleeping, then dreaming. She slipped away with the clouds, so that all we see of Tasha now are the gossamer flickers of mist dancing around Mount Hood.

Well, people die on these mountains. The few who do are only a fraction of the number who climb, who set out for summits and reach summits, and spin in the air on top of the world. Nearly a hundred people have died on Mount Rainier and its lower slopes and boulders in less than a hundred years. Three men died together on a two-thousand-foot slide there just a few years ago. One summer, a man fell two hundred feet off Mount Jefferson and died. A few weeks later, three people were crossing Mazama Glacier on Mount Adams. One man slipped; his friend, Bonnie Bronson, tried to stop his tumble. They slid together down the glacier out of control, and disappeared into a crevasse in the ice while Bronson's husband watched. Bronson broke her neck and died. A man from Colorado died recently, the same way.

In September of 1989, another accident. A college friend of mine, Roberta Mohrholz, was climbing on Mount Thompson, near Snoqualmie Pass in northern Washington. Roberta had climbed Mount McKinley and Mount Aconcagua in Argentina, and many of the Cascades. She had always seemed powerful to me, strong and durable. Roberta and her companion, a less experienced climber, were attempting to cross Mount Thompson on an unorthodox and dangerous route. She found herself stuck on a ledge far more narrow than she had expected it to be, unable to climb to safety like her companion, unable to move forward, unable or too afraid to take a step backward. And then she fell. She simply fell, in full view of a hiker below, a thousand feet down and down with a huge boulder falling beside her. It was a twirling cartwheel through space, a dive from the peak down through the air like the dive of a hawk to the grass. She fell so far and landed with such force that her boot was found but not her foot; she spread herself across the mountain like a fall of snow.

The highest peak of the Cascades—called Tahoma by the natives and Mount Bunyan by the whites who remember—usually is called Mount Rainier. "After the weather," joked James Stevens, "which is rainier there than in any other part of the country." Rainier frequently has winter seasons with snowfall exceeding a thousand inches; it set the national record for a season's snowfall in the winter of 1971–72, with drifts 1,122 inches deep at the Paradise Ranger Station. A viewpoint sign on the south side of the mountain, where logging roads spread up the skin of the hills like mange, has graffiti at the bottom: WE HOPE YOU ENJOY THE SPECTACULAR CLEARCUTS.

From a distance, the mountain is all primary colors: clear, uncorroded blue sky; dark-green, shadowed hills; a white heap glowing in the sun and as unnatural a shape against the air as a barrow mound. It slides along the horizon, first east and then west, first near and then far, as though slipping along the ground. Mountain men used to call Rainier "Old He," in deference to its grand authority over its view.

In winter, the conifers are loaded with snow in horizontal plates resting on the branches. They are tall bodies, and they look only slightly like trees—more like a crowd of giants caught in a storm. Round rocks in the rivers draining off Rainier scatter in mobs along the bank; after a fresh fall, each rock is coated with a high hat of snow.

Paradise Inn is the highest stopping place other than a tent inside Mount Rainier National Park. Paradise is on the south slope of the mountain, beneath the meadows, which themselves lie below the tongue of the Nisqually Glacier. Rainier has twenty-three large glaciers, counting Nisqually. Almost all the glacial ice in the continental United States is in the Cascade Mountains. The Nisqually Glacier has, over the decades of white visitation, shrunk and expanded up and down its trough. It spawns the Nisqually River, which runs down a groove of the mountain, grey with rock flour. From Paradise Inn you see the looming crest of Rainier to the immediate north; forested slopes to the west and east; the distant, deep Nisqually Valley to the south; and, past the valley, the toothy, snow-coated wall of the Tatoosh range.

The trails above Paradise, leading up to the glacier, are mostly made of asphalt. Where there is no asphalt, the carefully delineated walkways are coated with gravel and bordered by rope. They are also nearly vertical, and the altitude gain is so fast and the vista so big that vertigo replaces breathlessness. Every effort is made by the rangers at Rainier to make an arrogant mountain accessible to an untutored and varied public. Thus the asphalt trails, which stay relatively dry and unmuddied, and the polite exhortations at every turn to watch one's self, one's faults. But even trained and conscientious visitors fail; every year on Mount Rainier, the most ardent summit climbers leave thousands of pounds of human waste at high altitudes. The air is never warm there, the ultraviolet rays strong, so the waste doesn't rapidly decompose; it builds up beside the common trails in small piles like stupas dedicated to human shortsightedness.

The mountain itself can be buried in dark clouds any time of the year. And on many days, the land below falls away emerald and juicy, and water runs in streams out of the snowpack lying carelessly around. In the middle of the summer, the meadows, which spread in waves away and away from the trails below the glaciers, are bedewed with lilies and asters, buttercup and Indian paintbrush, and a dozen other blossoms, each of them small and precise like a drip of van Gogh. Tall, slim, noble firs, which have the soft, thick shape of a snow-laden tree even when they are green and fresh in July, march singly and in small groves up from the meadows.

In my guide to the plankton of Puget Sound—a slim, breathlessly enthusiastic book called *The Fertile Fjord*—the author Richard Strickland makes a most startling comparison. He is trying to help the reader understand how small plankton are, and in doing so he uses Mount Rainier. He includes a chart of powers of ten, the middle of which goes like this: A herring is ten times bigger than the biggest plankton; a salmon is ten times bigger than a herring; an orca is ten times bigger than a salmon; and so on. Mount Rainier, he adds, is ten times bigger than the Tacoma Narrows Bridge and Puget Sound is ten times bigger than Mount Rainier. A startling image, I find: the bridge— a long, dull, traffic-ridden thing—piled up against Rainier's angled slope. Rainier stacked butt to butt across the basin of the Sound. Then Strickland says, "It would take about one trillion large phytoplankton cells, 100 micrometers across, to occupy the same volume as an average six-foot man. The same number of humans could be stacked into a cone the volume of Mount Rainier."

Glaciers such as Nisqually are always noisy to one degree or another—grinding, moving, melting, freezing, shifting beneath tiny human feet, hiding lethal holes. The glaciers feed the meadows and the dozens of plants specific to this niche. Water runs out of the snowpack and across the trail in tiny streams. Glaciers also support hoary marmots—a large mammal shaped somewhat like a beaver without the flat tail, which stands like a sentinel and silently surveys your approach— and sometimes shrieks in alarm. (Daniel Mathews reports that marmots, voracious and greedy in their brief summer awakening, have been known to eat car parts.) So much life abounds in the snow, in the puddles of snow disappearing. Snow worms, up to an inch long, live inside the snowbanks and are eaten by birds, which in turn eat the algae plants that grow in and lightly color the snow, algae that eat the droppings and lost pollen of birds.

Easy to think of wildflowers—perfectly shaped, small, low, and brightly colored, living in the harsh climate of the slopes—as being tough things. But they are as frail as coral or egg yolk. Moving a rock completely destroys the area on which it lies. Stepping on the plants kills them. One of the rangers here, a tan, cheerful man, explained the meadow program to me: "It only takes six people crossing a meadow once to kill it. We call it a social trail." He pointed behind me to the wall, to the aerial maps of the meadows that plainly show the shortcuts people take: "It takes decades to repair a meadow even a little, and that means grading, and draining, and hauling in topsoil to be dropped from an airplane. We plant seedlings we've raised in a greenhouse, and then finally cover them with jute mats to protect them until they get established."

"It's such a labor-intensive process," he added. "I watch people go over the ropes and walk right across the mats. I'm not accusing all climbers, but they can be some of the worst offenders. Just yesterday I saw one of the most disheartening things I've seen since I started working here. Two climbers were coming down from Camp Muir on skis and when the snow ran out, they just kept going, skiing across the meadows." I asked him what the rangers can do. "Oh, we can give people a fifty-dollar ticket for 'damaging a natural resource,' but it's rarely done."

"What do people tell you when you point out the signs and ask them to get back on the trail?"

He smiled, a rueful, frustrated smile: "Oh, all kinds of things. They tell me they walk on the meadows to take photographs, to pick flowers. Or because their kids want a handful of snow. Sometimes it's just because the trail has water on it and they don't want to get their shoes wet."

As I walked out of Paradise Inn one cloudy summer day, I saw a group of people suddenly turn, shade their eyes, and point; I thought they'd seen an accident, or a rearing bear. But when I turned to look, I saw that all at once the veil of grey had parted and the mountain in all its arrogant mass had appeared above the meadows with shocking proximity.

Once all these mountains were part of a great chain, a great mass: the ancient prevolcanic Cascades, the Sierra Nevada in eastern California, and the Klamaths. The Klamaths include old rocks, perhaps the oldest rocks in Oregon. Peaks, ridges, and cliffs are only the latest variation these particular rocks are taking; they've already been sedimentary layers, magma, sea bottom. The plates beneath kept moving, basin and range, and the mountains separated into three, and for a time in the Eocene epoch, the Klamaths may have been a true island, with seawater passing on the east.

The rocks spread out like a puddle, in arcs, everything crammed up by erosion and glaciers and various eruptions. They have been faulted and folded and twisted upon themselves again and again, smashed and reshaped and kneaded like dough until you can't see where one era begins and another ends. Otherwise dry writers get excitable about the Klamaths, which are described variously as "scrambled" and "challenging" and "a chaotic mess." David Rains Wallace, author of one of the only books ever written just about the Klamaths, says they "are more like an entire, heavy cake that has been dropped on a previous one, splattering it all over the table."

A curiously retarded violence, geology: plate subduction and collision, malleable ridges of rock rising on magma currents, crunching neighbors, rolling upside down. I can squint at a mountain here and see the wrinkles and shadowed ridges for what they really are, the beautiful ruin of the earth's blast—a littered, lovely wreckage.

But I also see Adams Lake. Out of Coffee Creek in the Shasta–Trinity Forest of the Klamaths, the gravel road climbs past active placer mines and heaps of tailings. The trail to Adams Lake is a fast, steep climb with a big drop-off and a payoff at the top—at four thousand feet, among tall red and white firs, is the lake. It's nothing special in this lake-speckled country, a mere acre in size, very deep, very cold, filled with trout. I spent two days there one summer lying on a piece of hot slate by the water. My companion—there was no one else around—climbed one of the high, dry buttes that encircle Adams and got lost for a while in the dry, clean air, lost in the firs-on-firs, the high, thin sky, the burlap weave of cliff and valley.

The Klamaths' bizarre geology supports an extraordinary profusion of plant life, with more species in more different habitats than may be found anywhere else today. The principal trees are Douglas fir, Port Orford cedar, sugar pine, tan oak, mountain and western hemlocks, canyon live oak, the giant chinkapin, Pacific madrone, California laurel, and they occur in unexpected, even unexplainable combinations. Some stands have twelve, fifteen, in one case even seventeen conifer species mingled together. It is probably the most diverse and complex conifer forest in the world, top-heavy with variety. (Conifer forests are almost always dominated by one or two species.) The forest—and it is one forest, in spite of the constant divisions—is filled with endemics, species such as the Port Orford cedar tree that flourish here and grow nowhere else; some are relicts, left over only in the Klamaths when they've been long extinct everywhere else. The understory is dominated by the beautiful manzanita, and butterweed, wild roses, false Solomon's seal, starflower, and dogbane.

The most immediate reason for what Wallace calls the Klamaths' "promiscuity" is the relief of the landscape, the precipitous ups and downs and drops and falls of the mountains. One slice after the other falls away, and between each is a great crevasse; in the crevasses are streams and rivers fed by the runoff of the multiple, wrinkled cliffs, above overhangs and crumbling chunks of granite waiting for a winter fall. There are fires here every summer, some of them lingering and all of them sharp sculptors of the forest; every fire burns out some species, bypasses others, and creates a new schedule for succession in the forest. Flora from the north overlap flora from the south here, and the huge variety of rocks, the various soils, the abundance of minerals make so many soils that almost anything could grow *somewhere* in the Klamaths if the weather was right. And in a lot of parts of the Klamaths the weather is right; this island of mountains is filled with independent weather systems—warm and cold, dry and moist, windy and sheltered; there are south-facing cliffs that bake in the summer and freeze in the winter and keep almost no rain, and small draws that drip with dew all summer long and stay green and snowless all winter.

A fair amount of the soil of the Klamaths is the oddball dirt that derives from peridotite and serpentine rocks, which wind under, over, and through the complex faults and folds of the mountains. All along the roads of the Klamaths are views of serpentine. Half a hill might be covered in thick stands of green Douglas fir and ponderosa pine, and half, as though fenced against the forest, is bare, orange ground, with scattered, tired-looking trees. The casual viewer might assume she is seeing an old fire zone, an old logging area. (I always did.) But there's no slash, no ghostly grey trunks left by fire, no stumps. There is only an oval of coarse and reddened soil with a few trees clinging to it.

Serpentine, writes one geologist, is "a strange, greasy-looking rock that comes in various shades of green and may be soft enough to carve with a knife." Serpentine's slipperiness and its shalelike character make for frequent landslides. Its rocks are marked with slickenside, the scratches left on soft rocks by earth movements underground. Photosynthesis requires calcium, but serpentine soils are calcium poor. A great many species can't grow in such soil. In this moist and dewy climate, the reaction of plants of all kinds to these soils is that of the desert: The species are different and fewer, and they grow shorter and tougher and more slowly. The wood is sometimes tinged purple. Side by side in the Klamaths are stands of plants radically different from each other because one grows in serpentine soil and the other in more common soils. Because serpentine may intrude in the center of another kind of rock, there are even islands of plants—cat's-ears, pussytoes, daisies, and aster—radically different from all that surrounds them. Each is a specific variety not found in ordinary soils, not quite like the daisy or aster you would expect to find.

Because the plants grow more slowly and tend to be smaller, the serpentine regions are more open, and hotter. They are also drier in the long run since the openness leads to more evaporation, and there are fewer roots to retain groundwater. The exposed rocks hold sunlight, and the cycle feeds itself: Beginning as a wet desert, the serpentine region becomes a drier one, and then even fewer species can grow in it than before.

The Jeffrey pine is the totemic serpentine species. It is long evolved to calcium scarcity and direct sunlight. *Pinus jeffreyi* closely resembles the ponderosa pine; it is a tall, slender tree with bluish-green needles in clumps of threes. The rangers call it "gentle Jeffrey" because, unlike the ponderosa, you can stroke the Jeffrey's cones without pricking your fingers. The nicest thing about the Jeffrey pine is its odor, always noted, never agreed upon; if you crush the bark or twigs, they release a pungent perfume of lemon—or violets—or pineapple—or vanilla—or is it apples? The whole of the range seems the landed world of an old idea, this wild, rough, enduring forest. There is intelligence here, in this small, strange, heavily textured place; every rock, every canyon, every turn leads to something else.

Our summer cabin was in the center of the Klamaths, deep in the canyon of the Scott River, below the canyons of the Klamath River, fed by the myriad streams running off the ridges above.

Meals at the cabin were rarely more elaborate than corn chips and soda, with one exception. When Grandpa Doc was with us, he went fishing every morning before dawn.

One story told about fish around here concerns Captain the Honourable John Gordon, who sailed into the Columbia on the HMS *America* in September of 1845 to defend British territory—for about the last time. Perhaps he was a better sailor than fisherman, and perhaps he saw the future more clearly than his superiors, but Gordon declined to engage in battles either diplomatic or military. Instead, he returned to England and told his superiors that Oregon wasn't worth the struggle after all, because the salmon in the Columbia wouldn't rise to the fly.

But who needed flies back then? Everything from salmon and sturgeon to flounder, trout, crabs and lobsters, oysters, and cod were swarming in these waters, grown big and incautious. David Douglas took part in a sturgeon feast involving one fish more than ten feet long; the salmon sometimes weighed a hundred pounds each. They ran in the thousands and hundreds of thousands and when they spawned, up the rivers from the Pacific and up the streams from the rivers, they ran in the millions and tens of millions. Phoebe Judson spoke of "salmon time" in Puget Sound: "The bay was all aglitter and agleam with the shining beauties that were constantly springing from the waters in every direction, their silvery sides sparkling in the sunlight." The Clatsop tribe on the Columbia filled their huts with salmon, the way the Karuks hung lamprey eels to dry from every window and beam and tent pole, shoving them aside all winter long like beaded curtains. The Clatsop huts, wrote Frances Victor, had "salmon everywhere—on the fire, on the walls, overhead, dripping grease and smelling villainously, are salmon—nothing but salmon."

When miners first came here, they told of clouds of fish, rushing froth from the mad mating battles, horses that wouldn't cross but reared and bolted from the huge fish swarming the banks and biting at the horses' hooves. Even in the middle of this century, when we paddled through the water, they darted away by the dozens at the edge of our sight.

Grandpa was a very tall and slender man and utterly bald; he carried himself with an insouciant confidence and stood holding a high-ball in my parents' living room the same way he stood hip-deep in waders, holding a pole—always with the same loose strength. He cast for trout with flies he tied himself, and now and then my brother Bruce and I would rise early enough to scramble down to the riverbank with him, all alone and chilly in the bare light. He tried to get me to fish these rivers, though the fact that I was a girl didn't encourage him. I was never able to bait a hook without a flinch, and flinching annoyed him. He was a dentist, and he fixed our teeth in his dark, cold office on Saturdays, without an assistant and with no one else around; I began to flinch near him soon after my first visit.

We sat on rocks above and behind him, away from his long, sinewy casts, and watched the white line flicker out across the water, the float bobbing in the current until it sank all at once, taut. Then he would give the pole a few shakes, nothing more, and lean slightly back in his boots and reel in the fish. He silently measured the fingerlings against his big hand and tossed back the ones too young to keep.

I was hardly ever up that early, and I loved those rare, tender mornings. Mist rose off the soft surface of the river in tiny clouds, and a fish would leap, plop, gone. The rising sun shot hard, bright beams straight down the canyon east to west, bleeding in a muscular heat.

Grandpa never spoke. He swung his long arm over his head, swish, and flew his line like an arrow to the water.

My mother melted butter in a big cast-iron frying pan, and I washed the fish and handed them to Daddy to dry; sleepy Daddy smoked and gutted each one over a bucket with one slice of a knife. They were fried whole and eaten whole, without a fork; we would hold the transparent, lacy tail delicately in one hand and the fish's head in the other, careful of the teeth. The black eyes, stone-clear before cooking, turning milky white in the heat; Grandpa popped them out of his fish and ate them one by one. I nibbled all the flesh away like eating kernels off a corncob, from one end to the other and back, sitting outside on the porch in the early day, listening to the musical ratchet of the jays entreating their mates. And always the whispery voice of the river. If we were all quiet at once, we could hear the splash of another fish jumping, looking for flies.

There are few species in these rivers, compared to other fishing rivers; the cold winter temperatures give way to hot summer temperatures, the currents are rough, the ride is hard, and the fall from plateau, up to mountain, and down again takes its toll on fish. Almost all the fish in the rivers are anadromous, spawners—salmon and trout and sturgeon. But they ran: just like in the more northern waters, at Willamette, Celilo, Cascades, The Dalles. The Karuks who lived at Forks of Salmon and a dozen lesser falls stood on the rocks and caught the fish and eels by gill net and by hand, caught them by the hundreds.

Mining, road construction, dams, and logging have combined over the years against the fish—dams more than anything. The dams of the Snake and Columbia do not accommodate fish. The salmon and steelhead runs on the Trinity River south of the Klamath River dropped ninety percent in twenty years, after the Lewiston dam was built to divert water for irrigation in the Central Valley of California. Thanks to dams, the coho salmon run on the Snake River is now considered extinct. Many other runs in the region are endangered. Chinook are starting to return to the Klamath and its tributaries now, thanks to a joint project of the California Department of Fish and Game and the Karuk Indians. There are rearing ponds and the young fish are released throughout the system; they will eventually return, like all anadromous fish, to the place they were released—if they can get there.

"No one is allowed to fish in either the Klamath or the Salmon before the Salmon smoke," wrote Mary Arnold at the turn of the century. "When the night of the Salmon smoke is due to arrive, an old salmon is caught and brought up to the flat above the river. All the next day it burns over a slow fire. One of the old Indians tends the fire and guards the salmon. He must have fasted five days before the ceremonies commence. While the fire burns and the salmon smoke rises in the air, the Kot-e-meen and Pich-pichi Indians go into a large tent and sit there all day. That is, all the men. I think no women are allowed in the tent. The flap of the tent is carefully closed, for if anyone sees the smoke or catches a salmon in the river before the old salmon is entirely consumed, that person will not survive the year.

"His horse will slip on the trail and he and his horse will fall down the mountain and be crushed on the rocks below, or his boat will miss the landing and he will go over the Great Falls and be drowned, or a rattlesnake will get him, or he will be shot by an irate neighbor. Anyhow, something unpleasant will happen to him."

One afternoon when I was about ten years old, my brother and I were diving in the center of the river across from our beach. There was always a channel there, about fifteen feet deep, and the water had a green cast from the bloom of algae and the silt tossed up by the eddying currents. I was diving with a mask to the bottom when I found a rock as tall as me, resting at the base of the channel; the rock had a hollow in it, and in the hollow was a fish. Here was a fish bigger than any I'd seen—no trout for breakfast, not even a small salmon like the ones we sometimes had for supper, but a fish longer than my outstretched arms and as wide as my own young body, hovering half in and half out of a miniature cave and staring right into my eyes. A salmon about to spawn is corpulent, inflated, strange with the truck of breeding. A spawner has given up on a fish's ordinary worries and lies listless, preoccupied, anticipating his last brief, radiant season. This fish hovered that way, but there was nothing moribund about him. He simply didn't care about me at all. It was many years before I began to wonder if I'd been looking at one of the last of the large sturgeon in the Klamath system, a fish so big it would seem to burst these rocky, narrow streams.

I screamed for Bruce, lounging on the sand: Come see! We treaded water and talked, and decided, with a certain solid courage, to catch that fish for ourselves.

We didn't have rods, and I don't think we would have known quite what to do with them anyway. What we had, for some reason, was a rope, and while I hung over the sunken rock to keep the fish in sight, my brother swam back to fetch it. He was less fearless than I then, though we've long since traded places in the matter of nerve; I knew the onus of capture would be on me. He tied a knot to make a lariat and tossed it out.

The day was, like all those days, clear and hot and steady and still, smelling of clean water and green trees. I bobbed in the river with the current flowing around me slowly, flicking my feet now and then to stay in one place, and held the rough hemp in my hands. The rope trailed across the surface to Bruce, who sat on the beach with his heels dug in and the rope held tight in both his hands.

I took a deep breath and dove, down under where the bubbles rose one by one and sound thickened like a porridge in my ears. It was cold, and I sank down until I was face to face with a fish as big as myself. I was stung with a sharp sorrow, all alone with Most Sacred Old Man, King Fish, Salmon Spirit. He had probably taken and torn a dozen hard hooked flies in his time. I clung to his age and potency and grieved that I had to kill him: "O Supernatural Ones, O Swimmers," sang the Kwakiutl when they began to net the muscled salmon each season, "I beg you to protect me, Swimmer."

I couldn't possibly have caught such a thing, of course, but I didn't know that then; holding one long, long breath, I kicked closer, lariat at the ready, and he hung in the rock hole, waiting; I kicked even closer, with a final shiver of fear at last curling up my spine, and it wasn't until I brushed my hand against his scaly cheek that he shook his tail and was gone in one flicker, gone in the gold-green water for good.

When I was fourteen, I took my best friend Karen to the cabin with me. We planned to swim, sun, and sprawl on the couch in the cool upstairs, reading magazines. We opened the cabin and filled the pail and changed to our suits, then skipped down the path to find the boulders had moved. When Mary Arnold watched a winter storm come in, near the turn of the century, she wondered at the flood to come: "Big water, everyone said. This winter, big water." The winter I turned fourteen had been another winter of Big Water. The beach was narrowed, darker, the curve of whitewater just below a little closer. It was all a bit less hospitable, a bit less welcoming. We stared and mourned as we stood. We jumped from the rock to the sand, for the jumping of it, but nothing was ever the same.

So the heaviest pieces shift. My grandfather—who was not really my grandfather, but my grandmother's third husband and no relative at all—grew a brain tumor. Karen moved away. That fall, without warning or notice, Grandpa sold the cabin to a couple from Los Angeles as a vacation home. He sold it complete: with couches, silver pail, magazines, iron beds, trunks, and the folding Japanese screen. My grandmother rescued one frying pan and has never returned.

Mary Arnold wrote her book about the Rivers more than fifty years after she left, never to return. The moments captured there stayed clean and clear like bubbles in a fading sun. She remembered a hot summer evening when her best friend Mabel, like my friend Karen, sat with her on their cabin porch and watched the moon come up. An Indian friend, Les, taciturn and melancholy, arrived with his drum: "He sat against the house in the bright moonlight with his legs straight out in front of him. We could see the bald mountain back of the house quite clearly. For a time there was no sound but the beat of the drum, and then we heard the bark of a fox. The house and the fence and the garden and beyond them the dark outline of the chaparral stood out very sharp and clear in the moonlight, while above us towered the mountain." After a time, Les stopped drumming, thinking he had heard a step nearby. He wondered if a witch tracked him like the fox, and he left without a word, to buy a spell, pay for a prayer.

I stopped by the cabin in spring for the first time in nineteen years. I think I understand Mary Arnold's reluctance to make that final record. She knew there was no need to rush the Rivers into words; she knew that through the floods, the Rivers last.

In many miles there were no cars, only a single logging truck crossing the bridge by Kelsey Creek while I threw rocks into the water, and a single forest ranger riding a mower across the little square of grass by his station. It was a hot, yellow day, the river was low from a dry winter, the great humped stretches of basalt warm from the sun and smelling of mud and fish. I took my time getting to the cabin, but when I did, the crunch of last fall's oak leaves and scent of sugar pine and ivy were exactly what I desired, exactly as I wished. The cabin was closed up, like all these summer cabins are in spring; it's one reason I came to see it then and not later. I was worried a witch would track me through the trees.

Instead I found that the cabin was newly painted picnic red and had grown very small, like a doll's house—so small I don't know how it ever could have contained us. The brave, precarious deck was gone. The river was startlingly near, the bank had gone gentle and the water soft and slow. All alone there, with nothing to fear and no etiquette to preserve, I felt myself a trespasser and tiptoed away back up the driveway, to the road.

FOUR

There was so much gold scattered through the soil of the Northwest that it clung in tinsel to the roots of plants; there was so much gold in eastern Oregon, stones the size of plums rolled along the creeks; there was so much gold in the veins in central Idaho you could dig for months and still not find the end. People found gold when they stopped by a stream for a drink, or dug a posthole, or dowsed for water. A man named Orlo Steel sank a well on his property and it ran with gold; he panned his own drinking water and made a profit.

Driving Northwest back roads now, it's hard to imagine the chaos of the gold rush. (Although certain fresh clear-cuts put it in mind.) We call them gold miners, but the miners weren't looking for gold; they had no poetic appreciation for its dull malleability, for its various al-chemical virtues. They were mining money. If they'd thought they could sell it, they would have hauled hundred-pound bags of dirt and sacks of mud out of the hills; for all the damage they did, they might as well have done just that.

There are dozens of stories of treasure waiting to be found: lost mines, veins uncovered one day and buried by rock in a flood the next, caches of nuggets and gemstones hidden in the wilderness and never found. Thieves were said to have confessed on their deathbeds, giving directions to their squirreled wealth, but no one could ever find it; one member of a group of miners hid everyone's nuggets for safekeeping and then dropped dead without saying where. Whole streams were lost in floods—creeks where people claimed they'd seen emeralds, opals, rubies, and even diamonds lying on the bottom.

Towns and cities often grew haphazardly, bent around the strikes and claims and the roads used to haul the gold from the creek to the stores. Deeds were less than specific: They referred to " 'a fence post 100 feet to the north' or 'a dead tree on the bank of the creek.' "

There were mines and whole towns here in the most unlikely and bizarre turns of the canyon, shacks of seedy splendor perched where humans had perhaps never walked before, hung on the thin lips of cliffs and over gorges, soaking wet in the swamps, dangling over the draws. Streams were diverted, flumes built, massive pipes laid to demolish ancient terraces of prehistoric streams with water and wash the soil and gravel and sand down to fill the streambeds until it could be panned. "The force of the water is wonderful," wrote Albert Richardson in his travel adventure, *Beyond the Mississippi*, published in 1867. "The proprietor assured me that with these three little pipes he could cut down and wash away a section of hill twenty feet long, twenty wide and two hundred high, in twelve hours . . . the great hill melting to liquid and passing away through a wooden trough! It showed the miraculous power of water in changing the surface of the earth." Miles of soil were lost, hundreds of millions of cubic yards of gravel shook from the hillsides. The silt flowed down into the creek beds like snow, and the eroded, logged out, water-blasted hills shook and fell into the canyons. Miners spoke of having "turned the river."

"The trout turned on their sides and died," wrote Joaquin Miller, the self-styled itinerant poet. The Indians would come and silently watch the miners, he added, for hours, finally shrugging their shoulders and stalking away. Miller wondered, too, at these thousands of men wasting their health and youth in cold ravines for years. "Why we should tear up the earth, toil like gnomes from sun-up to sun-down, rain or sun, destroy the forests and pollute the rivers, was to them more than a mystery—it was a terror. I believe they accepted it as a curse, the work of evil spirits. . . . For my own part, I would abolish gold and silver, as a commercial medium, from the face of the earth."

During the gold rush, fires were set by the hundreds from neglected campfires, but more often on purpose: to destroy another man's claim, to clear trails, to drive game. Merry miners are said to have set slopes ablaze for recreation, to watch the forests burn through the night while they drank and danced.

National forests are still readily mined; all that is required is proof that an "ordinarily prudent man" would see fit to invest in a particular site. Such proof followed by active mining is sufficient for a patent, a deed of permanent, irrevocable ownership—deeds that sprinkle the forests here, even in the most remote and wild places. In 1948, a company applied for patents on twenty-three old lode claims in the Siskiyou Mountains north of the Klamath; the U.S. Forest Service protested and the company won the patents in court in 1954. In the next thirteen years, the company cut and sold a very profitable 6.5 million board feet of virgin timber on its mineral claim.

The Rogues were a collection of Indian tribes including the Takelma, the Dakubetedes, the Tututni, the Taltushtuntude, and others lumped together by the early explorers as a band of "rascals" intent on preventing white settlement. They roamed the upper Siskiyou forests, the banks of the Rogue and other rivers, from the lower summits to the rough coast. Rarely has a more determinedly genocidal campaign been waged in the United States than the one against the Rogues.

The first explorers, Hudson's Bay Company men such as Peter Ogden and the botanist David Douglas, liked the Rogue tribes; they found the tribes "kind and hospitable in the extreme," wrote Douglas. Then, in 1828, Jedediah Smith made the first overland trip from California with seventeen other men. They camped near the Umpqua and were attacked; fourteen whites died.

In 1846, one of the amendments to the Organic Laws of Oregon—which gave settlers the right to squat on land unclaimed by white men—

included this admonition: "The utmost good faith shall always be observed towards the Indians; their lands and property shall never be taken from them without consent." Such decency—the least of decencies of a conquering people—was almost never practiced; the best land was the land most likely to have been used by Indians in the first place. The settlers let hogs loose, and the hogs dug up the camas bulbs that the Indians ate, and they plowed under the grass the Indians used for seeds; some settlers even fenced in the already-cultivated patches of potatoes the Rogues raised, and they shot Indians who attempted to harvest their own crop. Said one man of another, "He shot Indians as he ate his dinner, plainly as a mere matter of course."

In 1849, a band of warriors attacked a party of miners in the Siskiyous and stole several pouches of gold dust. A large party led by Joe Lane treated with the Indians, and a considerable amount of stolen property was returned, including the pouches. But they were empty; the Rogues had no use for the yellow powder inside and had poured it into a stream. The army reacted by sending in Major Phil Kearny, who killed more than fifty Rogue men and captured thirty women and children.

From that time on, one depredation against the Indians followed another. Every response of the Indians—even calm ones—only brought them greater destruction. Peace conferences turned to slaughter, sleeping villages to abattoirs.

A dinner was held the night of July 25, 1852, public and festive, designed to honor the heroic efforts of the previous week. A man named J. W. Davenport offered a toast to the gathering:

> May your generous acts on this occasion, be honored throughout this Valley; may its emblematical influence excite the independence of our Union, and may you live to see the time when the Indians of Rogue River are extinct.

In 1853, miners captured several Indians in the woods, including a headman, and hung the chief with only a few terse comments; the others were released with their hands bound behind their backs and were shot as they ran away. Hanging was a favorite punishment for an Indian's being Indian. A group of miners brought a seven-year-old Indian boy to Jacksonville, Oregon, that summer; the boy was mobbed and hung.

For all that Joaquin Miller was a master of the half-truth, the stories he relates are so close to other truths, other events, that they have a certain veracity all their own. In his description of a winter mining gold on the Klamath, he writes of the small creeks freezing until the snow was deep and food scarce. The Indians, displaced from their riverbank villages, deprived of their stock food of deer and salmon, were starving. A group of miners—motivated, said Miller, by a story of connivery almost metaphorical in its falsehood—marched upon the hungry villagers, intent on ridding the river of the last of the "treacherous savages":

"Old squaws came out—bang! bang! bang! shot after shot, and they were pierced and fell, or turned to run. The whites, yelling, howling, screaming, were now among the lodges, shooting down at arm's length man, woman, or child. Some attempted the river, I should say, for I afterward saw streams of blood upon the ice, but not one escaped; nor was a hand raised in defense. . . . As we came up a man named 'Shon'— at least, that was all the name I knew for him—held up a baby by the leg, a naked, bony little thing, which he had dragged from under a lodge—held it up with one hand, and with the other blew its head to pieces with his pistol.

"I must stop here to say that this man Shon soon left camp, and was afterward hung by the Vigilance Committee near Lewiston, Idaho Territory; that he whined for his life like a puppy, and he died like a coward as he was. I chronicle this fact with a feeling of delight."

An Indian-hunter named Ben Wright was obsessed especially by the Modocs, but he was finally killed by Rogues: "He hated redmen and made 'good Indians' of them at every opportunity. Or, in the vernacular of the pioneer: 'sunned their moccasins.'" Wright collected noses and fingers from the people he killed and hung them like trophies. He was a dandy with long black curls like General Custer's locks, ringlets falling below his collar, a square, neat goatee. He made a grand feast of peace with Modoc leaders once, planning to poison them. When the Indians refused to eat until the white men did, he stood calmly, shot the leader point-blank, and dropped to the ground; at the signal of his shot, his friends hidden in the darkness killed all the remaining Indians. He returned to Yreka waving scalps, claiming to have been ambushed and to have won a great battle by dint of will and courage; "Captain Wright boasted on his return that he had made a *permanent* treaty with at least a thousand Indians."

Years later, Wright tried to ambush a peaceful meeting of Rogues the same way he had massacred the Modocs. He was found out and killed; some historians say the Rogues roasted his heart.

The Rogues, scattered in desperate bands in the mountains, began killing settlers in return. The settlers killed whole villages of Indians. On October 8, 1855, white settlers attacked a group of Rogues; they fired the huts and shot the Rogues as they ran outside. Eight men and fifteen women and children died. This was the final outrage. A band led by Te-cum-ton, called John by whites, responded the next day, pillaging the valley, burning every house, and ultimately killing eighteen white men, women, and children. Te-cum-ton refused to surrender, in spite of bloody retaliation, in spite of the fact that the population of Rogues had fallen from about eleven hundred three years earlier to only a few hundred now.

"You are a great chief," Te-cum-ton told an army colonel sent to treat with him. "So am I. This is my country. I was in it when these large trees were very small, not higher than my head. My heart is sick with fighting, but I want to live in my country. If the white people are willing I will go back to Deer Creek and live among them as I used to do; they can visit my camp, and I will visit theirs; but I will not lay down my arms and go with you on the reserve. I will fight. Goodby."

The last free Rogues, hungry, sickened by grief, almost without leaders, were captured in the summer of 1856. As punishment for their long resistance, they were forced to walk hundreds of miles to the new Grande Ronde Reservation in eastern Oregon, far from their land.

Te-cum-ton and his son were sent to the Presidio in San Francisco, accused of inciting the Indians, and began what would become a long tradition of imprisoning Indians on Alcatraz Island for resisting the momentum of the Oregon expansion.

The Rogues did eventually have a treaty—if one can truly speak of treating with prisoners. They received $60,000 for the remaining 2,180,000 acres of their land. (Almost four million acres had already been taken.) Included in the treaty was a payback of $15,000 to be given to the white settlers for Indian-caused damage to property that had belonged to the Indians in the first place.

The Rogues, along with a number of other bitterly reduced tribes, eventually moved to the Siletz Reservation, a huge place on the southern Oregon coast encompassing 1.3 million acres and stretching for 125 miles. But first a stretch here and there was taken, and then another—one small parcel was removed in order to build Oregon's first resort hotel, the Ocean House, in 1865. Within forty years of the establishment of the Siletz, it was reduced to 47,000 acres, but no matter—by then only a few hundred Indians remained.

The Northwest in which I was raised was almost wholly white. Its place names betray a curious preoccupation with other races; alongside such blank pioneer titles as Bull Shit Springs and Dog Turd Mountain are numerous Dead Indian roads and Dead Indian valleys and streams and hills. Near Waldport in Oregon is a Darky Creek; in the Siskiyou range is a peak long known as Nigger Ben Mountain. (The name was changed to Negro Ben in 1964.) Ridges with black basalt tops were called "niggerheads." The tribes, once the entire population, melted away into rarity. "The white race are to the red as sun to snow," wrote Frances Fuller Victor. Where there had been no whites, there was little else, and even now, as the percentage of Hispanic and Asian people in the Northwest's population creeps slowly upward, white it remains.

Blacks could be counted—and were, for a time—on the fingers of a few hands. In the entire century between 1870 and 1970, the number of black people in Oregon increased from .38 percent of the population to 1.26 percent; twenty years later, in 1990, blacks made up 1.6 percent of Oregon's people. It is a very slow wave. In Washington, 2.5 percent of the population is black; in Idaho, less than half of one percent are black—four thousand rare individuals, as common now as the slaves and free blacks of the Territory more than a hundred years ago.

The first black person I ever met was a slim young woman who lived up the street from our house when I was nine years old. She was the wife of an Air Force pilot stationed in the backwater base several miles away. They were, I believe, at that time the only black family in town, yet I never heard a whisper of notice. She kept a clean and precise little house surrounded by flowers, and she gave me piano lessons. I was impressed with the wall-to-wall carpeting, a luxury my own mother had not been able to afford, and the neat, oiled spinet in the living room. She taught me the simple abridged classical melodies my former teacher had insisted I learn, but after a few weeks of lessons, she announced a change. I remember her now as a lovely woman framed by careful black waves of hair, always cautiously dressed and courteous of bearing, and I remember the pleasant confusion when she introduced me to boogie-woogie. I found it very hard at first, the odd rhythm and off-center beat bouncing wildly from hand to hand. I used a funny little book with tunes called "Cowboy Boogie," and "Ice Cream Boogie." A black boogie man shaped like quarter notes danced on every page, pointing out the title. We spent a year together, one afternoon a week, and then they were transferred away and disappeared. Then there were only the Indians, the Karuks whom I hardly thought of as Indians at all and certainly not as exotics, and no one to teach me a crosswise left-hand beat.

Here in the Klamath region, the big and varied Klamath with its menu of climates, its valleys and palisades, lived the Karuks, the Yuroks, the various bands of Umpquas and Shastas, the Modocs, the Chilula and the Wintun, the Whilkut, Nongatl, and Wailaki; the Chastacosta, Achumawis, and other tribes lumped in as Rogues; the Konomihu, the

Okwanuchu, and Tolowas; the Takelma lived here, but only one survived to 1910; the Chimariko, long extinct, and Dakubetede and Tututni were here, and the Hupa, and up north—around the lake where the Klamath River rises and there are marshes full of tule and cattail and the Indian manna, *woca*—lived the Klamaths, also called Lutuamin, who called themselves the *Eukshikni Maklaks*, the People of the Lake. Some of these tribes, such as the Hupa and Yuroks and Karuks, were so culturally similar and lived so near to each other they seemed to be bands of one group, yet they spoke completely different languages. There were so many tribes that the Karuks believed the Great Spirit invented a new language whenever he camped for the night.

From the time of earliest contact, traders and trappers had noted differences among Indian tribes—variations of physiognomy, coloring, height. Theories to explain the many "nations" so distinct as to seem like different races ranged from the effect of weather and diet to the influence of latitude. On one point, though, almost all the early explorers agreed: The Indians of the coastal forests and valleys were far less appealing than the Indians of the Plains. Fishing cultures were generally considered inferior to the hunting cultures, the former feminine in its torpor, the latter masculine in its need. The Indians themselves were thought to be ugly, unkempt, fat, and lazy, and had little reason to spend their days stalking beaver hides for trade and trinkets. The lifestyle of the coast Indians lacked a certain Christian stress.

In the *Illustrated History of the State of Oregon*, H. K. Hines blamed environment for what he considered the disgusting condition of the Willamette Valley tribes. They lived "a life in the canoe instead of on horseback, and a living of fat, oily fish instead of alert and sinewy game. Hence they were short of stature; heavy and broad and fat of body; indolent and sluggish in movement; without alertness or perception of mind; indolent and inactive in all their habits; sleeping away nearly all but the little time that was requisite for them to throw their barbed harpoon into the shining side of the salmon that swam on the shoals and sands of the rivers and bays along which they thus droned away their meaningless life, and the few additional moments required to boil or roast it sufficiently to gratify their uncultured appetite." But such characteristics weren't all negative: Such gullible, well-fed creatures were also thought to be far more disposed to training, "more pliant and tractable." "I do not know any part of North America where the Natives could be civilized and instructed in morality and Religion at such a moderate expense and with so much facility as on the Banks of the Columbia River," wrote George Simpson.

Traders were driven to distraction by such tribes, apparently uninterested in money, unwilling to consider a distant future. "In affairs of trade," wrote one historian, "the natives impressed traders as being actively perverse," and that "two things about the natives especially warmed the trader's heart—his furs and his absence, particularly the latter." They were uncertain guides, inefficient beaver hunters, perfectly content to trade salmon for tobacco and smoke themselves into a giggly stupor. A historian dismissed the Indians of the Northwest in one sentence: "They are all savages; and they do not figure in the history of the country, over the destinies of which they have not exerted, and probably never will exert, any influence."

The Indians stumped the trappers with their lack of drive, but it was more than that. A life like that of the Karuks—a life of gambling and storytelling, broken only by deer and salmon ritual and medicine-making—was a life of sin, by virtue of its ease. How could such sloths and lotus-eaters go unpunished by a Calvinist God? The fur men and the miners—men called "people of the worst character, run-aways from Jails, and outcasts from Society"—were still subject to the puritan sensibilities of their society. It was right and correct to strive for a living, to go hungry if you were lazy and triumph if—and only if—triumph was earned by hard work.

The coast Indians behaved not so much incorrectly by white standards, but by the white concept of Indian standards gained from contact with the nomadic tribes. The contempt with which traders met the coast tribes, wrote Lewis Saum, was "not because they had wandered away from a *pastoral* or *agrarian* life, but rather because they had departed from what [was] considered a properly *Indian* existence." The tormenting flaws of the Plains Indians—aggression, bitter wars, a hostile territoriality—became virtues when the traders were confronted with tribes that seemed both tranquil and fatalistic.

The simple, solid Karuks lived in a small area, along the banks of the Klamath from the Seiad Valley down to Witchpec, most of them in the several dozen miles between Somes Bar and Happy Camp. The Karuk oriented themselves around the river, which ran like a winding thread through the center of the world, naming four directions: *karuk*, upriver; *yuruk*, downriver; *maruk*, away from the river uphill; and *saruk*, away from the river downhill.

The Karuks had little of the worldly ceremonial of the North Coast tribes such as the Haida and Kwakiutl, no lean, horseback grace. Their slightly more northern neighbors, the tribes of Upper Klamath Lake, lived in cold open country, surrounded by golden aspens and huge flocks of geese. Those tribes made petroglyphs—painted, pecked, and scraped into the volcanic rock. They drew people on horseback, chevrons, concentric circles, suns, birds in flight, feathers and lightning, lines like ocean waves where there was no ocean, lizards and fish bones, targets and huge murals. The banks of Klamath Lake are still scarred with these crosshatched, curvilinear stories. But not the Karuks: They were just fishermen and gamblers, smelling of eel, leaning on a tree beside the river, half-naked and pitch-tough. They lived almost in anarchy, with no chief, making good baskets but almost no pottery, their tools nothing more than an awl, a spoon, a special curved bone for crushing lice.

They lived in villages along the rivers, hunters and gatherers of fish and acorns. The Karuk people and their neighbors were great fishers of salmon, using weirs, gill nets made from the tough fibrous leaves of wild iris, dragnets, platforms, and bone-point harpoons. One single family might dry a ton of salmon in a year. Every family had a fishing hole, but one person could rent another's fishing hole for a percentage of catch.

They caught lampreys, haggy eellike fish with mouths that open like funnels and are lined with circles of horny teeth. At maturity it may be two and a half feet long but weigh only about two pounds.

Lampreys lived—and still live—in the Klamath and its neighbors by the fecund thousands, beside the occasional old-man sturgeon (the neighboring Hupa made glue from sturgeon heads) and the eulachon, an ugly fish with a large mouth and short fins and funny-looking stripes on its gills. *Eulachon* is a Chinook word for a fish commonly called the candlefish; it is so fat and dripping with oil that it can be dried and used as a lantern wick. The Karuks chewed milkweed, ate honey and larvae for treats, made jam and tea and a poultice for poison oak from manzanita, and cultivated almost no crop but tobacco.

Karuk women wove ceremonial clothes of shredded maple bark and basket hats for everyday wear. They sometimes cut hair by burning it with pitch. The men trained hunting dogs for the ritual stalking of deer and hibernating bear. Deer were sometimes caught by hanging a decoy deer head from a tree and catching the investigating deer in a noose hung from the tree. Deer were thought to be born again after they were eaten, to run back up the steep hillsides and mature until they were ready to be killed again. The Karuks shot ducks and grouse and quail with bow and arrow. But there was a strict kind of kosher here, too: They never ate frogs, gophers, wolf, fox, moles, bats, eagles, snakes, caterpillars, grasshoppers, dogs, vultures, blue jays, meadowlarks, wildcat, or fresh salmon and bear at the same time, and they never killed a coyote. Like so many tribes, the Karuks were great lovers of Coyote tales.

All the peoples of the Klamath were gamblers, addicted to guessing games and tests of skill like wrestling and darts, and they made bets of every kind. They were known to bet their mates, their children, their boats and fishing holes. The search for clearly defined material wealth, the bettering of another in a game, the careful apportioning of financial blame and obligation filled the days that were empty of the eternal search for food and shelter that dogged the Plains Indians all the day.

All wrongs could be exactly valued, even murder. "From what they tell us, killing people in this country is very expensive," wrote Mary Arnold of the Karuk system of debt. "You have to pay twenty-five dollars just for shooting at someone. If you hit him, it costs you fifty dollars. And if you are unfortunate enough to kill him, his relatives demand one hundred dollars." Though the Karuk people lived in small communities, all crimes were committed against individuals. There was no community crime, no community punishment. If you offended a taboo, then you would have bad luck or death; that fact was so obvious that no other punishment was needed. If you offended another person, you had a debt to pay, and if you didn't pay the debt, your creditor could kill you. Though it would cancel the immediate debt, murder wasn't a desirable end; it would only start a feud involving one's whole family. These debt feuds were the closest the Karuks got to war and could be ended only by the final settling of the debt by the survivors.

All wrongs, even indirect and accidental ones, had to be financially compensated. In the early days of white settlement, such compensation still took the form of deerskins or baskets, woodpecker scalps or obsidian blades. The Karuks used the common native currency of dentalia, hung in strings and measured against the tattoos every man had on his forearm for a ruler. A. L. Kroeber wrote that killing a man was worth fifteen strings of "money"; making a woman pregnant cost two or three strings; buying a boat was worth only two strings "of not very good shells." Later, as Mary Arnold found, cash became preeminent. Money was kept to show wealth, which conferred the only real status. Wealth was good, thrift was good, laziness and showing off were bad. Once wealthy, it was easy to stay wealthy, since the same wrong committed against a wealthy man cost more money than when committed against the poor. Once poor, it was hard to get rich. Debt slavery was practiced, sometimes through the proxy of one's child, and occasionally a person entered voluntary slavery for the simple sake of room and board.

Though there was no taboo against premarital sex, children born out of wedlock were a debt, and a bastard was someone "not paid for." Wives had to be bought, too; if the husband couldn't pay the marriage price, he could go "half-married" to his father-in-law and work off the debt. Divorce by either party created a complex divvying up of debts and credits, one partner to the other.

The Karuks were medicine-makers; medicine and debt were like twin poles of the world's magic. There were formulas for success in fishing and hunting, for love, for hate and revenge, for ease in childbirth, to grow hair, to stay young, to prevent or cure sexual problems or mistakes, to curse others and to be protected against curses and against witches. The latter were called *apruruwan*. Pains of all kinds were thought to be tangible objects pointed at both ends, short, colored black or red. An *apruruwan* might buy pains from other tribes, and might even be a doctor, sending pains into people so that she can make money by calling the pains back. Like everything else, formulas and medicines were bought and sold. Medicines, in fact, were thought not to work unless they were paid for; the universe was an encircling world of value. A small tribe of Indians, inventing money in the rainy woods and then counting every single thing in it and giving it a price: They kept neat oral lists of equivalence and discount. They ran their happy anarchic cornucopia as though it were a giant mall.

Essie, one of Mary Arnold and Mabel Reed's best friends among the Karuks, insisted on teaching the two unmarried women a love charm, an heirloom from her family worth a large sum of money. "I would have you know that this is not a plain, ordinary love song," wrote Arnold, "but a true love charm, and it is warranted to bring down any gentleman we have set our hearts on, no matter how great his disinclination. All either of us has to do is sing him this song and drop a few grains of dirt from a special ant hill in his coffee, and the deed is done. Very valuable knowledge, Essie considers it, for unprovided-for young ladies like ourselves."

The earliest white men to live in the Pacific Northwest now and then deserted their companions. A trapper would suddenly decide that the Indians, those well-fed, lazy, West Coast Indians, had the right idea, and would go to live with them. Some never returned. For the Karuks and their neighboring tribes around Mount Shasta, Joaquin Miller envisioned an idyll like the idyll dreamed of by the wandering trappers. It was "no less a project than the establishment of a sort of Indian Republic... a confederacy under the name of the United Tribes... a reservation in its fullest and most original sense." There no white men would enter without permission, and no Indian would leave; inside that bounteous, dramatic landscape, every need could be met: shelter, food, beauty, history, family. They would not be given money and nothing would be taken from them; they would simply be left alone, "to adopt civilization by degrees and as they saw fit. . . ." It was not to be.

So the Karuks, who still number three thousand in an area of eight thousand square miles, are making repairs on a shifting world. The Karuks were confused in the stream of time, and no wonder—they lived in a young mountain range among very old rocks, on the banks of a river cutting through backward.

FIVE

Boise is like the land; people who came here had big hopes, and big plans. In the varied lands surrounding Boise, you can move in a few short miles through the broad wheat plains, past isolated houses huddled behind cottonwood windbreaks, past barns and giant silver silos, seed companies, and tractors with columns of dust rising from under their big wheels like smoke. North of Boise are dry, steep canyons that break open into tree-covered hills, shallow quick streams that spread into marshes before they squeeze down other canyons. Meadows, hills, wheat, dust, trees, meadows: One seems to lead inevitably to another. I drive along the winding, steep, two-lane highways too fast, past the FROST HEAVES signs, my van leaning precariously in the curves, up and down until I reach another lumbering RV, another slow trailer too wide to pass.

People say mean things about Boise, and Idaho. (The poet Linda McAndrew calls it Idahohum.) One of my favorite postcards shows two men driving in a car with two shaggy dogs in the back seat. The caption is "Idaho Double-Date." People have always said mean things about Idaho, crawling over the hot, dusty southern basin and leaning ever forward, to the farther West. "In the raw new land of South Idaho it was shove and scrape, and if you had bad luck or lost your strength you were done for." So wrote Nancy Stringfellow, who is now eighty, of her childhood in Twin Falls, Idaho, "where the wind blows down like the hounds of hell."

Idaho was late settled, late to be a territory, a state, still an orphan of the West. In 1858, a travel writer, apparently serious, wrote, "Idaho is no chimera of the brain—*no terra incognita, no ignuus fatuus*—but an established fact." (Much later, after an extended visit to Idaho Territory, the same writer added: "Should we ever encounter an enemy, and his punishment be left to our decision, the sentence will be: 'Go, ride a fat, lazy, hard-trotting horse to Boise, and be forgiven.' ")

Teddy Roosevelt liked to hunt in the varied wilderness of Idaho. He was that kind of man who is eminently logical to himself, and almost incomprehensible to me: the hunter who loves the virgin wilderness and the kill at once, who in fact connects the two. If Mr. Roosevelt had been my passenger one night near Fossil, Oregon, when I drove past two perfect fawns standing like statues in the road, he would have wanted me to stop and collect them. Roosevelt once had a piece of great good luck on a hunting trip in the northern mountains in 1888. He was able to catch a water-shrew, "a rare little beast," he wrote in his memoir of the trip. "I instantly pounced and slew it; for I knew a friend in the Smithsonian at Washington who would have coveted it greatly." He skinned the animal and laid the treasure aside, while the night darkened and his Indian guide—"He was a good Indian, as Indians go," wrote Roosevelt—prepared the meal. In the process, the guide accidentally threw the skin on the fire and that was the end of the rare little shrew.

Because it is stuck between the open land of Washington and Oregon and the Continental Divide of the Rockies, Idaho gets left out. Is it Rocky Mountain country? Perhaps. Is it the Northwest? Perhaps. Is it anything, but Idaho?

The Northwest would be another kingdom—isolated, anarchic, raising itself up like a wolf child in the wilderness. The West's anarchy is another terra incognita; unfound, unexplored. It has a dual nature, murky, a vague combination of conservative and radical, pride and backwoods shame that would be more interesting if it were more examined. The Pacific Northwest is provincial and progressive in the same breath, conformist, regressive, excessively tolerant and intolerant by turns. It walks the conservative line and then elects a Democrat. We have a history of escape.

Not long ago, petitions for a new state circulated from Sandpoint, Idaho, through Spokane in eastern Washington and Coeur d'Alene in northern Idaho. The call was for a movement to form Columbia, the fifty-first state—the Wilderness State—out of eastern Washington, western Montana, and part of Idaho. Columbia's state animal would be, of course, the grizzly bear.

Secession isn't usually thought of as a tradition, but it is here—at least, attempts at seceding variously from the states and the Union itself have gone on since the first settlers came. It is Frederick Jackson Turner's fear come to life: The West breeds independence, and the Far West a kind of defiance.

In 1852, there was a bill to form a state of Shasta from what is now northern California and southern Oregon, out of anger at high taxes and poor mail service; the bill died in committee. In 1853, there was a call for the same area to form the state of Klamath; in 1854 and 1855, for the area to form the state of Jackson. In 1854, a group of men determined to prevent southern Oregon from joining the antislavery Union made a secession attempt; later, northern California was added to Oregon for the same purpose and a constitutional convention was called in 1857. In 1861, a secret society for secession, the Knights of the Golden Circle, was formed, and all through the 1860s there was talk of forming the Pacific Republic of Western States. The first mention of the state of Jefferson was in the 1890s. In 1908, eastern Washington and northern Idaho tried to form the state of Lincoln. Again in 1909 came an attempt to create the state of Siskiyou from the same northern California and southern Oregon area; and again in 1935 and 1940. In both 1915 and 1978, there were attempts to form a second California, called Alta California, from the sparsely populated, geographically defiant northern section.

In 1941, the Yreka Chamber of Commerce passed a resolution calling for a forty-ninth state to be formed from parts of northern

California and southern Oregon from roughly the fortieth to the forty-fourth parallel. A Proclamation of Independence was announced on November 27, 1941, declaring that regular and repeated secessions from the Union would occur every Thursday "until further notice." Cars were stopped on the main road through, Highway 99, and drivers were given informational pamphlets. A governor was elected, a flag was sewn, and rallies were held, complete with all-girl Drum and Bugle Corps. The momentum was high and mounting; it took the Japanese at Pearl Harbor to divert attention.

In places like Boise you can stop for a cup of coffee almost anywhere, even in a gun shop. I crossed the wide, empty Boise streets, the short buildings so far apart that whole chunks of sun seemed to fall between them, to a gun shop for breakfast, remembering the sporting-goods store on the main street of my hometown. The four high walls are covered with taxidermy, examples of size and prowess cut off at the neck: a moose, a buck with rack as wide as a park bench, a snarling, frozen bear. The center of the store is a U-shaped soda fountain, and around it, any time of the day, sit men—young and old, wearing cowboy hats and baseball caps, eating pastrami and tuna fish. If I can't find my father at the Elks Club, or the fire hall, or standing behind the counter at the hardware store, I know he'll be at Dan's Sporting Goods.

My companion at Moon's Cafe in Boise was a handsome, diffident man named Rick Ardinger, a Pittsburgh boy who dreamed of coming west. Rick found Pocatello, in eastern Idaho, then tried Albuquerque, and in 1977 moved back to Idaho City, a small town outside Boise where he feels permanently, and happily, settled. He has red hair, a bushy red beard, wire-rim glasses. Rick is a letterpress printer and, with his wife Rosemary, owner of Limberlost Press, one of the breed of small presses in the Northwest turning out handcrafted editions of poetry, journals, pioneer diaries. The evening before, Rick and Rosemary had hosted the poet Robert Creeley for a reading. It is Rick who gave me a copy of Nancy Stringfellow's memoir, a small, paperbound book he had set by hand, each copy bound singly, by hand. Nancy brought the love of serious reading to Boise in the form of a store called The Book Shop. She and her husband built a house that, her daughter Rosalie Sorrels writes, "looks like a bower and everywhere you put your foot a cloud of fragrance envelops you. The whole place seems to have grown from the ground."

We sat at a tiny table in the back, eating good, cheap food, and watched a succession of taciturn men examine shotguns and pistols. Hunting season was soon to start, and I could see boxes of ammunition pushed across the counter; a heavy-bellied man in a baseball cap sighted along a rifle toward the picture window at the far end of the narrow shop. We talked about the West's confusion, its adolescent ruminations on itself. "What is true for the West, is all most true in Idaho," Rick said, dipping into scrambled eggs. I could hear the murmur of men nearby, sipping good hot coffee, taking time. Idaho is isolated, Rick continued, running north and south the long way, split like a shingle by the Bitterroot Mountains. It is unclaimed, not quite set apart, but apart: Idaho is an orphan.

Idaho has a disproportion of millionaires; its conservatism and relative isolation seem to cushion the wealthy person seeking privacy and a big backyard. In 1980, Idaho had more millionaires per capita than any other state.

J. R. Simplot is one of the country's richest men, owner of one of the largest privately owned corporations in the world. His company employs ninety-five hundred people. Simplot sells McDonald's more than half its french fries. He is a symbol of Boise, and Idaho, not necessarily loved. When I was last in Boise, I stayed in a turn-of-the-century hotel in the center of downtown. Out my window I could see the western sky, a distant rivercourse, and a tall building right across the street, with big glass windows and a concrete sign as big as a small car: SIMPLOT.

J. R. Simplot is eighty-two now; he's lived in Idaho since he was a child. Simplot is a big, slow, sturdy man with a big, bald, freckled head. His voice has the drawl of a backcountry man, blunt and unpoetic.

We met in his thirteenth-floor office, the windowed walls open to the short, squat city below. The valley beyond was spacious and light, dry, speckled with trees following the winding course of the Boise River, up to the base of the soft, khaki-colored hills rising into the sun.

"I never wanted to live anywhere else—I know a good place when I find it. It's been good to me. And God, I've seen it come a long way. I started out with horses and farming, you know, and I know what you can get done with a couple or three teams of horses. I was a young fellow, didn't go to school, and I got to trading pigs and horses—I was a pretty good horse trader. Hogs got awful cheap, they got so cheap nobody wanted them. So my Dad and I built this hog pen and I bought six, seven hundred head of hogs, bought them for a dollar apiece, big ones, little ones. People just went out of the hog business, that's all. Anyway, I fed those hogs and in the spring I got a hot hog market. I sold those hogs and I got about seven hundred dollars, and I bought a hundred and twenty acres and went farming, and I was on my way.

"Then I started growing potatoes. They've really been good to me. The old boy I rented my farm from, he was alcoholic. And one day he and I bought this electric potato sorter, fifty-fifty. I beefed it up quite a bit and started sorting potatoes, my own and then I started sorting the neighbors', and I had a hell of a crew. It was the first electric sorter in the county. Well, he got drunk one day and he said, 'Jack, I think it's time to put it up.' Well, anyway, we got in a little argument, and I said, 'Hell, there's only one way to solve this thing, let's flip to see who owns this sorter.' So he pulled a dollar out of his pocket and threw it up in the air and I called it. And that put me in the potato business."

Boise looks prosperous and lucky and clean from Mr. Simplot's window; it has that charm of plenty, like the dark fields of potatoes on the outskirts: winding rows dug in the soft dirt and filled with thousands of ovaline russets and yellow finns and whites shiny in the afternoon sun. Simplot sat behind an enormous desk made from a single polished burl, rocked back and forth, laid his heavy, thick hands on the tabletop: "I got so big in the potato business I quit farming. In the thirties I built me some thirty warehouses, clear into Oregon. By 1940 I was probably the biggest shipper in Idaho. I got into dehydration, and that turned out to be the key to the whole thing, because I happened to have the only dryer when the war come on. They got a colonel out here and he said, 'You're going to go to work for Uncle Sam. You're gonna dry potatoes for him.' And I did, and I got big in the potato-drying business. And that led into the fertilizer business, and that led into the lumber business. Then, of course, we found out we could freeze french-fried potatoes, and that's just gotten bigger by the day.

"There was opportunities back then. What really made me was the fertilizer business, and then I got into the mining business. We came from nothing! Nobody used fertilizer when I started. I convinced myself by doing it. I got people to put phosphate on their hay, and that's the way we built the business. Well, honey, I've got some good mines. It's new money—you dig it out of the ground and sell it, it's all new money. And the farming business is the same way.

"I never went back to school. That's my whole thing. When we hire people we screen them, and we want the tops. If you walked in here today and said you only had gotten through the eighth grade, why, I don't think any of my people would even talk to you."

The company takes the leftover parts of the potato and mixes it with grain to feed cattle. Simplot also uses potato leavings to make ethanol, and the waste water from potato processing for irrigation. The cattle manure goes into methane production, and the company makes its own fertilizer from phosphate from its own mines. The potato muck left over from the ethanol is used to make food for tilapia fish, which are primarily turned into fillets for frozen dinners; the waste water from the tilapia tanks is run in to feed hyacinths, which pull the nitrogen out of the water and freshen it, to be fed back into the fish tanks. The hyacinths are fed to the cattle; the leavings from the fish-processing plant are mixed with the potato sludge and fed back to the fish. Now Simplot is moving into robotic fast-food cookers and computer chips.

"Did you ever go down to California? It's all plugged up and costs are awesome. And we got water. We're going to be providing all the power for the Southwest. I know, I'm in it. We've got the coal! We've got the water! You've just got to bring the coal to the water. We're growing, we're growing, this whole country is growing. And we're letting in a million or so people every year. Now, I know we've got a lot of Mexicans working for us, and I don't know if we could get along without them or not. But you start letting them in by the millions and pretty soon we're going to be in the same boat as they are."

His company is slowly moving into Honduras, Turkey, Poland, Germany: He wants to teach the potato-eating Poles how to grow potatoes the Simplot way; he calls it the New Frontier. He wants to build coal-fired power plants along the Snake River: "The future's not ours to see, but I see democracy is making the most progress in the world. It's going to change everything. Look at the military budget—it's awesome. Get rid of that and start putting it into our society. I can see what we can do with this system. We can build a utopia. We've got everything. I tell you, I think we're just getting started." The Simplot Company has a mandatory retirement age of sixty-five, without negotiation. Except for the boss. J. R. is still president and won't consider stepping down: "If I'd been working for the other guy, I'd have had to quit a long time ago! But I'm not. I'm working for me." He has been a horse-rider, skier, scuba diver all these years, and finally a bad hip has slowed him down: "I haven't had a sick day in my life; in all these years I haven't even had a pain! Nothing! It's hard to believe—but I can buy a part for this hip and get it fixed, and I'm gonna, next month."

We stood by the windows above the town, suspended in silence. Solid stone and brick buildings together on the floor of the valley, near the water, out of the winds, lit by sunshine; already the glass was beginning to reflect the fading light in tiny glints and squares. On a small coffee table surrounded by armchairs was a large, polished piece of jasper pulled from one of Simplot's mines; it was the size of a football.

"I like to see things grow. You've gotta have progress; that's what's built America. The marketplace is the best mousetrap." He points to the east, swings his meaty hands in an arc along the soft brown hills walling in the valley: "I bought all this land here. We've got lots of land, I'm a land-buyer and I just keep buying ranches. I've got the most beautiful cattle ranches you've ever seen, and I don't mean just one or two of them. They don't make a lot of money, but someday. Do you see that place up there? Someday my grandkids or my great-grandkids are gonna think that old sonuvabitch was pretty smart."

He lives on sixty acres of unnaturally green grass on the undulant khaki hills east of Boise; the thirty-by-fifty-five-foot American flag flying above his house used to flap and crackle so loudly in the night winds that his neighbors complained it kept them awake nights. He raised the flagpole to 150 feet, and now the flag snaps so high and bright the sound flies down the valley and is gone.

Suddenly he turns to me: "Well, how about you? You got a family?"

"Married, with three kids."

"No kidding?" He seems pleased. "Well, I'm proud of you, honey. That's America for you."

I would argue that the valley near Fossil Bowl is the prettiest place in Idaho. Fossil Bowl is a motocross course in Clarkia, a small town north and east of Moscow. The road in and out of Clarkia is a two-lane highway hemmed in by trees. One goes up and down this highway as though on a roller coaster, climbing between walls of white fir and ponderosa pine to a rise and dropping into a spreading canyon of fir and pine, again and again. It is like shooting down steel tracks into the curve, or sliding on a flume to a sea of trees, and at the bottom, before the next hill, the trees fill the sky. Log trucks spilling ragged chunks of bark blow by, and the road is littered with bark. When I went to Clarkia I was penned in, with one full log truck wobbling and wiggling its load just in front of me, and a sawdust truck behind, pressing close on the downgrades. The trucks travel both ways in this forest, going from different timber sales to different mills, each of which wants a certain size log of a certain kind of tree, in a strange Newcastle-ish procession. Every few moments, overbalanced log trucks passed us going the opposite direction, perilously close and knocking me sideways with their windy passage. There was, of course, no shoulder, only layers of trees on trees rising gracefully up and over the hills like wildflowers planted by some demented god.

South of Clarkia, the road crosses a spreading meadow dotted with the round silhouettes of deciduous trees, and cattle, each elements in a composition of texture. One sees short and tall; flat and rolling; pointed and soft. This meadow is what remains of a prehistoric lake, a flat-bottomed saucer inside the hills. Facing the meadow on the other side of the highway is the motocross course—a ragged ruin of torn dirt tracks; a steep, rutted hill dropping from a flat ridge to the ground, labeled DEVIL'S DROP; a few scattered course markers, with a sign, NEXT RACE, and no date. Before it was used for motocross, the course was used by snowmobiles. Behind a small trailer home is a crowded machine shop with a big sign visible from far down the road: BUZZARD'S ROOST MANUFACTURING TROPHIES. Out front of the shop, in the dusty, golden morning light, a thin man, smiling underneath blank black goggles, held the bright flare of a welding torch against a huge piece of machinery, an engine of some kind.

Francis Kienbaum has lived here since he was a child. It is his son who welds, his young second wife who works behind the desk in the trophy shop. And it is Francis who owns the fossil bed that gives Fossil Bowl its name.

"About '71, or '72, around in there, we were going to build this snowmobile race track," Francis told me. We were sitting outside on his little plank patio, a small, flat buttress in front of the faded blue trailer where Kienbaum and his family live. Between the patio furniture, bleached and dry from the seasons, and the highway was a sweet green lawn, with blooming pansies and a few short, arthritic apple trees. Francis Kienbaum, a handsome man with curly, greying hair and an easy manner, has told the story of his fossils a number of times, but he was perfectly willing to tell it again to a total stranger.

"I said, gosh, we can get plenty of dirt out of that bank over there. By golly, I want to dig in that bank over there. I just want to dig in that bank. Never did like that bank over there, anyway. So I got hold of a Cat, and I thought, This won't take long. I'm going to dig that sucker out. So the guy who was working on it, he worked until about five o'clock or so and then he stopped. And he said, 'Well, that's it, you just go ahead.' He'd pulled the bank down about eight or ten feet. So, about two or three in the morning, I'd dug down to that grey stuff, the ash, and I thought I'd hit some rock or something, but it broke away easily. So I just kicked the throttle in a notch, and it didn't take that long. I pushed it all around the track in big piles—for the number one and number two turns. And it wasn't quite light yet and I was done over there. I wasn't even aware those fossils were there—I'd spread them all over the turns there.

"I think a week went by. I was really busy. Another guy came over, was talking to me, and he said, 'Gosh, darn, there's sure a lot of leaves over there. You know that?' And I said, 'Oh, yeah, there's a lot of leaves.' I didn't give it a thought. And a few more days went by, and I had a little more work to do, and I went over there and saw all these black leaves. There was all kinds of them all over the place. I can't believe it! I knew there was some kind of a fossil leaf. They were just everywhere. So I thought about it, and I thought, Ah, hell, fossils. Nobody gives a damn about fossils anymore. So I waited a day or two and finally I thought I'd better call the university. So then some professor from the University of Idaho came over, and he looked around, and he said, 'Oh, my goodness. Such a deal.'

"As soon as they saw it, they knew what it was. One guy halfway accused me of trying to destroy the find. There wasn't anything like it in the country, maybe in the world. And that's it.

"They've found a hundred and twenty-five different varieties of leaves. Also insects, fish, and then this kind of minnow—I don't know what the hell it's called. Some kind of salmon, twenty-four inches long. Then those—what do they call them? Diatoms.

"We get people spring through fall. At first there was quite a few, and then it slacked off. Now it's picking up considerably. We do high school, grade school tour groups. There's a little money in it. It pays for the diesel and the grader work to keep the site clean. I used to dig in it all the time and I never got anything done. Because you can find something every time. You can carve it like soap and save them real good."

Over the light, thick soil, crossing myriad tracks, is the bed itself, a mere bank cut into the hill. The top of the bank is a torn edge of grass and the exposed roots of pine trees loose in the air where, day by day, hunters have pulled down the soil. Almost every rock, every layer of this bed holds a fossil. In twenty years, perhaps four feet of the bank is gone.

I had never found a fossil before that private hour, never tried, and I may never again. I've always hoped simply to find a fossil, a bit of the impenetrable past handed to the present, cast off a trail in the path of my next step. I vaguely imagined, when I thought of it, turning over a rock in the woods and finding the outline of a beetle, a fish, a fly or leaf. I thought it should be easy, like that. The discovery of a fossil is the most undeserved grace; it seems almost ungrateful to search for it. But I searched, with the clumsiness of the amateur, hardly knowing for what I searched. The dirt was crumbly, made of paper-thin layers of dark-grey ash that felt like crayon wax, and an ochre clay. The opened bank was like a cabinet lined with secret drawers and boxes; small pieces of it in shapes like blocks fell loose into my hands. I picked with a small kitchen knife, and pulled out flat rocks, broke off the layers with my hands, and again and again I found parts of a maple leaf, a whole black silhouette of birch. Grasshoppers bolted from my step with a whir. The air was hot, still, smoky with dust. When I turned around, I could see the silent valley, a few wisps of cloud, the golden dome of autumn coming down.

When I was done, splotched with the clay dust and sweating in the sun, I saw the Kienbaums' little girl nearby, a delicate blonde child with a sly smile. She was standing alone on the edge of the empty motocross course with a stroller, methodically loading the seat of the stroller with handfuls of dirt clods. She had dust on her blue pinafore. As I drove out slowly, back to the road, she was struggling to push her full load back home, up the silted path that held the wheels of the stroller tight. I slowed when I passed her and she turned to look, her face breaking with a proud, self-conscious smile.

Between Boise and Lewiston is a rock formation known by the Nez Percé as the Heart of the Monster. The monster was dismembered by

Coyote in a great battle. Each body part became a different tribe of people, growing up wherever Coyote threw the pieces. In the end he squeezed all that was left, the heart, and the drops of blood became the Nez Percé. They lived in north-central Idaho and nearby areas of Oregon and Washington, so that the intersection of the three states is near the center of their ancestral land. Frances Fuller Victor describes the Nez Percé as "lounging about, full of impertinence, and very Indian altogether."

The man we know as Chief Joseph was in fact the younger Joseph. He wasn't named Joseph, but Hinmahtooyahlatkekht, which means Thunder Traveling to Loftier Mountain Heights. Nor was he a chief, because the Nez Percé didn't have a chief.

The Nez Percé were bamboozled by the same combination of circumstances that conquered other tribes: a white negotiator who interpreted as he saw fit, a tribal representative who negotiated only as he saw fit, and most importantly, a tribal structure so unlike the white concept of government as to be incomprehensible to the whites who hoped to usurp it.

The white leader was Governor Isaac I. Stevens, still praised as a man of fairness, even greatness, but such claims seem rooted in the fact that he didn't treat the Nez Percé as badly as other whites had treated other tribes. He came to the tribe with a single purpose: to obtain their lands and move them elsewhere; he did so primarily through cunning rather than warfare. The "representative" with whom Stevens worked was a young man named Hollolsotelote. He converted to Protestantism in his youth and in all ways seems to have been enchanted by the whites he met. When he became an adult, he took the name Lawyer.

The Nez Percé lived in bands, with band leaders who spoke for no one but their own small groups. There were no chiefs, in the white definition of the word. In the long run, the treaty between Stevens and Lawyer may have been a better deal than any other the Nez Percé could have had, but again, this begs the question. The Nez Percé paid in plenty.

The Nez Percé had a reservation encompassing most of their original land. Gold was discovered on that land in 1860, and within a few years the reservation was reduced to a tenth of its original size. Lawyer, for reasons now murky in time, was thought by Governor Stevens to be the chief of all his people, empowered to sign for the entire tribe. Stevens had every reason to want to believe this, and there is evidence that Lawyer enjoyed the status and made little effort to convince Stevens otherwise. Stevens certainly ignored the protests of a number of other Nez Percé band leaders, and leaders of the Palouse tribe as well, some of whose lands were called Nez Percé and included in the treaty by the whites. Stevens held all the Indians accountable to Lawyer's signature. So a man named Lawyer, as the historian Alvin Josephy points out, was responsible for "a fine legalistic point of great consequence." But the other Nez Percé never accepted Lawyer's signature as binding on them. Their refusal was considered tantamount to a crime by Stevens.

Most of the Nez Percé unhappily began to gather together stock and supplies to follow Stevens' order to move closer together on more distant land. But Hinmahtooyahlatkekht's band eventually went to ground in Montana, crossed through what is now Yellowstone, through Crow lands and north to Canada, racing from the army. After they were captured, the tribe was taken to Oklahoma (Stevens had promised them Idaho), and there another half of the remaining Nez Percé died of disease, including all the babies.

On the way from Boise to Lewiston, I stopped at White Bird Battlefield, where the first battle of the short-lived and doomed Nez Percé War of 1877 was fought. That time the Indians won. The plaque by the road praises the attacking army.

All the way from Hermiston, Oregon, in the bright sunlight near the bend of the Columbia, down through the northeastern dry lands and through the valley of the Grande Ronde, down and east to Boise—all the way I feel a swollen sense of hope, the kind of irrational optimism that doesn't give a damn if it's unwarranted. I find one thing after the other. South of Pendleton, a single-engine plane sits half in the trees, cockeyed by the road. The plane's engine is open and cables are dangling down; a man has his head buried in the machinery. A young couple sitting nearby between a parked car and a tiny dome tent are holding hands and watching the mechanic silently. I see all this at fifty miles an hour, shooting over a pass. A few miles later, a girl canters a horse up a steep hill, her ponytail and her pony's tail bouncing together in the overbright, panting sun. I pass signs reading ROADSIDE ATTRACTION AHEAD. Once, twice, three different times, but never anything more, never the special attraction itself.

The young barley heads are yellowish-green and tangled together every which way in the sun like grasshoppers swarming and ready to leap. Fields as soft and puffy as rising leavened dough, mounds and bubbles and gentle folds of soil. The swirls of tan wheat alternate with the dark-brown fertile rows of a fallow field. Who cares for reason? sings the heart; who needs a point for contentment? As I head into Mountain Time, the corn is as high as an elephant's eye, and I'm in love.

I am seduced by this land, by the repeated and immortal belief that a good life can be led in this big, broad land. Of course, it's a lie; times are hard here. But the land—there is a sensation in this land, land that is fertile and moist in the shadows of the stream courses, yellow and light in the open plains, bright in the sun. The land will provide, says the heart's voice, the schools will be big and clean and safe, and there will be church on Sunday, and picnics, and you will be able to afford a decent home and a good lawn and have the chance to know your neighbors. You can have a good life here; the land says you can.

When the first settlers crossed overland, a hundred forty years ago, they stumbled into this place with a sense of wonder. "Camped in one of the lovliest valleys in the world called Grand Round," wrote Lucia Lorain Williams of her own crossing in 1851. "It resembled an enchanted valley, as we wound around the hill before descending into it. Found plenty of Cayuse Indians." But these first settlers were bound for the greener, warmer, wetter Willamette Valley. It would be another decade and more before the wave returned in smaller measure, and farmers left the Willamette Valley for the Grand Ronde and the country of the Palouse. These settlers, wrote one disapproving missionary, were "tinctured with rationalism." They trusted, like me, the land and the hazy golden light, the steady rivers and the protective wall of the basalt mountains that grow out of the plains. And one by one the ranches failed, the farms died, the families starved or froze or died of loneliness, or moved.

I was heading, eventually, for the Whitman Mission, the closest thing to a pilgrimage I wanted to make. Solemn, almost ceremonial pilgrimages are commonplace here—out-of-the-way journeys to graves and memorials, the sites of shipwrecks and ghost towns, totem poles and battlefields. The white journey to Indian roots is almost a duty to some, an acknowledgment of wrongs done, sins sinned, forgiveness asked. In the process, a shiny-cheeked sense of virtue is achieved. Without forgiveness, the pilgrim feels forgiven—as though the dead victims know your steps. The grave of Hinmahtooyahlatkekht is in northeastern Washington. It is one of the more popular pilgrimage sites for those so inclined. I've been nearby more than once, but never there. I wonder sometimes if my refusal to visit the grave of a man I admire, regardless of race, is a kind of reverse pilgrimage. What am I guilty of other than luck and an easy birth?

The Whitman Mission is west of Walla Walla near the border between Washington and Oregon. The name of this place has always been Waiilatpu, which means Land of the Rye Grass. This is bottomland, with green fields and yellow fields of waving rye, huge ricks of square hay bales and intricately woven fence. Cottonwood trees hide the winding river. I paid my dollar and entered the cool, small room.

There are mannequins of Cayuse Indians and the missionaries—Marcus and Narcissa Whitman—in the center of the display room. The diorama is inadvertently flavored with suspicion and reserve. Perhaps it is the still faces, the frozen plastic hand reaching tentatively up. Both white and Indian are in their own traditional dress, and the Cayuse are so much more handsomely and finely dressed, their jackets and shifts decorated with elegant rows of beadwork.

The Passage, furs and gold, and the land brought settlers, but somewhere in the sequence, the Protestant missionaries and Catholic priests helped pave the way. "I would delight to know that in this desolate spot, where the prowling cannibal now lurks in the forest, hung round with human bones and with human scalps, the temples of justice and the temples of God were reared, and man made sensible of the beneficent intentions of his creator." So spoke a Senator Bailies in 1822, extolling the virtue of mission work on the frontier. On seeing the Indians in the Willamette Valley, one preacher wrote that he would make them into "herdsmen, users of soap, tee-totalers, hymn-singers, monogamists, and newspaper-readers."

There was an almost total lack of irony or doubt in the minds of the missionaries. They had concerns about their effectiveness, fear that they might not save each soul, but never doubt as to the correctness of the mission. The Protestant missions lasted only thirteen years—from 1834 to 1847. (It was really the Whitman killings that ended the Protestant work.) The Catholics arrived a short while later, in 1838, and stayed until 1850, only twelve years. But in many cases the Catholics were more successful, in part because there was a kind of superstitious, mystical affinity between the Catholics and the Indians. Between Catholics and Protestants were suspicion and hostility.

The Indians of the Columbia Plateau had a myth about strange men who would come with a book, and how the world would change after that. It was a good prophecy, a promise of a kind of heaven, a transformation, a time when the Indians would stop migrating and suffering the cycles of hunger and have plenty every year. And then the missionaries came, bearing a book they claimed to be the One, the Single Book; they came with hoes and a promise of plentiful food and an end, forever, to the Indian migrations. (This last promise they kept.) Then the Catholics showed up, with the same Book and a different teaching, accusing the Protestants of being impostors. The bickering confused the Indians, who had always, in their oral history, spoken of one Book. How could there by two Teachings?

Narcissa Whitman and Eliza Spalding, another missionary wife, were the first white women to cross the country overland. The Whitmans came with a calling, a vocation of faith and confession, came into a dangerous, unsettled land. They carried with them books, tools, strong wills, a stronger faith, and a dangerous naïveté. Their innocent expectations proved fatal, not only to the Whitmans themselves but to their hoped-for converts. Marcus Whitman himself wrote that he didn't expect the Indians to survive white settlement, but he believed that settlement was inevitable—was, in the Christian scheme, a good thing in spite of its harm. As time passed, he actively encouraged passing immigrants—making a profit, in fact, by selling them supplies at prices considered high even by the inflated economy of the frontier.

Marcus Whitman, like many of the missionaries, was bitterly disappointed that the Cayuse and the neighboring Nez Percé didn't take quickly to his teaching—either his religious teaching or his cultural ideas. Small groups of Palouse, Cayuse, and Walla Walla Indians occasionally attacked passing wagon trains. He insulted the Cayuse men to the point of blows when he expressed disgust at their sin, frustration at their recidivism. (Writes one historian of Marcus Whitman, "His stubbornness and impatience saved him from being a paragon of virtue.") The Cayuse, even after many years in close proximity, considered Narcissa arrogant, proud, and superior. So did some of the passing immigrants. She, in turn, disliked the "filthy" Indians and longed for home, especially after her two-year-old daughter, Alice Narcissa, drowned in the river nearby. One gets the feeling that the Cayuse never did understand the Whitmans' purpose in building the mission, and that the Whitmans never understood the Cayuse reluctance to embrace a foreign culture. The Whitman Mission became a stop on the Oregon Trail; it wasn't long before children orphaned on the journey were deposited in the Whitmans' care. In 1840, Joseph Meek left his two-year-old daughter, Helen Mar Meek, the child of an alliance with a Nez Percé woman, with Narcissa. Eventually the mission had a mill and other buildings, with more than seventy people staying more or less permanently. The Whitmans were so busy with children and the running of the mission business that they had little time for teaching religion.

The Cayuse, like all tribes, had seen disease. The winter of 1779–80 was known as Smallpox-Used-Them-Up Winter, a single season in which the Plains tribes were devastated and the Nez Percé and Cayuse sharply reduced. When Lewis and Clark passed by, in 1805, not only smallpox was prevalent, but also tuberculosis, measles, and syphilis.

A measles epidemic came to Waiilatpu with the wagons in the fall of 1847. Because the white people had some immunity and the Indians had none, Whitman was able to nurse most of the whites back to health, while the Indians died. In less than two months, half the Cayuse died—two hundred people. More than half of the children died. The Indians began to think they were being poisoned by Whitman's medicine. Nor was it such a strange thought: Since their arrival, the mission staff had poisoned Indian dogs with wolf bait and secretly filled the garden melons with emetic medicine to discourage stealing. One rumor held that a healthy Cayuse man went to the mission, feigning illness; he died the next day under Whitman's care.

The whole of the story of Marcus and Narcissa Whitman reads like one long, sad mistake. It has, of course, been read otherwise; most histories of Waiilatpu extol the Whitmans' noble work, decry the Cayuse, without questioning the rightness of the Whitmans' very presence. We tell each other histories, big and small, the way we recite "The Night Before Christmas" on Christmas Eve, like a ritual. They all suffer the same error, these stories, these histories: They are simple. They are simple, straightforward things, pure and heroic and uncomplicated. So the neat stories of the missions. The ambivalence of the Whitman Mission, the role of the Whitmans themselves, are there to find. Perhaps it takes this long, this much distance, these many generations, to bring that darker reading to bear.

The Cayuse tradition held that a medicine man or shaman should be rewarded for success, and pay with his life if he failed in his cure. Marcus Whitman saw many examples of this during his tenure, especially after the white sicknesses arrived in the country and many more of the tribe were ill. Another reason the Cayuse felt compelled to kill the Whitmans was their prophecy. Either the promise of a heavenly destiny was wrong or the Whitmans weren't the promised bearers of the Book. But it was also possible for the Cayuse to take action because Marcus Whitman seemed to have the power of the shaman, the ability to control and to kill. Since the Cayuse themselves didn't have a shaman strong enough to counter him, Whitman would have to be killed.

Marcus Whitman was warned to get away, but he returned and presided over the funeral of an Indian child, another measles victim. He was killed shortly afterward, on November 29, 1847, by a ritual axe blow to the head. Over the next few days, thirteen other people died, including Narcissa, who was shot. (Two, including Helen Meek, died from the measles.) After the Whitmans' eleven years of labor at Waiilatpu, twenty-one Nez Percé and one Cayuse had been converted to Christianity. What a great price was paid for those few. To the Indians of the Pacific Northwest, the so-called massacre wasn't a massacre at all. It was more like a skirmish in a long, undeclared war.

The deaths of the Whitmans, writes the historian Malcolm Clark, "was a grievous event, but an event less important to this history than the use to which it subsequently was put." The Whitmans were considered by the other whites in the region to be "victims of savage superstition, jealousy, and wrath." The official National Park Service history of Waiilatpu, sold in the little gift shop at the mission, states, "today, the story of the Whitmans serves to inspire all people who would pursue the way of high principles and ideals."

At the desk sat a handsome broad-shouldered woman, with a dark, wide face. I asked her if she was Cayuse.

She smiled politely. "Yes, I am," she said, with hesitation in her voice, but as I explained myself, my questions, she relaxed and began to talk. Her name was Marjorie Williams-Waheneka, and she was, she said, "Full-blood—Cayuse, Yakima, and Warm Springs—Paiute and Nez Percé." She spent her childhood on the Umatilla Reservation some miles south of the mission site, then moved to Seattle, returning to the reservation when her grandmother died. She is the only Native American on the staff of the Whitman Mission, where she has worked since 1980: "I'm the only one who has survived, anyway."

"I first saw this place in 1978, 1979. My grandmother brought some of her work, her beadwork and baskets, to show. A lot of what they had didn't sit right with me. I was offended—it seemed like everywhere you looked it was the killings—the 'massacre'—and I didn't like that word." It was only in the 1970s, after the site was developed and the neat walkways and the tall white tombstone pillar were built, that the National Park Service began to recruit tribal involvement in the exhibits. But even then, Marjorie explained, they had to justify all their recommendations. She is frustrated by the slow changes she sees, but also by the unwillingness of people on the reservation to get involved in, or even visit, the site.

It wasn't easy, she added, for all the visitors or even all the staff to get used to a Cayuse working there: "I get very frustrated and angry sometimes at how naïve people are. They tend to group Indian peoples into one. I had a visitor from Massachusetts who told me he had just been through the Nez Percé Center, and he said, 'But I didn't see any tipis.' And I said, 'Those went out in the late 1800s.' And he said, 'They did? I thought Indians just lived in tipis.' The biggest thing I've noticed is that people don't really remember what happened here, just, 'Isn't this where the Indians killed the missionaries?'" Marjorie stays at the mission because she wants to educate people and stay in touch with her own culture. She is also on an organizing committee for the Oregon Trail Interpretive Center being developed on reservation lands; it will be the first time the Native American version of the Oregon Trail migration is presented. But at work she wears the tan uniform and badge of the Park Service.

The death of the Whitmans led immediately and directly to the formation of a territorial government in the Northwest, and to a series of battles ever after known as the Cayuse War. Even after the abducted prisoners were rescued, a tentative peace reached, even after five possibly innocent Cayuse warriors were turned over to be hanged, payments were extracted. H.A.G. Lee, the Superintendent of Indian Affairs, and the governor of the Territory declared the Cayuse land forfeit: "In consideration of the barbarous and insufferable conduct of the Cayuse Indians, as portrayed in the massacre of the American families at Waiilatpu, and the subsequent course of hostilities against the Americans generally; and with a view to inflict upon them a just and proper punishment, as well as to secure and protect our fellow citizens, immigrating from the United States to this territory ... I, H.A.G. Lee, Superin't of Indian Affairs, hereby declare the territory of said Cayuse Indians forfeited by them, and justly subject to be occupied and held by American citizens, resident in Oregon." The settlers also made a formal demand for recognition and protection from the United States from "ungrateful Indian savagery." The Whitmans had been killed in the hope of saving a tribe. In that one blow of the axe, the tribe lost almost everything it had left.

"A lot of people don't realize it, but this is where we began," said Marjorie. "This is where our ancestors were. I find this place real peaceful. What happened here happened long before I came into the world. It's our beginning, right here." In the bucolic, gardenlike fields of the mission stands a tall, white obelisk memorial for the fourteen people killed here by Indians. There is nothing, not even a plaque, in memory of the Cayuse who died before and after.

A few miles east of Lewiston, Idaho, on the Clearwater River, is Lapwai, the site of Henry Harmon Spalding's mission for the Nez Percé. Henry and Eliza Spalding came west with the Whitmans. Eliza Spalding's baby was the second child born of American parents in the Pacific Northwest, after the Whitmans' daughter, who had drowned at the age of two. The Spaldings left after the Whitmans' death, but Henry later returned, and died here.

Henry Harmon Spalding was genuinely alarmed about the Indians' decline. He wrote a formal report on the Indians west of the Cascades, and it is little more than a list of numbers with comments: "Numbers rapidly diminishing. . . . Whiskey and Venerial Disease is doing its fatal work and in a few years there will be none left to tell the tale. . . . There are but few of them." Yet he blamed the Indians for their own loss, almost subconsciously; in letter after letter, he detailed their sorry, sick, and hungry state, their need for medicine, food, and land, and then complained of their flawed characters, their lack of an understanding of their own original sin.

He was a well-intentioned and utterly bemused man, himself illegitimate and eternally ashamed. He loved the Indians almost against his own will. He assumed that the Indians would take his word for the reason the Sabbath should be kept, and keep it; he assumed that if they were told to stop swearing, to give up gambling, to ignore the dictates of the medicine man, they would. He ordered them not to lie, quarrel, or fight, not to indulge in the infuriating behavior called "Indian-giving" (the last "very evil in its tendency," he wrote). "It is true they never forget a kindness," Spalding added, "but often make it an occasion to ask another," puzzled by a behavior he seemed never to have witnessed in a white man. But there was more: Polygamy was one thing, but the trait that seemed most to discourage Spalding was "an apparent disregard for the rights of white men." In a prophetic aside, Spalding wrote in a letter some time before the murder of Whitman—and, nearly, himself: "I have no evidence but to suppose that a vast majority of them would look on with indifference, and see our dwelling burnt to the ground and our heads severed from our bodies. I cannot reconcile this seeming want of gratitude with their many encouraging characteristics."

Spalding sometimes whipped the Indians himself. Once he offered a reward for the killing of the Indians' dogs, because the dogs harried the sheep with which he hoped to make the Indians farmers. As the missionaries left, the Oregon Trail settlers arrived. The remaining Indians were short of food; they stole cattle, chickens, potatoes. It was common pioneer justice to punish stealing severely. Dr. Elijah White describes in his letters a man who killed an ox to feed the remnants of his starving tribe, who was made to pay as a fine his rifle and eight horses—his only hope of more food.

Spalding shared the frustrations of all the missionaries, who spent themselves in the effort to convert and then doubted the truth of conversions. Asa Bowen Smith, working at the mission in Kamiah, Oregon, lamented that the Indians seemed to accept the church and baptism happily and with apparent innocence, but did not appear, somehow, to be true Christians. "It is possible that he may be a child of God; but *I* certainly should not have dared to place the seal of the covenant upon him," he wrote in a letter to his superiors at the board of missions in Boston. "The most favorable that I can speak of him is, that he gives but doubtful evidence of piety—He has no clear views of the nature of sin or of the plan of salvation & I fear that he has never been made sensible of the vileness of his own heart." What folly; what hopeless idiocy. Smith had no clear sense himself of what he wanted from the man of whom he wrote. But he felt there'd been no conversion in the heart, no true rejection of what came before or embrace of what would come. Why, he wondered, did the Indians in their savage state feel no shame? Why did they have no need for confession when they obviously had so very much to confess?

Asa Smith ends this particular letter with a complaint about Henry Spalding: "Mr. Sp. has been in the habit of dwelling much on their wicked practices, such as fighting, stealing, adultery, lying, medicine, juggling, gambling &c. & the Indians very generally seem to think that sin consists only in such practices & if they leave them off & are strict in religious worship, this is all that is required of them." He quotes another man as saying, "Mr. Sp. had got so that he did nothing but whip Indians & kill dogs."

The northern Paiute, who occupied the huge bare land south and west of the Snake River Plain, thought that white men were descended from rattlesnakes, who are greedy and bite people who want to share their territory: "Just because they were snakes and came here, the white people took everything away. They asked the Indians where they had come from. That's why they took everything and told the Indians to go way out in the mountains and live."

The Clearwater River canyon, where Spalding's mission was built and where Lewiston now lies, is green and flat, flat-banked, with dry, dove-colored hills. In the late fall rain, the smell is utterly fresh. White turkeys trot stupidly beside the road, purple wattles swaying with each step. A flock of five black birds, their wingtips white as though dipped in paint, feed on a dead raccoon beside the road. Above Lewiston, the hills rise to an alarming height, a varying shade of brown dry as bones, tufted with short, spare grass and cobbled with crumbled dirt. I can see them as large, whole things, mounds of clay ridged and dented, worked by the fingers of giant hands. Between the town and the hills lies the

Clearwater, emptying into the Snake, crossed by grain barges and train trestles.

This is also the home of the Lewis and Clark Visitor Center, an open-air building with trim grounds, a statue of Sacajawea, and murals depicting the great journey that started the opening of the land. At ten o'clock on a late fall night, I sat on the banks of the Snake River, on a bench by the center. I had been playing miniature golf in Clarkston, Washington, across the river from Lewiston. One of the holes on the course was marked by a totem pole made of plastic, bearing a yellow happy face. Across the wide, still water, the round hills were so barely visible and soft that at first I thought they were clouds lying close to the earth.

Barges carrying lumber, sawdust, or grain can now cross all the way from the mouth of the Columbia to Lewiston, can slide down the domesticated Columbia from Idaho to the Pacific. The river rapids that so daunted Lewis and Clark are almost gone. They've been gone a long time, but long before that, the Columbia River swam with ships.

The Oregon Steam Navigation Company ran both steamships and rail lines, reaching eventually from Portland up to Umatilla and later, on to Boise City. The trips were regular and frequent, always leaving Portland at the exotic hour of five in the morning on "comfortable and capacious" steamboats. They were also expensive: A single fare from Portland to Lewiston, which took almost three days, was sixty dollars, and that didn't include either meals or a bed. The boats stopped for a rail portage around the falls at The Dalles, the Cascades, Celilo. Above Celilo, wrote Samuel Bowles, passengers rode a boat "with large state-rooms, long and wide cabins, various and well-served meals." Charles Nordhoff recommended sleeping on board the night before and rising around six, by which time the ship was under way and Mount Hood was visible on the horizon. Seeing Mount Hood from the deck of the ship, seeing wilderness in a cocoon of safety, Bowles called it "the great snow peak of Oregon, its Shasta, its Rainier, its Mont Blanc," and gave the sight second place in his list of the best natural scenes in the country, behind Yosemite.

These were first-class trips, taken not only for business by settlers and miners but also by many as vacations, larks, and adventures. The tourist industry grabbed first at the Columbia River and then at the coast, where a number of hotels and spas catered to the upper classes. Visitors frolicked in the summer, wading and fishing, and rode horseback through the strange forests, toured Indian villages, and climbed mountains. The scenery was "lush," "Edenic," "paradisiacal," a "constant succession of wild and picturesque scenery." It was a trip through an evolving land, evolving from steep palisades to rolling hills, sharp cliffs to tree-covered hills, banks and beaches, and evolving from the primitive to the controlled. (Nordhoff, after praising the landscape, adds, "I should like to have seen the rugged cliffs relieved here and there by the softness of smooth lawns, and some evidences that man had conquered even this rude and resisting nature.")

"Steam, gas, women and wine are the ruling powers of Oregon," wrote C. Aubrey Angelo, and especially he meant steam. Barges plow across the Columbia without encountering a single difficult passage now, plow up, and up to the Snake, to Lewiston, to the dry inland basin from the sea, as though nothing had ever stood in their way, as though no one else had ever lived where the water runs now, as though no one had ever fished, or sung, or copulated, or died, under the surface of the docile dammed-up water.

When Seathl, the Duwamish chief who gave his name to the city of Seattle, spoke at the final signing of a reservation treaty, he reminded the white men that his people believed in eternal life. "When the last Red Man shall have perished, and the memory of my tribe becomes a myth among the White Men, these shores will swim with the invisible dead of my tribe," he said. "When your children's children think themselves alone in the field, the store, the stop upon the highway, or in the silence of the pathless woods, they will not be alone. In all the earth there is no place dedicated to solitude. At night when the streets of your cities and villages are silent and you think them deserted, they will throng with the returning hosts that once filled them and still love this beautiful land. The White Man will never be alone."

Two small fishing boats, dark shapes on dark, slowly moved down the river while I sat on its banks. I could hear the fishermen calling quietly to each other. The air stank of pulp. To the south, straight over the dammed, dead Snake, I could see the bridge from Idaho to Washington, lined with globes of light, and over it, hung magically in the air, the golden arch of a McDonald's.

SIX

Everything grows here. Iris, sunflowers, rhododendrons and azalea, roses, and a million other flowers. Oregon grows ninety-eight percent of the American filbert crop (those are hazelnuts to you) and Washington grows the other two percent. Most are exported to Europe, especially to those fussy German torte bakers. The first apple seeds arrived as a joke, slipped in the pocket of Lieutenant Aemilius Simpson's jacket by a friendly lady. They stayed there, around Cape Horn and up the coast for months, undiscovered, until the good Aemilius arrived. Equally in fun, he planted them. Now Washington is the nation's number-one producer of apples—and of hops, though it's apples that the wise tourist seeks at roadside stands. Those ubiquitous five-nubbed Red Delicious, and Golden Delicious and Jonathans, Newtons and Romes and Granny Smiths and varieties antique and new you've never heard of before: Winter Banana and Look No Further, Gloria Mundi, Bellflower and Northern Spy, Spitzenberg and Grimes Golden and King of Thompkins. In the Depression, when the market failed, it was Washington apple growers who encouraged the poor to sell apples on street corners. The orchard owners cut their trees down for firewood.

Asparagus grows here, and kiwifruit, peppermint and spearmint, alfalfa, and flower bulbs. Meadows of grain are headed and heavy in summer, and in the hazy afternoons give off their own tawny light, silky like the light of gems. On the back roads in the valleys, unmarked intersections pass fields of onion and fescue and broccoli, vineyards and acres of green pepper, corn, and cauliflower, acres of tulip and rose. We grow Christmas trees, too: Between Oregon and Washington, more than eleven million Christmas trees are cut each year. All through the rolling valleys they run over the hills, lines of furry, cone-shaped trees in rows from smallest to largest, like marching soldiers.

Berries—you want berries? Bunchberry and cloudberry (sometimes called baked-apple berry), gooseberry and dangleberry, serviceberry, snowberry. I prefer the delicate, flaky thimbleberry hidden under spreading, hairy leaves in shady woods, its delectable flavor known only to a few. Winterberry and inkberry, deerberry, the buffaloberry (called rabbitberry by some), lemonade berry and marionberry, four types of mulberries, the partridgeberry (also known as twinberry), the checkerberry (also called boxberry, or pigeonberry, or teaberry), and the nannyberry (called wild raisin), eight kinds of cranberries, square miles of blackberries, endless acres of blueberries.

When I ask my husband what he sees in the weather forecast he is reading, he looks up and says, "How many ways can you say rain?" It is the rain that makes the berries, after all. It rains, said one settler on his way to California after a single winter in the Willamette Valley, "more than twelve months in the year." Sometimes the rain falls horizontally here, sideways to the ground; it rains a little some days, a lot on others, hard and light, steadily, in drizzles, warm and cold. The really wild storms that bang into the coast are called "timber-rattlers." The rain here is bleak and enduring, but umbrellas are considered the refuge of a coward. It rains in September and June, December and July, but mostly it rains in the winter, when the air is cold and the storms build up over the mountain ranges into towering sacks of water. Here it rains while the sun shines. Here I can see the edge of weather, the line between the shifts of climate and season, dancing on the land before my eyes. I dash through rush-hour traffic in late October and come round a bend at full speed into a sphere of peachy light, the freeway a band of metal reflecting the rain flying into my windshield. The dome of sudden light on the other side of this brief and local rain is thick and syrupy and insistent, radiant above, slippery and mirrored below. I am flying down a tunnel of light, gliding out of storm and into calm. In less than a mile, less than a moment, the sky clears, the rain is gone, and the road is dry, and far away I can see fog lap up the peaks like dove-colored lakes, sooty clouds creep far away across the valley, full of turmoil.

I drive for days on the Olympic Peninsula in an old Ford pickup truck, drive in dark, unceasing rain, sleeping secretly in the cold camper in back, on the silent streets of small towns. Tree-lined, shiny black roads slathered with falling water, water running in streams along the road, water spreading in puddles and rivulets and ponds, water cascading against the truck in splashes like fistfuls of water thrown by a hidden hand. The windshield wipers throw cups of water off the glass; I peer through the small, circular space each swipe makes.

The weather has a way of evening out. West of the Cascades, where it rains a lot, it rarely snows. East of the Cascades, where it rains little, it snows a lot. (On the mountains themselves, in the spine between west and east, rain and snow combine and fall so hard and heavy there's a kind of snow called "Cascade cement.") There are rain sinks, and rain shadows: valleys and hills a few miles apart with climates as different as different latitudes. The most dramatic is Sequim, a prosperous town on the northern edge of the Olympic National Forest. Sequim is about ten miles from a part of the Olympic Mountains where rain pours down all winter in solid feet. But Sequim gets less than twenty inches of rain a year; the farmers there have to irrigate. Small cacti grow on the hills.

Today, late November, is a light and cloudless day, chilly, dry. Yesterday it rained all day and night without end. There is no predicting, no certain combination of weather and day but that it rains on all our parades.

An army surgeon at Cape Disappointment on the mouth of the Columbia River kept weather records every day of his tenure. On April 7, 1871, he wrote only this: "Tremendous rain and hail, full of alarming consequences." Sir Francis Drake complained of the "most vile, thicke, and stinking fogges." A settler wrote that the winters were "extremely irksome and disagreeable." When a melancholy trapper would now and then drink enough rum to get the courage to kill himself, it was called a "Northwester's death."

That long-suffering pair, Meriwether Lewis and William Clark, spent one very long winter at a place called Fort Clatsop, near present-day Astoria, Oregon. From Astoria's hills, you can see clear down the widening mouth of the Columbia and out to the ocean, and up the river to follow the undulant wakes of ships the same color as the water. Lewis and Clark camped back in the woods.

It rained so much inside the huge hemlocks and spruce where they stayed that their fort—a solid square of huge logs and shakes—disappeared in a few years, melted into the ground like so much ice cream. It rained all but twelve days the winter they were here, and only half of those twelve showed sun. Clark, ever assiduous, kept a daily journal. "Every man as wet as water could make them all the last night and to day all day as the rain continued all day," he wrote, stuttering a little with the damp. "A Tremendious wind from the S.W. about 3 oClock this morning with Lightineng and hard claps of Thunder, and Hail . . . rained with great violence. . . . It would be distressing to See our Situation, all wet and colde."

As the days wore on like rags, Clark spent less time on the climate, wasting fewer words. The men were "all wet and colde," and they were bored. They had no liquor, and even the "lude" Chinook women were off-limits, thanks to venereal disease. They entertained themselves by drying out the gunpowder, making maps, and preparing the countless elk hides, using the brains for tannin. He sent some of the men down the coastline to make salt, others into the woods for food—they killed 131 elk between December 1 and March 20, and ate little else. On February 7, 1806, a now-sarcastic leader wrote, "This evening we had what I call an excellent supper it consisted of a marrowbone a piece and a brisket of boiled Elk that had the appearance of a little fat on it. this for Fort Clatsop is living in high stile."

Clark began to speak of "The rain &c.," and to say that it "rained last night as usial." Lewis, less of the record-keeper, wrote on January 4: "Nothing interesting occured today," and to drive in the point, on the twenty-ninth of the same month he wrote only, "Nothing worthy of notice occurred today." Clark was sick and at the same time raring to be gone, a young man on a big trip and ready to tell it, stuck in the mud by the endless rains and rough water. "O! how horriable it the day," he penned.

By the middle of the last century, Oregonians were called "moss-backs" and "webfeet" by their visitors, but in fact it rains no more in the heavily populated trough between the Coast Range and the Cascades than it does in many places. The difference is that here in the farthest Northwest, a year's worth of rain falls in six months. The springs are bright, falls hazy and warm, and the summers dry, hot, clear. The winters are something else. And west of the Coast Range it rains far more, and in the summer, too. "T'aint weather, it's a disease," the loggers used to say. Up there in the woods, the tree crowns and volcanoes grab the mist and clouds and wring them dry, literally tearing drops from a fog as though tearing strips from a bolt of fabric. A word is required for the dry, sunny, snowy land east of the Cascades, which is after all most of the Northwest: With most of the land and few of the people, there are sometimes three hundred cloudless days a year. (And the wind races down the canyons full of snow.) A word, too, for the impact of mechanical life on our winters here: The Columbia River used to freeze solid, as did the Willamette—solid enough to drive cars across. With all the dams on the river now, it will probably never happen again.

It rains most in the Olympic forests and on the coasts, and it seems to rain more near the mouth of the Columbia than any spot on earth. Cape Disappointment, on the Washington side of the Columbia River across the mouth from Astoria, gets enough heavy fog every year to shroud almost one of every three days, and the worst months are August and September, when all the rest of the Northwest is basking in sunshine and hoping for rain. Though it often seems dank near Astoria, it is by no means the foggiest place around: Stampede Pass in Washington gets 252 full days of heavy fog a year. The help-wanted and real-estate ads in the Portland newspaper extol life on the coast for a lot of good reasons, but now and then I see an ad pointing out that one should move to the coast because summer is coming. I have a travel-magazine cover story on Astoria, and in every one of the photographs, the freshly painted Victorian homes and the well-kept gardens are in full sun, against a backdrop of deep-blue sky. It's an inviting prospect, that well-kempt town on a hill above the blue Pacific. Every year in Astoria, there are fewer than fifty clear days, and 239 cloudy ones.

The Coast Guard runs a lifeboat school at Cape Disappointment, a neat, whitewashed institution populated by big young men with military haircuts, waddling down the steep roads in orange survival suits, smiling; they know how many hundred ships have sunk nearby. Fishermen call this part of the river "the graveyard." When the *William and Ann* arrived in 1823 with David Douglas, the ship sighted the mouth on February 12, in winds "a thousand times worse than Cape Horn." It then lay to for six long weeks, unable to pass the mouth because of the currents and the waves. They watched the churning water and calculated tides until April 7 before they could pass in. Four years later, the *William and Ann* was back, and she sank in the mouth of the Columbia with all aboard. When Dr. and Mrs. White (she of the "deep and abiding interest" in the Columbia) arrived at its mouth, their ship took half a day to pass through in good conditions. (The captain, she remembered, was "becoming more desperate and determined, continually fortifying his wavering courage by deep quaffs of brandy.") The Whites would lose much to the river: Their adopted son George and their eleven-month-old infant son Jason would drown in the Columbia; Mrs. White herself nearly died in the canoe accident that killed Jason.

The mouth of the Columbia opens like the mouth of a tuba and the water pours in and out in a great waxing and waning tide, like the tuba's blast squeezed down a long, narrow pipe. The salt and the sweet waters churn together in a violent wedding of demands. Lewis and Clark thought they'd reached the ocean when they were near Pillar Rock—"Great joy in camp we are in view of the Ocian." In fact, Pillar Rock is several miles from the mouth of the river, but the river there spreads so, widens and rolls and breaks so, they concluded—rightly, in a way—that they had arrived.

The woods leaning over the ocean are full of alders and spruce, ferns and salal and seagrasses, lush and mossy, sliding down the doughy hillsides into swamps and sloughs. Every creek feeds acres of moist and shadowed bottomland with dark green cow-heaven grass, homes peeling in the wet wind, trailers hidden under oaks. The neat vacation houses have names like "Lo! Tide" and "Weather 'n' Heights." Alders grow in thickets, slender, lacy, but even in the sun, the colors are quiet and earthen, rust and lilac and aqua and many shades of grey. Pussy willows bud early here, and the shore pines grow strange in the sandy soil. Private slash piles and giant stumps burn in the winter rains here, on and on through the night. Tiny reddish flames flicker in the ragged piles of wet branches and bark, smoke trickling through the grey air in a sweet, melancholic cloud.

On the Long Beach Peninsula, in the southwestern corner of Washington, tiny towns spring up clean and green. On the inside edge of the peninsula are the huge tidal flats of Willapa Bay, grower of oysters that once commanded fifty dollars a plate in San Francisco's gold rush. Half of Washington's oysters grow in this one bay (about five million pounds), hung on strings or sown in baskets, along with shrimp, crab, clams. I was picnicking with my family near the flats one summer, all of us sprawled in the warm sand above the waterline. The hard mudflats smelled of sea, and shell, and trickles of water still ran through their ripples at low tide. We had been there about an hour when we caught sight of a line of people coming toward us, seeming to march out of the ocean a mile away. They all wore slickers, orange or yellow, and walked with high steps, lifting their waders out of the sucking mud. They were oyster pickers, a crew gone out to gather bags full of fresh meat. As the line grew closer, I could see first that they were all men, about two dozen of them, and then that they were all dark-haired and dark-skinned, and finally that they were Hispanic. They passed us one by one by one, smiling tired smiles, each with a bag of sharp shells banging against his knees.

The coastal towns have go-cart tracks and video arcades, clam-chowder shops and Mom's Pies for the summer mobs out for Indian bingo, beach races. The Oregon coast is restricted, but the beaches of Washington are dirty and hard, traced with tire tracks and mire and never silent. At any time, in any weather, old Mustangs and station wagons and pickups run up and down the twenty-eight-mile length of Long Beach, the WORLD'S LONGEST DRIVABLE BEACH, going nowhere, splattering the sea foam. Men with chain saws slice up the giant bleached logs of driftwood for their woodstoves and toss them in the back of pickup trucks parked conveniently on the sand.

The Oregon coast is a study in relief. Just following the road can give one vertigo. From below, when the highway skirts the water, the weather is grey and misty and cold; halfway up the cliff, five miles away, the car breaks into a burst of sun and the land below is pearl-white. The easy, simple sea rolls in foamy and ruffled to a crescent of camel sand, and the mist is mere shreds of light. Everything from single rocks to single trees is outsize, overlarge, bizarre and solitary and old. A bank of clouds on the horizon seems without definition, out west as far as west can go, and the sun turns it into a dreamy cloud of gold. Tillamook and its neighbors, where the cheese is made, smells of fresh manure instead of sea. Cow manure washing off the hills into the bay in heavy rain brings the bacterial count of the water so high that shellfish harvests are closed ten or twelve times every year.

All of Oregon's beaches are public, every foot, so that one can walk from California to Washington and never tread on private land. One takes caution on the beaches here, watching tides, scooting out of the range of the tossing logs and sneaker waves that kill a dozen or so people every year. Oregon was the first state to make its beaches public, in a sweeping declaration by Governor Oswald West in 1913. He declared that all beaches were public highways, as they were by proxy and use, because the forests were too thick and the hillsides too steep and rocky for travel. There was no complete coast highway until 1936, and people, horses, wagons, cars waited at one end or another of every long, flat stretch for the tide to go out.

A woman I know runs a hotel on the coast, in one of the more popular seaside towns. She says that visitors from out of state always want to know "what part of the beach is theirs." When she says, "All of it, all you see," they don't believe her. They take their blankets below the hotel and stay there, and, I imagine, dart disapproving glances at the locals straying up and down the length of the soft white sand, crossing boundaries.

It's the opposite for me. A few years ago, I was hiking along a high, sandy path near China Beach, south of Monterey in California. Lots of people were out; it was a fine summer day and the small bay far below was calm and its water almost transparent. All at once I came to a fence, a high cyclone fence obstructing the path. On the fence was a NO TRESPASSING sign, and for the longest moment, I couldn't figure it out. I thought for a brief minute that someone had broken the law, had decided in a fit of anarchy and selfishness to take possession of the beach. I could see the path zigzagging down to the water's edge, and far below a small, sandy beach with a few bodies spread across it. A hundred yards above the beach stood a house, full of the arrogant windows facing west that beach houses have. It was only when my friend, who lived nearby, motioned me onto a fork in the path that I realized the beach there was truly private. It was *owned*, a concept I still find slightly askew.

Astoria, the oldest settlement west of the Rockies, immortalized by Washington Irving, was meant to be a huge shipping port, a megalopolis of the coast, a city to rival the cities of the long-lost East. Astoria seems never to have been taken seriously. The Astorians "must be content to live on hope, kisses, clams and salmon," said the nineteenth-century travel writer C. Aubrey Angelo, who reported that, after all, some of the salmon were seventy-five to ninety pounds each, so the fate wasn't quite as bad as might be expected. The first canning factory opened in Astoria in 1864. The Chinese were big in the fledgling canning business, working on labor-intensive assembly lines—one cut off the head, the other definned and disemboweled, then the fish was bled out in a vat and washed several times, then another person chopped it up and again another chopped it smaller, steadily smaller; the pieces were soaked in brine and then stuffed in cans. By the end of the 1880s, Portland had the second largest Chinese population in the country, second only to San Francisco's, and it wasn't just railways: Salmon had a lot to do with it.

Houses still dangle from the hillsides in Astoria, and the Columbia

Maritime Museum is always busy, and so is the Merry Time Museum Tavern. You can still hear yodeling on the radio here, a remnant of the many Scandinavians who came to work as fishermen. You can still climb the faded Astoria Column hundreds of feet high with what may be the world's wettest view.

When I was last in Astoria, late in the spring, I was caught in a rain so traditional, so relentless and drenching and ceaseless, I felt borne back to history. I was melting like Lewis and Clark's muddy fort. There were so many drops of water in every inch of air that it was like walking through something solid, like walking into the spray of a sprinkler, caught by surprise. And after a while I enjoyed it, watching the dark, iron sky break and slither about, and the river turn the color and texture of jade. A friend of mine calls these sleeting rains, where the drops are so heavy and pregnant they elongate as they fall, "celestial threads." There were shadows under each little, rolling wave. People hunched over in yellow slickers fished from every half-rotten pier or boulder, and they were catching. The lichen-coated trees get brighter in the rain, an aquarium sea-green fuzzy against the dark russet forest. The red bark and bush are warmer, the fields greener in the rain; it adds to the great endurance of the landscape for me. No vista is the same twice, because the sky is never the same twice here, the light never repeats. And there's no point in trying to stay dry. There's nowhere to walk, no place to stand. Mist clings to the hillsides like torn tissue, and when it has finally passed, a calm settles over the hills and trees—a satisfied, moistened calm. Ah, everything sighs. Aaah.

A bridge flies from Astoria across the river to Washington. (People are always asking the toll-takers what the name of "that island" is, over the water.) The Astoria Bridge is a gleeful crescent, leaping up from Oregon in an improbable curve, to make way for the tallest ships, the widest barges, before it drops down again flat to finish the trip along the river's surface. On the waterfront by the broken-down, ruined wharves are rows of ragged pilings coupled to their own reflections, doubled, dark, and wet. Hairy circles on the river's surface swirl water of a slightly different color, marking the treacherous shallows, the shifting, malevolent sandbars. Navigational charts of the Columbia's mouth are polka-dotted with the yellow warning marks of sandbars, which disappear in the higher tides like ghosts, sliding under an inch of water until they look like nothing more than another section of still and cloudy water. I was driving from Washington to Oregon, across the bridge in a pounding, eternal rain. I saw slate-grey water on either side, a slate-grey sky that met the water in a vague, half-discerned line at eye level, the green skeleton of the bridge structure fading into fog above, and the shiny grey pavement of road below disappearing into the twisted cloud in front. And nothing else was visible, until I crossed the endless water and could see a vague outline of hills and the ghostly ramp of the climbing bridge rising into the air.

It rains enough here to give us a good silver thaw every few years, what the weather types call a "glaze": Rain falls through relatively warm air, hits a frozen surface, and turns to ice almost at once. Layer by transparent layer, the ice builds up. You wake in the morning not to the blanketing silence known in your heart as snow, but to the creaking of tree limbs and the splintering groan of whole trees falling, the crash of sliding cars and the sputter of downed power lines. No one goes anywhere. We have had friends who came for an evening, stay for the weekend; one Christmas I played Trivial Pursuit with my mother-in-law by candlelight for two days, watching my maple trees collapse under the weight of the solid, gorgeous rain. I lived one winter in a house in the central Willamette Valley, a little house with a huge, old willow tree off to one side. One morning I woke to find my neighborhood encased in sheen hard as a rock and slick as a griddle. The willow tree, with its frilly branches hanging in a cup above the ground, was a sculpture: a bright, giant haystack of ice. I wanted to slip inside it, look out at a white diamond world from inside the bell jar of willow, soft willow transformed to tinkling, crystal glass. But I was past seven months pregnant, cumbersome, awkward. I couldn't step outside my own door without crawling.

Puget Sound sits in the rainy embrace of the Pacific Ocean on one side and the Cascade chain on the other. The Sound is surrounded by cities— Vancouver and Victoria in British Columbia, Seattle and its wildly spreading suburbs in Washington—and filled with the San Juan Islands. Most of the islands are rocky and uninhabited, or thick with the short, stubborn pines that grow in the incessant winter winds; quite a few belong to a bird preserve, and flocks flit through its puzzle pieces unmolested. It's a hoary myth, the number of San Juans—most literature says 172, but maps don't bear it out, especially considering how low and shallow many of the islands are, scrubbed by tides and coated with barnacles. The naturalist Floyd Schmoe counted meticulously and found around eighty, give or take a few of what he called "rocks." But, he pointed out in his gentle correction, it is "after all a matter of quality and not quantity." The continental shore and the islands were once completely forested, the trees crowding down to the water, "as if they were courting their fate, coming down from the mountains far and near to offer themselves to the axe," wrote John Muir.

A few of the islands are populated, only a few: old military posts turned to towns, served by the ferries, their harbors are crowded with sailboats white and trim in their slips. Britain wanted the San Juans, even when every other boundary claim was satisfied. The center of the Sound hadn't been clearly surveyed in 1842, when the outline of Washington state was drawn, and the Treaty of 1846 included nothing more certain than a reference to the center of the main channel of the Strait of Juan de Fuca between Vancouver Island and Washington. Unfortunately, the San Juan Islands form a clump in the center of Puget Sound, and a small channel runs north and south on either side of that clump. England, of course, meant the eastern channel; the United States, naturally, presumed it referred to the western channel. So each drew a border, one pulling all the San Juans into the States, the other pulling them all into British Columbia. A compromise splitting the difference, proposed by a British captain named James Charles Prevost, was sternly rejected by the Americans, who had every intention of keeping the

Sound for democracy. So the islands were shared, with relative comfort, for a surprising number of years, until the infamous Pig War erupted in 1859 and a delicate military truce had to be hashed out. Ten years later, the English and the Americans agreed to arbitration over their multiple disputes, and Kaiser Wilhelm made the decision: United States, approximately 80, Great Britain, 0. Washington even holds a tiny tip of what is otherwise a peninsula of British Columbia jutting just far enough below the international boundary to fall inside the state.

The Sound is a glacial remnant connected to the Pacific by the strait of that Greek who called himself Juan de Fuca. The high, ragged line of the Olympic Mountains fills the south view from the Sound like a wall. They stand like a seawall of sorts—a tide stopper to end all tides. Betty MacDonald thought the mountains looked down on her like heavy-chested matrons. "I felt the resisting power of that wild country so strongly that I was almost afraid to look back for fear the road would have closed behind me," she wrote.

The Sound is filled with the little eddies of introduction that take place between salt water and the heavier, sweeter fresh water of incoming streams and the long winter rains. It is an estuary and it is also a fjord— a deep, ovaline bowl with steep sides called sills. Puget Sound extends north around Vancouver Island, where it meets the Strait of Georgia, and south into the tortured fingers of Hood Canal. The water looks fresh, like rainfall, but tastes salty and sour and cold, full of tides and subtides, undertows and currents and thermoclines fathoms thick.

The rain sometimes sits on top of Puget Sound like a lens, a balanced layer skimming across the top for a few moments or days. River water flows into the Sound in plumes, spreading fans entraining bottom water with it toward the ocean. Winds excite the surface water, pulling up water from beneath; more bottom water flows in from the sea to replace the entrained water flowing outward. The layers of salt and fresh, cool and cold—the temperature varies little from summer to winter—seaward and landward are blended and separated in a constant cycle, like thread being pulled from a skein and sorted by nimble fingers.

Cold water holds oxygen, fertilizing the Sound, which blossoms with so much of so many different kinds and sizes of life that it seems like God's neglected garden, an unplowed heap of volunteers bursting out of the humectant soil of the sea. The list is poetry: lobster, scallops, abalone, sea cucumbers and sea urchins, loons, tufted puffins, and bald eagles, crabs of every kind, tunicates, basking sharks, skates and anemones, swans and geese, sea stars, kelp trees and jellyfish, perch, coho and chinook and Pacific salmon, sea lions and Pacific seals, oysters, sponges, minke and grey and humpback whales, rockfish, giant nudibranchs, flounder, sole, sand dabs, lingcod, orcas that run under the surface in pods and leap in front of the ferries with apparent delight, octopuses, sablefish, dolphins, clams, sculpin, "barnacles like tiny snow-covered volcanoes clustered on the pilings beneath the water." The littleneck clam used to occur in such numbers that the siphon valves of burrowing neighbors would touch, emerging from the tidal bottom side by side with that truculent, naked clam's kiss so welcome to clammers. Edward F. Ricketts wrote that, before the Depression, he could feed several hungry people with the clams found in a few shovelfuls of submarine silt.

On the upper eastern corner of the Olympics, where Puget Sound turns directly south and becomes Hood Canal, is Port Townsend. The whole hilltop town seems to be engulfed at its front by the Sound. Gulls stand on the point in a crowd, facing one direction like commuters waiting silently for the subway. The air has the liquid dead smell of the sea, of seaweed, shells, the bodies of a billion creatures drying in the sun. Mount Baker, which is properly called Kulshan, and the smaller Mount Shuksan turn copper in the afternoon, and the big, boxy ferries chug across the water. Far to the southeast, on a clear day, you can see the slumping cone of Rainier, slowly melting.

Puget Sound was recommended to 1800s-era tourists as a good place for "people who like to go to sea without getting seasick." People have sailed here a long time, ducking between the islands so small and numerous and similar that one blends into another. Murray Morgan talks about escaping minor legal scrapes and impending disaster "by catching the night boat to Victoria." "We sailed through a passageway of mile upon mile of dark green trees coming down to the water's edge on both sides of us," wrote Burgess Cogill in her memoir of a childhood on a sailing schooner. "There were endless islands, small, large, medium, all covered by trees and darkly green. To one small girl, there was never such a lovely sight or another place on earth of so many tree-covered, evergreen islands, so many tugs bustling their tows of logs."

Puget Sound now has the world's largest ferry system, so busy that you have to get reservations ahead of time on hot summer weekends. The long, white ships are crammed with cars, bulldozers, motorcycles, kayaks, bicycles, semis with lumber and freight, and hundreds of people. I've shared ferries with black-jacketed motorcycle gangs, golden young Californians on a northern lark, and groups of bicyclists. The bicycles are lined up in a row at the front of the ferry, and if one falls over, down, down, down the row they all fall over like dominoes. The ferry docks have a dozen lanes, each numbered, each leading to a particular ferry, a particular island. In the lines of cars, people pull out lawn chairs and card tables, or perch in the back of pickup trucks with books and coolers, sipping Cokes, petting their panting dogs, catching a few rays.

One summer day I waited four hours for a ferry to Friday Harbor, the one town to speak of on San Juan Island. First two, then four, then a dozen people began to pace the length of an empty lane, tossing a softball back and forth, or lobbing Frisbees. A couple carried chairs to the edge of the water, and turned into the sun. A young man walked up and down between the cars, juggling for children.

The silky blue water shifted in long, mild swells away from the heavy boat, and wrinkled like old skin all around us. I took a seat with several other cheerful people, under the chain at the prow, sitting cross-legged on the cold iron in a chill wind. Someone nearby yelled, "Man overboard!" and everybody laughed. It's an old joke on the ferries, especially up here at the front, a few feet from the unguarded edge. Next to me, a family sat piled on top of each other, hugging against the cold. They were on their way to visit "Sis," who lives on a sailboat on the far side of San Juan Island. Another couple—she five months pregnant—were bicycling from one bed-and-breakfast to another, across the islands. Once you've paid to get on the ferry system, once you've entered the islands, the ferries are free, no matter how many ways you traverse back and forth. The engines chattered endlessly, deep and strong. People grew silent in the rumble, pulled out tattered paperbacks. A young woman leaned on the dusty hood of a maroon sports car nearby, pulled a forbidden beer from her cooler, and drank a long draft, squinting and grinning into the wind. In front of the ferry, a flock of gulls circled and landed on what seemed a random patch of water, like workers on a coffee break; they were riding the oscillations of a kelp bed. The wild mounds of unnamed islands were flat against the marbled sky, floating above the water as though on oil—a thin, fine line of mist at the surface. I leaned against the rusted chain, shivering on the snubby prow, nodding to the reggae steel-drum engine beat.

The city of Seattle, so says Murray Morgan, enjoyed a brief life as the city of Duwamps. It was finally named after a Duwamish chief of controversial reputation who lived on the coastline of Puget Sound. His name was Seathl, or Steatl, or perhaps Stealth. Seathl was friendly to whites, became a Catholic, and ended up representing the loosely knit tribes of Puget Sound for lack of a more definitively elected representative. He required that a tribute be levied to him for the use of his name. The mention of a dead man's name disturbed his peace in the next world, and he required payment in advance for this future stress.

What began as Alki (and is still called Alki, or West Seattle) moved a little north, across Elliott Bay, to take advantage of better access to the water. But that new village (named for the chief) quickly filled the flat waterside and built on the hills, and it wasn't long before the hills were in the way.

"The streets were so steep that members of the Seattle Symphony, who had to climb three blocks to reach their practice hall from the place where they stored their instruments, arrived winded, and sometimes rehearsals were over before all the horn players caught their breath," begins Murray Morgan's classic history of Seattle, *Skid Road*. "The musicians rigged a pulley to carry the instruments uphill, so that strangers in town were sometimes startled to have a cello or tuba swoop past them up the street." The three largest hills—Denny, Dearborn, and Jackson—blocked north-south expansion. They were just too steep, leaning up into the cloudy sky at a daunting angle. So at the turn of the century, sluices were built, just as they were built for mining, and week by week the hills were washed away. Ten million cubic yards of dirt disappeared in the muddy waves and was carted and rolled to the tidal flats, and Seattle got wider and flatter. But it didn't get any calmer.

Vice was a ruling element; the population argued over whether Seattle should be "open"—which meant a regulated red-light district—or "closed." The great Pantages chain of theaters began in Seattle, with burlesque shows catering to the gamblers and shanghai artists who lived down near the water. Arguments led to graft, political and financial corruption, recall elections, indictments, and finally riots. Seattle enjoyed entwined and strange politics, suffered endless strikes and strike-breaking—and the first general strike in the United States, in 1919—plus street fighting and widespread head-busting. The whole state was referred to as the "Soviet of Washington." After World War II, things settled down: "For years, there wasn't a good riot," wrote Morgan. A poor laundry-truck driver from Seattle named Dave Beck became head of the International Teamsters Union. He held considerable power with his union's vote and his pension funds, before he was convicted of tax evasion and sent to McNeil Island penitentiary.

What is now the Seattle waterfront, much of it built on dead, dredged-out hills, is prosperous and busy, and behind it rises Pike Place Market, a wide, layered, steep market of stairs, produce, fish, and kitsch. The Seattle police ride mountain bikes on their patrols near Pike Place. Inside the market, fish sellers toss whole fish over the heads of the customers, the signs are neon and the architecture California beachfront. At Pike Place are fast-food Chinese-noodle and frozen-yogurt joints, imported batik, African masks, "real shrunken heads," Japanese fishing globes, saltwater taffy, hand-painted greeting cards, dried flowers, strange fruits, fringed leather purses, wind-up toys from Taiwan, earrings and beaded necklaces, glass paperweights made from volcanic ash.

The Olympics are veiled in the distance across the flat bay, where you can spy cruising ships and ferries, and now and then, very occasionally, the small, surprising pipe of a nuclear submarine peering up from below.

These days, nearly a half-billion gallons of industrial effluent flow into Puget Sound every day. Another 175 million gallons of sewage effluent drain into the waters. From the ferries, the powerboats, the nuclear submarines, and the merchant-marine ships, another two million gallons of motor oil are dumped into Puget Sound every year.

"I think Elliott Bay's actually gotten cleaner," one local marine biologist told me. "In the last few years, everyone's gotten on the environmental bandwagon to clean things up. There are many, many pollutants still in Puget Sound, but I think a lot of it is because the pollutants are lodged in the bottom sediments—things like the heavy metals and some bad toxins. As for dredging—dredging's been a fact of life for a lot of years. The land the Seattle waterfront is on was dredged out of Denny Hill and washed into Elliott Bay."

Elsewhere in Seattle, houses are disappearing into the equity boom; by the thousands, people have escaped wearier cities to buy in Seattle. Real estate prices climb, the schools worsen, the traffic is unmanageable, employment erratic. The rain is not quite clean anymore. The Space Needle, that 1950s-style tower of souvenirs, slowly spins around with one load after the other, turning from the expanse of water, the vague mountains, to the now-rounded hills, the lake dotted with sailboats, the freeways thick with cars, the sprawling suburbs, the exclusive island neighborhoods across the bay. Now the crescent of sand in front of Alki holds a pint-size Statue of Liberty and an obelisk dedicated to the original landing party. (It names the men and the children; the women are simply called "wife.") Today commercial development outside the city boundaries rivals that of Los Angeles, but for the distant hazy cone of Rainier. Mobile-home lots, minimarts, drive-ins, hairdressers, and banks are all crammed together and connected by concrete and a crowded four-lane road. FOR SALE OR LEASE. BUILD TO SUIT. The roads are already named 168th Street, or 214th Street, even where the trees still rise up from empty, untouched land. All ready to go.

"Your God makes your people wax strong every day. Soon they will fill all the land. Our people are ebbing away like a rapidly receding tide that will never return." So said Seathl, perhaps seeing for a moment the dreamy vision of a vast metropolis creeping over his land. "Why should I mourn at the untimely fate of my people? Tribe follows tribe and nation follows nation, like the waves of the sea. It is the order of nature, and regret is useless. Your time of decay may be distant, but it will surely come, for even the White Man whose God walked and talked with him as friend with friend cannot be exempt from the common destiny. We may be brothers after all. We will see."

Point Whitney is near the Dosewallips River, called "the Dosey" by the locals. (And the Stillaguamish River is called "the Stilly.") The point is at the end of a shady road sliding between huge madrones, gentle undulant trees with an almost silken, salmon-colored bark. They are, a friend of mine said once, "salamanders with branches." It leads down from the highway to the water—a small, protected harbor inside the long refuge of Hood Canal. On one July afternoon, it was balmy and calm and seemed almost unpopulated; beneath a sign forbidding clamming and outlining the specific times and seasons in which shellfish could be gathered, was a sloping, rock-lined beach, stubbled with smashed and broken oyster shell. The buildings of the shellfish laboratory are separated by enormous tanks, and dripping hoses, pipes and puddles both muddy and clear. In a long, low building near the water, a catwalk extends between rows of vats, teeming with geoduck and other larvae. Behind the beach, in a stagnant bowl, is a fragrant pond, slimy at its edges and thick and still with clouds of algae growing like hair in the sun-heated water.

Lynn Goodwin, a marine scientist at the Point Whitney Shellfish Laboratory operated by the state of Washington, has the unlined, open face of a happy man. He looks younger and stronger than fifty-one, with curly brown-grey hair, mustache, the permanent tan of an outdoorsman. He was wearing a T-shirt, shorts, and sandals when we met;

his T-shirt said GEODUCK STATE. (On a doorway inside the lab, I saw a bumper sticker: Go, GEODUCKS!) Geoducks—pronounced *gooey-ducks*—are giant clams, bizarre and slightly comical creatures whose existence is hardly believed by people outside the region. Geoducks have the oval, shell-encased bodies common to clams, though much larger—the average weight is several pounds, and the record is sixteen pounds, less than a quarter of which is shell. They are extraordinarily long-lived: Geoducks commonly live beyond 150 years.

Geoducks don't dig—they don't even move, but live encased several feet under the substrate, in tidal beds and deeper. The neck, a siphon with two tubes for exchanging water in and out, can expand and shrink several feet. The buried geoduck reaches all the way up through the sea bottom to the sea and its attendant plankton. The neck is a tough, ringed muscle, the body fatty, fleshy, fruitily sweet meat prized for chowders, fritters, and sushi. The body is soft, but the siphon needs to be pounded and beaten like tough steak, flattened and shredded to soften. The first step is to throw the geoducks into hot water a moment, until the skin of the siphon bubbles and blisters. Then the skin peels off in a single piece, "like a used condom," Lynn told me. Lynn Goodwin's specialty is geoducks.

"When the white people first came here, they started using them like the natives up to the 1920s and 1930s, when the numbers started to go down and the season was closed for a while. In about 1966, we started examining the deep areas in Puget Sound with scuba gear, and we found millions and millions and millions of them. That's where the main body is, and all we see is the upper fringe of the population. If you dug up everything in a geoduck area and weighed it, they'd be the dominant animal, weight-wise.

"There are no permits written for geoduck, but it's heavily regulated. The number of participants is strictly limited. We lease beds of geoducks, and they're purchased by individual fishermen by the highest bid at auction. The person who puts the most money down gets a lease for a certain period of time to remove geoducks from that tract. We give them an estimate of what's there, and then they have a ceiling that they can't exceed."

In a downstairs office, Lynn found a model geoduck made from ceramic and carefully painted; it reminded me somehow of all the sculpted seagulls and whales lining gift-shop windows throughout the Sound.

He held up the model in both hands: "Now this—this is the Arnold Schwarzenegger of geoducks. This is what geoducks strive to become." As a kind of game, a staff member will sometimes line up several mature geoducks along a desk. Over a half hour's time, the geoducks open and drop their siphons, blindly reaching for the water that isn't there until the necks reach almost to the floor.

"And then," Lynn explained, "if you walk by and tap them lightly with a ruler"—he mimed the tap in the air by the desk—"they just curl right up, just like that." I was laughing, helplessly lost in an unspoken series of phallic jokes. He could tell—he's worked at the lab for twenty years. "You know how we measure them?" he asks. "No." "You stroke them, down the length, stimulate them, see, and they expand," and he softly, gently, strokes the air.

One of Lynn's experiments now concerns predation of geoduck larvae in the free waters of Puget Sound. He led me out of the laboratory into the hot sun, where two biology students in shorts and Wellington boots were shoveling sand in and out of wooden troughs. Each box, Lynn explained, held a discrete number of larvae and a species of predator, such as snails and crabs. The two are mingled for a few days, and then the gallons of sand are raked and sifted through wire mesh to count the remaining larvae—white commas barely bigger than grains of sand. (The surviving larvae are simply thrown off the beach into the water for a second chance.) The students invited me to help find the half-dozen moon snails buried in one trough.

I stood in summer sun in a muddy puddle, and plunged my hand into the damp, cool sand. It was a blind and somehow eerie search, a creep through darkness and the silt of sand and larvae, and then the sudden touch of a snail's skin, slick and soft.

The moon snail, *Polinices draconis*, is a heavy slug of meat as big as a cantaloupe, which fills itself with water until it has expanded several times larger than its own shell. In danger, the water can be spit out holes along the edge of the snail's foot, until the snail shrinks enough to hide, but it will die after a short while in that position, all curled up, smothering, like a claustrophobe in a stalled elevator. The moon snail crawls not over but through the substratum of Puget Sound, an omnivore that eats live clams and mussels, dead fish, and its own brothers and sisters. Once, diving in the Sound, I came across a moon snail out during the day, in shallow water. It was a pink mother-of-pearl, the size of a large honeydew melon, a few sharp horns wavering at what I took to be its head. When I lifted it from the gravel floor, its foot almost encased the small, grapefruit-size shell, but within a minute or so, the flesh began to shrink, the foot to scallop into a ruffle, sinking back inside.

I'd been snorkeling on the surface of Puget Sound, in a protected corner inside one of its fingers. A seal was darting about several dozen yards away, peering up quickly with dark hound eyes and then diving again. The eelgrass below bent with the pull of the tide, mats of algae with crabs darting beneath hovering flounder. Below me on the bay floor, I could see a sunflower star so big it looked inflated by a pump. I counted twenty-nine bright-orange arms. A moment later, I found a bigger sea star, a different variety in pale pink, with a mere five arms, but each as long as my calf.

As I expected, I had only to swim a few dozen yards before I saw a jellyfish, a soft ivory cloud with a pink inner ring, and lavender tentacles, bobbing up and down seductively. "Whoever frequents wharves, piers, and floats, especially at not-quite-respectable hours, will be certain to see some," wrote Ed Ricketts in his book *Between Pacific Tides*, the granddaddy guide to West Coast tidal life. Ricketts digresses in his manuscript when he comes to jellyfish, since they aren't properly tidal creatures, but finds it "a pity" not to mention them a moment: "In quiet bays in Puget Sound and British Columbia the jellyfish, *Aurelia*, nearly colorless, except for its four horse-shoe-shaped brown gonads, sometimes occurs in such immense numbers that it is impossible to dip an oar without striking several of the beautiful pulsating animals. A boat seems to glide through a sea of jellyfish rather than through water."

The beating globe I can see is solitary and framed by the dark water as though in a spotlight; it is only a few yards below and to the side, but it seems as far away as a mirage, as far away as a planet swinging in orbit.

Sometimes the silt near the shoreline gets churned up, by too many divers or a sudden storm knocking the layers of water about. But the visibility in the Sound drops dramatically and predictably every spring and summer. I don't mean to imply that there is any pattern worth relying on from day to day; the magnificent blooms of phytoplankton and zooplankton that thicken Puget Sound can rise in a day and leave in a day; one spot can be turgid with them while a hundred yards away the water is glassy and clean. Almost ninety percent of the flourishing plankton growth in the Sound takes place between April and August.

The largest of planktons is ten times smaller than a herring, and most are far smaller than that. The blooms that magically appear and disappear all season long are blooms of the most tenacious and minimal creatures, myriad varieties of diatoms, rotifers, flagellates, and others. They are plants and animals stripped bare of excess, like competitive swimmers shorn of every hair and tweezed of every brow. The living plankton grows in thick millions, and even then there is more dead material than alive; the dead scraps of skeletons, feces, and shed cilia fall so thickly they are called "marine snow."

In the winter, when the plankton dies out and the cold temperature holds the oxygen in, Puget Sound's water clears. (The air is warmer in the summer, and the water is a little warmer, but Puget Sound is always cold.) As often as not, it rains, or the sky turns into a grey glare and meets the flat, grey, glaring water without a break, so that the world is a sphere in which I form the center. The water is like space, not mist, or fog, but a solid, flat white, broken only by the sharp, tiny, black lines of a single duck, or an almost-sunken log floating out with the tide.

Along the billowy floor of Hood Canal, the diver follows the dipping movement of the eelgrass, the scattered anemones like plush carpet over the sharp, oyster-coated rocks. (The shellfish are there for the taking; on the rocky banks of popular dive spots are shared campfires, and the divers come up hands full and toss the shells whole on the coals.

The best description of the experience comes from Burgess Cogill's memory of her girlhood: "Stuffed to the gills with steamed clams, the rest of the day could have been part of an alcoholic's lost weekend for all it mattered.")

When I keep my eyes open and pay attention, I can see the twin ovals of geoduck siphons in the soft silt between the rocks. They are the size of dimes, no bigger, and the edges ripple as I watch; a rush of water from my hand and they slip away. I find inexplicable things, enigmas, everyone does: a bright-orange shred with rippled edges, a curled green leafy thing, unclear whether it is plant or animal, alive or dead. A diver told me he found a full-grown dead harbor seal in about twenty-five feet of water, covered with feeding crabs.

One fall day, I was diving in Hood Canal, the southernmost arm of the Sound. I expected the water to be reasonably clear, but some element or other had been at work: There were dancing bits of weed and tissue and unidentified flotsam in every cubic foot of water. All the yellowish particles clinging to the eelgrass came loose and floated around me in a cloud, each mote dancing like hovering gnats waiting above the summer lawns, the distance disappearing in a brown curtain, the water's surface twenty feet up visible only by a stronger, brownish light. I felt like I was sliding through snow at night, on a smooth road, suspended and even and steady and the tires humming into the black. In such a fog, what is near is made suddenly dead-clear; in the snow at night, a deer, a sign, a companion's softened face. Under me I could see a blade of eelgrass, and a two-inch blood-red crab scuttling out of sight; the world retreated and left only a small frame, an empty oyster shell turning in the backwash of my fin, a white anemone waving hungry fronds.

At Point Whitney, the dark water receded to infinity. Bright speckles of light like white radials bounced off my mask and broke into geometric patterns around me. Odd scraps of weed and tissue without apparent organization passed by, floating in the space of green water, not rising, not falling. Sometimes in deep water I'm caught by visceral, leg-dangling shark fears that mean somehow more than sharks. I am caught up in the strangeness of where I am, the size. But that day at

Point Whitney, I felt surrounded by fertility. It was like being plunged into a culture medium, a womb. I was feeling a generative intimacy with the water, an abrupt fetal memory almost embarrassingly immediate. I was paddling through a soup of milt and roe, copulation determined and steady on every side. Geoducks and anemones, like a lot of marine creatures, reproduce by spewing clouds of sperm into the water. I caught a mouthful of salt water, a teaspoon mouthful overflowing with seed.

Roland Anderson is a baby-faced, pink-cheeked man. He is a baby-faced malacologist—a student of mollusks. His specialty is the octopus, and his choice of terrain is one of the best for his chosen creature; the octopuses in Puget Sound are the biggest in the world.

The basement laboratory of the Seattle Aquarium, where Roland works, is cold the way only wet, underground concrete can be cold. The walls are lined with tanks covering several sets of shelves along the walls and in the center of the room. He led me around, with a little paternal pride in the tank inhabitants. In one corner, several abalone clung to a glass tank front, flesh the color of butternut squash, purplish shells lined with hairy black tentacles. In the tank next door, a giant nudibranch—essentially, a very large snail without a shell—was slowly chewing up a sea pen, an almost immobile animal shaped like a bright orange-feathered quill pen. More sea pens wavered in water nearby, more golden than their dying peer. In other tanks scattered around the room were green anemones, lobster and balletic, tentative shrimps, and fish of various kinds. On a bottom shelf was a tank filled with wildly churning brine shrimp looking as though they were an experiment in Brownian motion. But it was the octopuses I'd come to see.

Why, I wondered, did they grow so big here?

"Puget Sound is a very rich area," said Roland. "I'm not sure I'd go so far as to call it unique—it's comparable to the fjords of Norway, or New Zealand, or Chile. It's all a matter of food—here we have optimum conditions. Puget Sound is a reverse fjord, because the glaciers came in at the open end of Puget Sound and stopped at the closed end.

Normally in a fjord, the glaciers start at the head of the bay and go out. Fjords typically have sills that don't come to the surface. Now, Puget Sound has sills, but they weren't left by the glaciers. Puget Sound has a lot of nutrition because there are a lot of rivers running into it, and some flushing action because of the tides. But the nutrition tends to stay in the Sound because of these sills. We have a lot of plankton and a lot of plankton-lovers, on up the food chain to the top.

"Plus, it's a stable environment. The octopuses don't have to migrate, and they don't have to spend energy keeping themselves warm or cold. One thing about octopuses is that they have a very short life span—our Giant Pacific octopus grows to a hundred pounds in three to five years. Compare that to a tropical octopus, which grows to adulthood in six months—they're a lot smaller, and they live only six months. Basically, you think of tropical animals as living fast and furiously; colder animals live longer. I strongly suspect some of the longest-lived animals on earth live deep, deep in the cold ocean."

The largest octopus officially on record weighed 117 pounds and had a tentacle spread of twenty-eight feet. The typical octopus even in Puget Sound is considerably smaller—perhaps sixty pounds with a reach more like twelve or fifteen feet. But that's not a small octopus, whether encountered in a tank or at nighttime, darting past with the octopuses' peculiar, inimitable glide. "The actual spread depends on how much you pull it—it's rubbery flesh, there are no bones or anything, so you can pull it as wide as you want. People forget, too, that everything looks bigger under water—and people have a tendency to exaggerate, anyhow. We went and got an octopus in the bay here, which divers had seen. They said it must be two hundred pounds and have suckers twelve inches across. We pulled it out. It was big—it was eighty-three pounds."

The male octopus has a sexual organ, called a hectocotylus, located on the tip of his third right tentacle. The hectocotylus enlarges for breeding, and after suitable posturing and displays of machismo, he inserts it into the mantle cavity of the female. The pair may then sit in one or more mating positions for as long as an hour before parting. ("It knows sex, but it does not get excited about it," writes one biologist of the octopus.) Octopuses mate only once; shortly after the encounter, the male dies. The female harbors the fertilized eggs a while, then hangs them inside her den in strings that look rather like rice kernels, or "a long bunch of sultana grapes in miniature," as Ed Ricketts wrote. She may lay a few thousand or as many as 150,000 eggs or more, depending on the species. The female, who starves herself throughout the brooding period, dies soon after the eggs hatch. She dies, and her little octopus infants, considerably smaller than the nail on your little toe, drift with the currents for a while, being snatched by the plankton feeders and swimming to new grounds.

On the shelf above the tank of brine shrimp is a tank with a single inhabitant—an eighteen-month-old Giant Pacific octopus. The tank, like all the octopus tanks at the aquarium, is kept closed by a long strip of black Velcro, one of the only locks an octopus (which can live out of water for about half an hour) can't seem to pick. "Octopuses are great escape artists," Roland explained, while we watched the male crawl across the glass a foot away. "They can escape through a hole about the size of the diameter of their eye, which is also about the size of their beak. They have no skeleton; they're limited only by the size of the beak and eye. In one case I know about, the tanks were all adjacent to each other, and all the octopus had to do to get a free crab was climb from one tank to the one next door. We had an octopus that was trained to get out and get into a rolling tank, which was then taken out into the public, and then we'd take it back, and it would climb out and get back into its own tank. Everyone has an octopus named Houdini because they can get out of almost anything; you practically have to have the tanks hermetically sealed to keep them in.

"It's pretty easy to catch one, though. A lot of the ones we've gotten recently were just under the piers here—you just pick the little ones up and put them in a bag. The hundred-pound ones are a little bit harder. They have grip strength and pulling strength—they can't push on anything, but they can pull as long as they want."

The octopus in front of us, its body about as big as a human head, slid sucker by sucker very quickly back and forth, back and forth, more elastic and pliable than the water itself. Each sucker on each tentacle seemed independently alive, and in fact the octopus—the smartest mollusk by far—has a strangely decentralized brain. The muscles of the tentacles and the color-changing apparatus of the skin are innervated directly; there is not a long neural path from a central brain to an arm. Its skin was a rusty red, its continual movements so supple and complex—and so daringly lovely—I couldn't follow them, couldn't count the linear progression of musculature from inch to inch.

"Red is usually considered the color of anger and frustration," said Roland. "But that's anthropomorphic. This guy's always hungry, and he always will be. He associates us with food." Octopuses have highly variable and individual behavior, but like all good biologists, Roland is averse to guessing at motive and thought: "You'll hear various comments about how smart they are. They are certainly the smartest invertebrate animal. But you have to remember that an octopus is related to a clam, and a clam is not very smart. I'd say octopuses are somewhat less intelligent than a mouse or rat, but they can learn. They can do labyrinths, they can learn how to open jars and push buttons to get food.

"I'm doing research on octopus behavior. One of the things I've noticed is that you bring different octopuses into the aquarium and they behave differently—some are sort of shy and retiring, some are very aggressive, and others are just sort of devil-may-care and bland. Now, 'personality,' of course, is also an anthropomorphic term.

"They're the bane of my life. They're always squirting you with water, escaping so you come in the next day and find them dead on the floor. They get out and can't get back. I like the fact that everyone seems to be intrigued by them—they're so alien. You look at depictions of the octopus in movies and they're always giant monsters attacking people."

Octopuses do bite, with their parrotlike beaks, although you might handle one a hundred times without a single problem. Divers all over the world like to pick them up, balance them on their arms, or their heads, and have a photo taken with the tentacles hanging in front of their face like a Medusa's hair. (One fellow I know was doing this when the octopus suddenly grabbed his mask and snorkel and dashed away with them.) But it's a risky business. "All octopuses have venom. The Giant Pacific seems very loath to bite, but there have been cases in the aquarium—I don't know any cases in the wild. But the little octopus we have here, *rubescens*, is very prone to bite, and can have a nasty effect. We have a person here who was bitten by one ten or fifteen years ago, and she still has a scar."

On the other side of the cold, dank-smelling room is a tank holding a female *rubescens*, about the size of an orange and hugging the far wall. *Rubescens* is the most common octopus on the West Coast, and it occurs in huge numbers in Puget Sound. This species likes to live in beer bottles when free, compressing itself in. (It's worth picking up the bottles one finds along the Sound floor; in the daytime, a diver can often see an octopus inside, improbably swollen to fill the space, eye balefully glaring at the disturbance.)

"Watch," Roland commanded, and I turned in time to see him grab a tiny crab, no bigger than a quarter, from a small box and drop it into the tank. Octopuses have paralytic and digestive enzymes, and some species also have a radula, a drill for opening shells and injecting toxins. The very second the crab hit the water of the tank, the round animal opened and flew, saillike, upon it, winding her many arms about it and tugging it into her embrace before retreating up and backward into a small box to dine.

I had never been diving at night in Puget Sound—the best time to see not only octopus but much more. A diver I know says the best night-diving he's ever done was off Port Angeles, in the Strait of Juan de Fuca, at three in the morning. "There were abalone everywhere," he said. "You just pick 'em up and put 'em in your bag. Here's one, and here's one—they're everywhere."

I drove up to Jorsted Creek, a small stream falling into the west side of Hood Canal, on a very black night in a pelting, constant rain. I followed my headlights through the wet dark the way I follow my dive lamp through the dark water, suspended in a small bubble of light. I climbed down a muddy, slippery slope of rocks, leaves, and tangled roots to a small gravel beach. There were no stars or moon, only the sooty, palpable sky and the rain falling, swishing through the drooping cedars over my head and into the water. I couldn't tell, except by the dip of my toe, where the gravel ended and the water began. The drops pattered on the surface and my little flashlight caught the small cups of their impact. Far away, I could see the black silhouette of a fir-covered point, and a few distant, tiny, smeared lights.

I was hoping for octopus. The rain had made a lens of the first few feet, a mixture of salt ocean and fresh water mingling to oily distortion, like Vaseline smeared on my mask. In the clear, deeper water, I could see the startled crabs, the soles, and open, hungry anemones on their night hunt. But no octopus came that night. I was embraced instead by moon jellies. Oh, moon jelly, a name to spread on one's evening toast and eat bite by tiny bite. Transparent white cups, like the top half of a coffee cup but rounded on the bottom, hung before me. They seemed to have no structure at all, to be as frail as soap bubbles, to be made out of tissue, or fog: small shells of sea, floating, turning themselves almost inside-out with each pulse, collapsing in the hard wash of my hand movements, righting themselves again.

SEVEN

In the first years of white habitation, no labor was more important than clearing the land of the ubiquitous trees. Every foot of encroachment was a relief, a possible garden, a home.

The phrase *cabin fever* came from these woods, after all. The very first sawmill in the Pacific Northwest was closed more than once for lack of a market or transport for the logs. It was built in 1827 in what is now Camas in southern Washington, north of the Hudson's Bay Company headquarters at Fort Vancouver. The mill was powered by water and used the labor of the "Kanakas," Hawaiian men brought over to the new frontier. The little mill turned out timber at the rate of three thousand board feet a day (equal to a five-foot-diameter, sixteen-foot log, far less than a whole tree might contain). The mill was able to supply all the local needs, with excess. The unfortunate local tradition of exporting trees began with that mill, which sent its excess wood to Hawaii and elsewhere in the Pacific. Twenty years later, the Territory was exporting five million board feet of timber a year, most of it cut from this area.

What mornings those must have been, cold and wet with the mists of the night and winter. Coffee-skinned men with the frizzy black hair of the native Hawaiian, men raised on the papaya and the canoe, waiting for the dim sun to climb above the looming woods. Was it hard for them to leave their rough beds to face that work each day? To stand, arms crossed in defiance, alone among an alien cornucopia? Or did they feel a positive pleasure in the work, hook their thumbs in their belts, and lean back to follow the line of an asymmetric, unapologetic Douglas fir, knowing it would fall and they would fell it? What a satisfying scrape as the saw teeth bit through the bark, what a lovely crash when it finally hit the ground.

The effort began almost with a vengeance against the forested arrogance of the land. In the latter part of the 1800s, Charles Nordhoff traveled to Puget Sound and Port Townsend, a popular shipping place for timber: "You may hear one man pitying another for the confession that he made no more than a hundred million last year. It is feet of lumber they are speaking of; and when you see the monstrous piles of sawdust which encumber the mill ports, the vast quantities of waste stuff they burn, and the huge rafts of timber which are towed down to the mills . . . you will not longer wonder that they talk of millions."

There were no trails, no stores, no towns, no signs of all that had been left behind. But here was a place where a man with muscle and a sharp saw needed only an acre and one tree. One tree! One single tree was all it took for a house and a barn, and enough left over to fence two acres; one single tree filled a schooner with shingles; one single tree was turned into a mile of railroad ties. Sizable streams were fitted with splash dams, tricky contraptions of wire and logs, and the trees were rolled in while the water backed up and flooded its banks. When the dam was opened, the straining water burst down the streambed, pulling logs with it in a wild flood down the hillside. They invented flumes greased with tallow, and skid roads made of logs laid side by side to slide other logs along.

Nordhoff wrote with admiration of the men "who are busily turning these forests into lumber." It might take an entire day to clear a space in which to drop a single redwood tree; they were, for all their size, fragile, and sometimes broke apart on impact, destroying the length of the log. Their fall had to be cushioned—by the branches and slash cut from other trees, by the mud and bog of the wet woods. They fell, remembered Stewart Holbrook with the kind of nostalgia reserved for natural disasters, with a sound "like a hurricane being born." The trees were so big that special saws had to be employed in the mills to cut them small enough for the usual circular saws to reach; others were split with wedges and even blown into pieces with dynamite. "It is a kind of jungle," he wrote, "and the loggers, when they have felled a number of trees, set fire to the brush in order to clear the ground before they attempt to draw the logs to the water." The trees were cut off twelve and fourteen feet above the ground, and the stump left, or burned; then only the straight, unbranching middle of the trunk—the "body wood"—was used, sometimes only a few dozen feet of it. The upper sections—thinner and knotted—were left behind to rot. In fact, it was better for the forest that all this mess was left behind to nourish the soil and the seedlings to come. The more efficient methods of modern clear-cutting steal or burn the leftover material. Still, it's estimated that for every foot of lumber that made it to market, two feet were left behind.

Regarding naturalists, the cranky trapper Peter Skene Ogden had, as usual, strong words. He was sometimes required by his employer, the Hudson's Bay Company, to take scientists with him into the wilderness. At the beginning of one such trip, Ogden wrote, "five more Gent. as follows 2 in quest of Flowers 2 killing all the Birds in the Columbia & 1 in quest of rocks and stones all these bucks . . . are a perfect nuisance." But even Ogden, who frequently seemed to like no one and nothing at all, liked David Douglas, who was described by one friend as "the most sociable, kindly and endearing of men—a sturdy little Scot," and by another, the "happiest of mortals."

David Douglas was a person blessed by both circumstance and temperament. He is the Douglas of the Douglas fir, of course, already half-forgotten here in every other way. His journals are among the most important documents ever written about the early Pacific Northwest.

Douglas was born in Scotland in 1799, attended school until he was eleven years old, and then was apprenticed as a gardener. He was a very shy, retiring fellow, but single-minded about botany, the only subject that wholly caught his catholic attention. When he was twenty-one, Douglas went to work first for the Botanical Garden of Glasgow, and then for the Horticultural Society of London, at that time the penultimate garden of the exotic. The Horticultural Society owned a thirty-three-acre tract in Chiswick, planted with thousands of roses, fruit trees, and flowers brought from around the world by botanical explorers. Douglas, then twenty-four, was assigned to go to China, but a break in diplomatic relations canceled the trip. Instead, he traveled to the eastern United States and studied not only the local flora but plants brought to New England from the Pacific by Lewis and Clark. With the Anglo-Saxon's patient view of empire, Douglas also collected acorns from the largest and stoutest varieties of oaks he could find, planning to plant a grove for a future navy. One man-of-war battleship favored by sailors then required two thousand trees of at least a hundred years in age.

Douglas was never happy in Britain again, never able to relax in the society of the wealthy collectors. He could not stop imagining the unimaginable world he had yet to see. Six months after his return home, Douglas left on the *William and Ann* for the Pacific Northwest, under the protection of the Hudson's Bay Company.

When he landed months later on the banks of the Columbia, he found the scenery "sublimely grand" but was far more interested in the plants. In his journal, he wrote of the thickness of tall, dark trees, the pleasure of ground beneath his feet, and: "Immediately on stepping out of the boat we found *Rubus spectabilis* and *Gaultheria shallon* growing close to the water's edge." This ingenuousness pervades his extensive, detailed writings, as do the Latinate names; he witnessed the subtle variation of the landscape and the startling aspects of never-considered plants with a reserved ecstasy, writing on one occasion only that he had "found some very fine pebbles."

Douglas had been warned about "privation" in the Northwest. When he arrived, there were perhaps four hundred white men in the entire region. He adjusted magnificently and with little complaint, living variously in a cedar-bark hut, a deerskin lodge, a tent, and out of doors, traveling far and often alone, collecting samples endlessly. Douglas learned to shoot birds on the wing and lit his pipe with a magnifying glass and sunlight. David Douglas traveled more miles in this "country so exceedingly interesting," and to more new places, than almost any other explorer, without intending to explore at all.

In 1826 alone, Douglas traveled more than four thousand miles throughout what is now Oregon and Washington. Reading his diaries, it is hard to imagine anyone surviving one of his expeditions, let alone several years of them. More than once, Douglas lost months' worth of samples, in storms and in rushing rivers, and on his trek to Russia, he lost more than four hundred samples, his journal, and nearly his life in a whirlpool. He lost most of his vision here, too, through worsening ophthalmia exacerbated by alternating glare and dust. He traveled throughout the year, stopping at a Hudson's Bay fort for the dead of winter only with great reluctance. He regularly forded rivers thick with ice, sometimes dozens of times in a day, and marched off on the other side on makeshift snowshoes, sleeping in snowbanks and under fir trees, eating berries, roots, dried fish, and beaver meat. Twice he was forced to eat his horse, and at least once, to his own dismay and scientific censure, the sample skins of animals he'd shot to take home to his colleagues.

David Douglas was probably the first white man to climb the daunting Blue Mountains of eastern Oregon, and he did so in the arduous weather of a thunder-and-lightning storm; he spent the night on a peak in the open weather, cold and without food, frustrated by his slow pace and the rains dampening his precious samples. That night he wrote, "If I have any zeal, for once and the first time it began to cool." He helped map the Umpqua drainage ("that very partially known country called 'Clamite' "), traveled up the Columbia to its northern reaches, walked overland across the northern Rockies, and, on his last trip to the Northwest, tried to walk to Siberia. He wrote every day, under the most difficult circumstances, and often without a candle; when there was no other light, he would write by the flame of a burning piece of resinous wood.

Archibald Menzies, the surgeon-naturalist who had come to the area with Vancouver earlier, discovered what would come to be called the Douglas fir. But David Douglas was the first to retrieve cones and seeds to take home to England. He thought it "one of the most striking and truly graceful objects in Nature," measuring the diameter and length of fallen trees, climbing the trees he could scale, shooting cones off with his gun when he couldn't find any on the ground.

He was remarkably liberal about the Indians, considering the attitudes of his fellows, and though he professed pleasure in the occasional glimpse of "a Christian countenance," he never attempted to correct the Indians' way of life. The Columbia tribes called him "the Grass Man" because he was unlike anything else they'd seen: not a trapper or trader, not a sailor or hunter, not a man of medicine or a farmer or a trickster. He spent his days crawling across the forest floor, or gazing into its upper stories, and was wont to bribe the Indians with tobacco to climb an immense tree and bring down some cones.

In three separate trips to the Pacific Northwest, David Douglas was able to introduce almost two hundred species of plants to England, among them trees, shrubs, roses, orchids, and berries. (Some of the plants he sent back to England had flakes of gold clinging to their roots, but Douglas wasn't interested in gold.) He found the evening primrose, the lupine, the delicate ocean spray, the noble fir, the white fir, and the Sitka spruce, many varieties of rhododendron, and the only native peony in North America.

For months he searched, and asked every trapper and hunter and Indian he met to join the search, for a strange tree whose cone he had seen; against all botanical expectations, the pine appeared to exude a sweet sap like that of sugar maples. Finally, trusting in native descriptions, he struck south with a small group of fur trappers to the dangerous Umpqua region in southwestern Oregon, a wholly wild, unwelcoming thickness populated by pointedly hostile natives. It was one of his more difficult trips, during which he was forced to run from a grizzly bear, fell into a ravine and broke ribs while hunting deer, and narrowly escaped a band of angry Indians.

"The fact plainly this," wrote Douglas one evening, "all hungry and no means of cooking a little of our stock; travelled thirty-three miles, drenched and bleached with rain and sleet, chilled with a piercing north wind; and then to finish the day experienced the cooling, comfortless consolation of lying down wet without supper or fire. On such occasions I am liable to become very fretful." But in spite of everything, he found his "much-wished-for Pine," the immense and lovely sugar pine, growing on what is now Sugar Pine Ridge by the thousands, growing casually like weeds over the wet hills.

But we change when we change the land, and Douglas changed, too. By the time of his last trip, in the winter of 1832–33, Douglas had grown a little weary of the Northwest. He hated his brief returns to England, where he was publicly lauded for his contributions but couldn't make a living as anything more than a gardener. He had been to Hawaii and Monterey, and studied the Galápagos, and felt there was much to be done. He spent most of the third trip doing astronomical and magnetic observations, in spite of his poor eyesight. But the Northwest was different. He noted the terrible depopulation of the Indians from illness, the increasing hostility of the survivors, and then he almost died of fever himself. There was, he wrote, "too much civilization."

The forest, for all its fertile strength, could only be a wrong thing, because it was a raw thing, the unwanted barrier to what each one wanted to believe was a God-given place. The small clearing, the new farm, was right in the midst of it, not only because it meant home, but because it meant change. The delicious landscape Douglas loved was incomplete without the hand of man. Finishing it required an extraordinary amount of work, because all that was immediate and true about the land had to be removed. Not only must the trees go, but the rapids, the rocks, the course of streams, the wildlife, the natives, and the height of hills. This sculpting of the wilderness, which David Douglas aided and despised, is literally the creation of the frontier. The frontier requires passage and settlement to be a frontier at all—to be new land undergoing its first use. More than the journey, more than travail, it is reconstruction of the landscape that is the experience of the pioneer. Only much later do the great-great-grandchildren fly over the land to see how scrabbled and torn it has become. Only later are there cities, freeways, garbage heaps. The endless logging roads wiggle across the unwalked land, like ribbons of flatworms embedded in the ground. David Douglas could see the future coming.

When his dream of walking to Siberia, and from there back to

England, failed in a whirlpool, Douglas returned to the Columbia, recovered, and finally left for another trip to Hawaii. He was thirty-six years old. There he marched around the Big Island's volcanoes for weeks, writing and taking notes and delighting in the endless number of surprising plants. Even now his death can excite scholars to argument: Was it an accident or murder? (His celebrated gentle character had grown irascible with time.) Either way, after all his time in a deadly wilderness, David Douglas died by falling into a bullock pit and being gored and trampled to death.

Frederick Weyerhaeuser emigrated to the United States from Germany in 1852 while still a teenager; within a few years, he was running a timber conglomerate in Minnesota. Weyerhaeuser was an immensely hard-working man, rarely leaving the office except to sleep and now and then impregnate his wife with one of his seven children. He was strong enough to carry 120-pound sacks of wheat on each shoulder, drank a quart of buttermilk a day, and regularly quoted from *Poor Richard's Alamanack*. He was a beekeeper by hobby and a tree-buyer by trade. "He said he liked to buy trees when it was raining and sell them when the sun shone. But, said his son, 'I cannot remember that he ever sold any, no matter what the weather was.'" What Frederick Weyerhaeuser sold was timber, not trees.

In St. Paul, Weyerhaeuser had a neighbor named James J. Hill. (J. J. Hill was the father-in-law of Sam Hill, the eccentric builder of a reproduction of Stonehenge on the Columbia River.) It happened that Jim Hill took over the Northern Pacific Railroad Company in 1896, a company that had received one of the grandest examples of congressional largess in American history. The United States Congress had granted the Northern Pacific 25,600 acres of land for every mile of rail built to the West. In 1900, Weyerhaeuser and fifteen partners—none of whom lived in the Northwest—bought 900,000 acres of largely unseen and unsurveyed land from James Hill, all of it land granted to Hill's railroad. They paid six dollars an acre, and shortly after the deal, one of the members of the syndicate told a press conference, "We bought this timber not to look at but to cut."

(Some of the land given to the Northern Pacific Railroad included the slopes and fields of Mount Rainier. When Mount Rainier National Park was created, the United States decided it might be a good idea to own the land on which the park stood. The Northern Pacific—and James J. Hill—traded every acre on Rainier for an acre of carefully chosen, unclaimed land elsewhere in the Northwest. The exchange of rocks and wildflowers for virgin forest only increased the value of the land Weyerhaeuser was soon to buy. In his confessional book, *Looters of the Public Domain*, S. A. D. Puter claims with unnecessary hyperbole that James Hill told the United States Congress to create Mount Rainier National Park just so he could profitably divest himself of the land. But then, Puter calls himself "King of the Oregon Land Fraud Ring.")

Within a few months, the Weyerhaeuser Company began separating out the rest of its poorly timbered sections and buying up the small private tracts of good timber between the acres of original railroad land. It was a heady, rapid business: Within three years, the company owned 1.3 million acres of forest, most of it in enormous, unbroken tracts. That number grew to more than two million acres in Oregon, Washington, and Idaho. Meanwhile, Frederick left cold St. Paul and moved to southern California.

Frederick Weyerhaeuser died a very wealthy man. In a thinly veiled reference to Weyerhaeuser, President Theodore Roosevelt once excoriated men who "skin the country and go somewhere else." But Weyerhaeuser did most, and perhaps all, of his skinning legally, and in large part with the help of the United States Congress. The company grew so big that in 1969 it was able to buy outright almost two million acres in a single plot of land crossing central and western Arkansas into eastern Oklahoma. Weyerhaeuser has plants in most states and several countries—especially in the Far East markets, where log exports receive such a lucrative price—and has diversified into real estate and housing development, disposable diapers and nursery stock, chemical production and packaging. The University of Washington's College of Forest Resources, which trains foresters, is sometimes called the University of Weyerhaeuser. Mill closures and layoffs may hurt the towns near Weyerhaeuser holdings—the company employs 45,000 people—but not the company itself, which is still run by Weyerhaeusers, earns ten billion dollars a year, and is now the world's largest private timber owner. One out of five of its logs is exported, primarily to Asian markets. The company no longer owns any old-growth timber. ("That's all harvested," I was told by a company spokesman.) The few acres of old-growth trees the company had left were destroyed in the eruption of Mount St. Helens in 1989. The lower acres of blown-down timber were salvaged, but in a move reminiscent of old Hill's Rainier deal, the upper acres were sold to the United States, to be incorporated in the Mount St. Helens National Monument. Weyerhaeuser's enormous wild forest holdings have been transformed, in less than a century, to fields of trees as smooth and unvaried as a lawn.

Frederick Weyerhaeuser wasn't the only timber baron to get rich off railroads. Congress offered several land grants. For every mile of track laid between the Siskiyou Mountains and Portland, a railroad company would receive 12,800 acres. It was nothing as effortless or sudden as Weyerhaeuser's purchase of the Northern Pacific lands, but still it was a sweetheart deal. The Umpqua and Siskiyou ranges proved shockingly difficult for rail building, and one company after the other made failed attempts to finish the line, which ultimately took more than twenty years to build. The Southern Pacific Railroad had leased the southern end of the O & C (Oregon and California) line, a massive effort that held land throughout western Oregon. Southern Pacific failed to abide by the naïve demands of the congressional grant that the acreage be sold to "actual settlers," in small plots, for no more than $2.50 an acre. (Better deals—irresistible deals—abounded, most of them involving logging huge parcels flat as quickly as possible.) The government ordered Southern Pacific to divest to the government in 1913; the Bureau of Land Management (BLM) took over those O & C lands in 1947. But Southern Pacific sued and won an additional four million dollars in compensation.

Under the earlier Timber and Stone Act, early settlers could buy

160-acre parcels if they would live on and work the land. Entrepreneurs enlisted hundreds of dummy buyers, wined and dined them and often paid for their vacations, for the mere act of putting their signatures on a sworn statement of their intent to farm the land. Walter McCulloch, in his encyclopedic dictionary of logging slang, writes this under the entry *Public Domain*: "Excursion trains were run from the mid-west cities bringing out hordes of vacationers, each of whom put down a 12 x 14 inch doll's house on a quarter section of public domain timber land, then swore he had put a 12 x 14 cabin on his claim. The quarter section was then sold for $1 to the real estate speculator who had thoughtfully furnished the cabin and the trip. Timberlands were later sold to lumber outfits at fabulous profits." Some loggers just bought what was called a "rubber 40": the right to log a forty-acre parcel, which was then logged as far as they could go, until they ran out of trees or got caught.

The Weyerhaeuser Company dedicated the nation's first tree farm in 1941, promoting the science of tree-raising with an enormous and careful advertising campaign. In 1965, the company logged its own second-growth timber for the first time. In little more than a lifetime, an impenetrable forest had officially become a crop. In a few decades, the region was pockmarked with more than thirty-one thousand such farms covering more than seventy-seven million acres. Now almost every road in the Pacific Northwest passes alternately from clear-cuts to new growth to open slash fields. The signs say PLANTED 1977 or PLANTED 1986, and on the ridge behind, Douglas fir, each tree exactly the same height and color as its neighbor, the same shape, crawls back away from the road and over the hillside like fungus.

Weyerhaeuser, in fact, calls itself "the tree-growing company," and still blankets television with expensive commercials. In these ads, healthy young men jog through cathedrals of tall pines. Young people plant seedlings of Douglas fir on a sunny hill, the snowy peaks of the Cascades in the distance. They smile with uplifted faces at their own good work, like pioneers planting corn in the newly turned ground. A forester wearing a convincing white lab coat explains patiently to the camera how important the future of the forests is to Weyerhaeuser. But of course it is the future of tree farms that matters to Weyerhaeuser, not the little bit of chaotic, decadent forest still left.

Several years ago, my husband and I were backpacking along logging roads in a southern arm of these woods, looking for a rumored, secret hot springs. We left the car and dropped down a dirt road into a valley that had been half-logged decades before; the old stumps were softened with moss and new fir trees were growing in the cuts. The soil was springy with humus, mild and pale. We were following the directions given us by a friend, but nothing seemed right; turns didn't come when we expected them, the landmarks didn't follow.

We walked across a logged acre and followed the road into forest again, crossing between two standing fields of mature trees. We decided we'd lost our way and were about to turn around, talking quietly about where we would camp that night, when we followed a curve in the road and saw, like a frame frozen on the screen, three men. They wore hunting clothes: orange caps, down vests, boots. There was something immediately strange about the way they stood, staring at the two of us, loaded down with packs. Three men, older than we, silent. I took in the tension and the strangeness, the incongruity that I couldn't quite define in one glimpse, and then saw with a hot startle the small, dead doe lying bloody beside them and the great crossbow dangling from one man's hand. I saw the still tableau and then realized that not only was the deer a doe, but it was not hunting season, not by months. No one spoke, and I was suddenly afraid, with the shark fear of being caught in a big, empty place without hope of rescue, without anyone to hear a shout for help. They stared at us and we stared at them, all in a few seconds' time, and we kept walking without a word, not slowing our pace for a moment. I smiled, and nodded to the man with the crossbow, and kept walking. My shoulder blades itched as we put them behind our backs; under my pack I could feel that tight, tense place between them where the arrow fit. We turned another corner and crossed out from between the standing trees into another stumpy field, blooming with wildflowers and grass.

We waited there a long time, until we heard the gunning of a truck engine and its long whine up the hill, and then we waited some more. In the open field, as the day passed, there were great clots of sun falling in the late afternoon; behind us, between ourselves and our car, was a grey, dim wall of trees. There were no sounds but the buzz of insects and the occasional cry of a bird. No cars, no voices, no deer hungry for grass in the twilight. When we finally lifted our packs and walked slowly back through the fir trees, the men were gone and the deer was gone and there was nothing but a dark patch of blood on the grass. It was getting dark by then and the clear-cut near the road looked ashen with age and weary, overrun with rodents and rotting logs. We wound back up the valley rim and drove away.

Even driving on a sunny afternoon, staying on the road, passing the occasional logging truck, I feel the nearness of the forest mind. Throughout the deep woods are footprints, and the potential for strange encounters. The prints are much longer than a human's foot, much wider, often shaped in a vague hourglass, with four and five toes; the tracks are often slightly pigeon-toed. The prints are very unlike a bear's, and bears are the only other large mammal around. These prints have been found singly and doubly, in snow and mud and moist leaves, along trails, stream banks and in the most obscure, untraveled meadows and woods: tens of thousands of prints in more than 125,000 square miles of territory in the Pacific Northwest. (The otherwise-sober David Thompson found the first seen by whites in Alberta in 1811, a fourteen-inch, five-toed clawed footprint.) They have been found pounded into soil to a depth not possible to obtain with the weight of several humans, and they are of different feet, with varying toe lengths and strides.

There is one film of a Sasquatch, taken October 20, 1967, at Bluff Creek, a tributary of the Klamath River on the California side, by two hunters, Bob Gimlin and Roger Patterson. Even the most serious Sasquatch hunters tend to discount this film now, though I'm not the only one who was transfixed at a vulnerable age by the image. I saw it in a covert look in my father's forbidden *True* magazine, which reported the incident with flat, undoubting prose. I remember vividly a black-robed, broad-shouldered creature emerging from dark woods into the bright sun of a grassy meadow, turning ever so slightly toward the camera, one arm back to swing forward in the next step. It is a picture of an animal cautious but without fear, near to home, willing to be seen. In the film she—for breasts can be seen shadowed on the chest—crosses along the edge of woods and grass and then disappears into the trees, unhurried.

Reports of "sightings" of this LUHB—or large unknown hairy biped, as its fans are fond of calling it—are on record by the thousands. On the slope of Mount St. Helens, in 1924, a group of miners fired at a strange creature, which seemed to be injured, but ran away. That night, their shack was pounded and pummeled with fists and rocks in a riotous attack that lasted till daybreak. Every few months, reports come in of single prints seven by fourteen inches long, or a series of prints marching out of the Blue Mountains onto semifrozen ground near Walla Walla, Washington. People, all kinds of people, of all ages, see a giant, dark-furred creature walking upright, swinging long, powerful arms with the confidence of a man at home. There are two different accounts of Sasquatch walking up to hunters and appropriating their deer carcass; in one account, the hunters were "very annoyed." The general impression of the observers, writes one collector of stories, is "of a huge man that can move with the speed and economy of a trained athlete." In 1967, a logger saw three creatures of different sizes pulling up boulders in an Oregon wood and eating the rodents hidden beneath.

Something's going on here, enough to convince a few people—rangers, campers, sheriff's deputies. In the *Environmental Atlas of Washington*, the U.S. Army Corps of Engineers lists Sasquatch as an indigenous species; Skamania County in Washington prohibits killing Sasquatch: The county tried to make it a felony punishable by five years' imprisonment, but when they found that a county government didn't have the power to dictate felonious crimes, they changed it to a gross misdemeanor, with a year in the county jail and a thousand-dollar fine.

The Indians never doubted the large unknown hairy biped. Virtually every tribe here carries a legend of hairy giants in the trees. In

Puget Sound, they were *tse-at-ko*; in the Blue Mountains of northeastern Oregon, they were *stiya-hama*. To the Fraser River tribes of British Columbia, they were the *sas-kets*—later, to us, the Sasquatch. They are *Omah* to the Hupas, *Seeahtiks* to the Clallams and Quinaults, who considered them an intermediate stage of evolution between animal and human. They are the *Bukwus*, or "Wild Man"; they are *Bokbokwalli-nooksiway*, "Cannibal Woman," and *Matah kagmi*, and *Dzoonokwa*, or "Wild Woman." They are the "little choppers" and the "tree-strikers." The Indian Sasquatch is a nocturnal creature, dark in color, with shining eyes. He has been described as "very good looking." He whistles. He steals food, tricks the unsuspecting but is never aggressive, and the sight of him can make you go crazy.

One of Sasquatch's greatest advocates, a serious anthropologist named Grover Krantz, gives chiding advice to those who would hope to prove the creature's existence. Like many believers, he discounts the absence of natural corpses as evidence that the species doesn't exist, pointing out how rare it is to find a bear or mountain lion dead of natural causes, undisturbed by carrion eaters. To his own dismay, Krantz thinks a "specimen" is the only way to protect Sasquatch. He explains in his writings why a shotgun won't work, and what part to cut off if you ever do manage to kill one. ("Any part would suffice," he says, "but the head would be the best.")

I have never seen Sasquatch, though I can't blame him for that; it's hard for me to imagine a circumstance in which he would want to be seen by me. The world in which he ruled, and grew scarce for whatever reason of environment or temperament, has itself grown scarce.

In the end, for all the sympathy I hold for Sasquatch, it's the disbelievers I pity most. They who can readily dismiss him have lost something more than gullibility. It has nothing to do with the number or quality of footprints, with photographs or nesting sites, height and stride ratios, or food sources—at least, belief or lack of it in Sasquatch has nothing to do with those things for me. People who can argue over them have already lost a little sympathy with the woods, and true disbelievers have lost their own mammalian vigilance about the greater earth. There isn't any mourning in their disbelief. That is their biggest loss, because if Sasquatch is proven false beyond a shadow of doubt, I will mourn his unlived life for a long time. Until shown otherwise, I walk here with a certain kind of caution, a bracing, apprehensive hope. Walking the high Siskiyous, in the Sawtooth, in the dark Olympics, up steep, muddy buttes away from the empty, winding road, I let myself believe that I might be undeservingly blessed by a moment's glimpse.

In June of 1972, very early in the morning, several loggers returned to their work site east of Eugene, Oregon, a clearing they had logged flat the day before. They found there, standing in the midst of the crumpled, fallen trunks, a very tall, brown, hairy creature, staring about himself. "It seemed," one reported later, "to be just looking around in total amazement." When the creature noticed the loggers, it slipped silently into the woods behind, and left, one might guess, to report this new and devastating development to its kin.

EIGHT

If only Captain Cook's men hadn't been cold enough on the damp coast near Nootka Sound to trade a few baubles for some sea otter fur, the West might have become a different Eden altogether. That simple transaction rang like a shot around the world: rang with the sound of money boxes and cannon. Cook's men took the furs to Canton eventually, expecting nothing; unlike the Russians, who'd known about otter fur for quite a while, the English seemed to have little understanding of the fur's value elsewhere in the world. The Nootka Sound Indians considered the fur a status symbol, but not much in the way of a bargaining chip until the results of Cook's voyage became clear. In 1784, Cook's account of his voyages was published, including the prices paid for sea otter furs in China. The first commercial fur trader showed up at Nootka in 1785.

The Indians learned not long after the whites what a prize the fur could be to the strange new visitors, and they began to raise the price. The whites began searching for undiscovered tribes who had not yet been "corrupted" by a profit motive, in order to find the cheapest possible source. The Indians sold the whites furs, for beads and cloth and iron, and the whites took the furs to China and sold them for silk, tea, and porcelains to be taken back to Boston. Profit depended on exploration, and exploration was bought with fur profits.

Meriwether Lewis described the sea otter as being as large as "a common mastive dog" with a coat in good shape, "perfectly black and glossy. it is the riches and I think the most delicious fur in the world at least I cannot form an idea of any more so. it is deep thick silkey in the extreem and strong." In the first years of trade, the otters were almost tame, and would swim almost to the trapper's hand. William Sturgis said that he found almost nothing more attractive than a "full grown prime skin which has been stretched before drying." He would rather gaze on such a thing "than half the pictures stuck up for an exhibition"; they were, he felt, "excepting a beautiful woman and a lovely infant ... the most attractive natural objects that can be placed before him."

The sea otter was trapped into near-nothingness in a mere twenty-five years, almost extinct by the beginning of the 1800s, by which time at least half a million otters had died. A skin brought twenty-five, thirty, and even forty dollars in Canton in the late 1700s; as they grew scarcer, the price rose, encouraging continued trapping. By the end of the trade, the price had climbed to as much as two thousand dollars for a single pelt. When the sea otter became too hard to find, around 1810, trappers started hunting beaver.

Beaver had proved a successful trade on the East Coast, and later, in the Great Lakes, long before the northwestern territories began to open. It was a natural shift, then, for the traders to seek the same product in the West. The standard barter on the northwestern frontier—until it disappeared and was replaced by gold—was the beaver pelt. The currency was called "made-beaver"; one made-beaver was the equivalent value of a single prime, cured adult beaver skin. The first coins minted here were made-beaver tokens. In 1733 a single made-beaver was worth one and a half pounds of gunpowder, or two pounds of sugar; it equaled a gallon of brandy, four spoons, twenty fishhooks, or a pair of stockings. Beaver was good for meat, for pelts, for the miracle of castoreum; beaver oil was even used on calk boots as waterproofing.

The Hudson's Bay Company, a British venture chartered by the king on May 2, 1670, entered the North American continent "with practically absolute power over their domain." In fact, it had all the authority of an independent, mobile, and foraging government, striking out across land long claimed by aborigines as though no one had ever set foot in it. The officials of the Hudson's Bay Company had the power to arrest and punish criminals, divide inheritances, and even, history adds, to declare war, a right not exactly exercised. The Hudson's Bay Company had the chance to control and harvest every resource in an enormous virgin region, and to administer the laws of the king and the territory as the company's leaders saw fit. They had only to pay a small tribute to the king, who, after all, already had the tribute of the enormous country held in his name: precisely, two elk and two black beaver at his pleasure. Before very long, the initials HBC were said to stand for "Here Before Christ."

The fur trappers and politically minded capitalists of the Hudson's Bay, who had covered the fur land of the East Coast with their trappers, were officially called a "Company of Gentleman Adventurers." They were maritime traders, aristocrats, diplomats, and inland fur traders; a few individuals played several roles. The North West Company was first in the Pacific Northwest, ahead of the Hudson's Bay by almost twenty years. American ships had traveled the coast and the rivers for decades before that. But the Adventurers had great momentum. It was the avowed intention of the Hudson's Bay Company to turn the perimeter of the vast Oregon country, by fierce and exhaustive trapping of beaver and otter, into a "fur desert" that would stop and starve the interloping American fur traders working inland. The HBC planned " 'to hunt as bare as possible all the Country South of the Columbia and West of the Mountains.' "

Dr. John McLoughlin was chief factor for the HBC at Fort Vancouver. He is commonly called "the Father of Oregon," and it was written of him that he had "that balance so rare: the balance of toughness and grace" that characterized the region. He is called "the veery Christ of Northwest occupation" in the *History of British Columbia*. There are few pictures of McLoughlin, all taken late in life. His wild white hair melts into stiff muttonchops around a downturned mouth. He had small bright, fanatic eyes and a weathered, pouchy face, and he wore stiff, high-necked jackets and high black hats. He looks zealous and single-minded and of what I would call a high moral fiber.

By all accounts he was a sober, fair man, kind, mannerly, dignified, but with a violent nature. He thought the Northwest soil poor and thin, somehow seeing the surrounding trees and jungle thickness as the rank weed of bad land. He was perpetually dissatisfied with his supplies and suppliers, and he often complained that he was not appreciated. At least one assassination attempt was made on McLoughlin. But he was widely regarded as a grand host, serving dinner on china plates on tables covered with linen tablecloths.

The Chinooks had been the first Columbia River tribe to see Robert Gray enter its mouth and were most profoundly affected by the presence of the HBC traders. One of their early white visitors was the painter Paul Kane, who traveled overland with the HBC to the Pacific coast expressly to make a visual record of the strange new land. He complained of the impossibility of learning Chinook, and then commented that the language he was unable to learn was hardly worth learning anyway, because it had no words "conveying gratitude or thanks." Kane could not understand the "horrible harsh spluttering" language, their "extremely filthy" habits, their "laziness." The Chinook in return resisted the efforts of this strange, solitary white to capture their images on paper and make off with them—thought to be a lethal act among the Chinooks.

Kane well represents the double standard of the whites on the Columbia River. It is with some relief that Kane describes a funeral, approving of the elaborate proceedings he witnessed and the Chinook belief in life after death. A few paragraphs later, he describes with annoyance the trouble and risk to which he had to go to rob a Chinook grave and obtain a skull for shipment back east.

By 1830, the lower Columbia River Indians were dead or dying. Disease brought by the whites would eventually kill three of every four Indians near Fort Vancouver. Outside the walls, the winter rains of 1830 fell and the remaining Indians huddled close by. "The Indians who were frightened at the mortality amongst them came in numbers to camp alongside of us," wrote McLoughlin in his official report on November 24 that year, "giving as a reason that if they died they knew we would bury them. Most reluctantly on our part we were obliged to drive them away."

George Simpson was the titular head of the Hudson's Bay Company holdings in North America, no small job. His reach was great and, think some historians, so was his character. But the historian Malcolm Clark calls Simpson a "small-souled" man, a man with power but no poetry in his soul. Simpson thought the Indians of the Columbia and the Far North would only work for what he called the "philosophy of rum," the one item of a licentious life not otherwise available. At first the Indians thought drunkenness in white men a disgusting trait. But thanks to the fur trapper's habit of tipping Indians with rum when they brought in pelts, the Indians soon craved liquor. The fur men liked the method; when rum was involved, prices paid for furs were lower, the number available higher. In spite of its success, Simpson didn't like the use of rum; it somehow offended his Christian belief. He hoped to find a more temperate bribe, and suggested instead that the trappers should tip with clothing and European products: "We must encourage the Consumption of Woolens and other useful British Manufactures which will in due time become necessary to the Natives from habit . . ."

Jedediah Smith kept a pet beaver, decked out with a scarlet collar and given to traveling around on Jed's shoulder. A lot of the mountain men liked the beaver, somewhat against better judgment. "Their curiosity exceeded our own and often proved fatal to them," wrote Alexander Ross, noting without emotion that on a good day, his team could catch sixty mature animals. A Rocky Mountain trapper wrote, "When the beaver are cut [trapped] they will twist their foot off. They won't bite it off. They are the most harmless thing in the world. They are just like a little baby. Catch a beaver and touch it and it will just turn up its head; a little one will just turn up and cry like a little baby. I hated to kill them, but says I, 'it is $5.'"

On one single day near the Bitterroot Mountains in Idaho, Ross and his men took 155 skins; in one season, on one river, they killed five thousand beaver. The HBC sold three million pelts in a twenty-four-year period, and many millions over the course of a single century: beaver and ermine and mink, bear and bear cub, lynx, elk, fox, muskrat, musk ox, rabbit, raccoon and badger, wolf and wolverine, and panther.

The trappers roamed the land relentlessly, starting with the Columbia, which once was full of otter. They sought the cardinal clues of downed trees and chewed bark, and set dozens of traps every day. (The steel trap reached its zenith in 1823. Ice chisels and spears were suddenly obsolete, and so, not coincidentally, was the beaver.) Ross writes of a place where 148 poplars had been brought down by beaver in an area less than a hundred yards square. The usual method involved a set of traps along a bank where beaver-chewed limbs and trees were found, places called "come ashores" on streams and rivers. A metal hinge trap was hooked to a log and the log then was sunk a few inches or a foot beneath the surface of the water. A few feet above the spot, the hunters hung a stick coated with "beaver bate"—castoreum.

The castor, or bark, stone assumed among the fur men something of the value the Rosetta Stone assumed among certain alchemists of Europe. It is not stone, but a pear-shaped gland in the genitals of both male and female beaver. The HBC exported castoreum by the ton, as well as pelts; it was used as musk in perfume and was thought to be a powerful curative for fevers, mental illness, epilepsy, headaches, tuberculosis. How many times have humans assigned healing strength to the slime and goo of lower animals? The beaver died for his stone in the same way the sperm whale died for his spermaceti; the skin and meat were a fine thing, but the magic, the mystery, lay in the unexplained cyst not found in people, which was therefore something humans must want.

Meriwether Lewis gives explicit instructions for preparing the "bate" from the castor stone, specifying the addition of "half a nutmeg, a douzen or 15 grains of cloves and thirty grains of cinimon finely pulverized, stir them well together and then add as much ardent sperits to the composition as will reduce it to the consistency [of] mustard prepared for the table." Such a concoction grew stronger with time if kept from the air in a tight pouch. To reach the delighting scent, a beaver would forgo all caution and leap for the stick, using the sunken log as a support. Trapped, the beaver dove, and then tried to tear its own foot off in order to escape; to prevent this, the trappers would hook the trap to a rock on shore, so that when the beaver dove, the entire contraption of trap and rock dove with him, and the beaver would—eventually—drown.

If the water rose very much from storm or snowmelt, the beaver would drift over the trap completely; but if the water dropped, the beaver couldn't dive and consequently couldn't drown. It then had its leisure in which to chew off a toe or an entire foot, and escape. Ross recorded on a typical day that his men's traps yielded fifty-two dead beaver, along with eight feet and seven toes that had been chewed off, and fifteen beaver washed away.

Peter Skene Ogden, "subtle as a fist," was a born fur man, with great physical endurance and a dour, morose nature. He traveled and mapped much of the country east and south of the more amenable Columbia basin, because he wasn't much good for anything else—and he was very good at running trapping expeditions. He seems to have been in a bad mood for most of his life, and nothing more properly suited a bad mood in the early 1800s than traveling through Snake Indian country.

He was born in 1794, the son of the Honourable Isaac Ogden, judge of the Admiralty Court at Quebec; the elder Ogden had left New England for Canada just to be able to retain his British citizenship. Peter had been trained as a lawyer, but he had a high, squeaky voice (a disadvantage at the bar) and a restless, difficult personality. He had joined the North West Company, the Canadian competitor to the Hudson's Bay, at the age of about fifteen as a clerk; by the time he was twenty-six, he was a full partner. "My legal primer is that necessity has no laws," he was fond of saying. Before he made partner, he'd left the relative civility of his father's life for the wild Columbia basin.

Ogden was "one of the more unprincipled" trappers working for North West when the company was absorbed, at the behest of the British government, into Hudson's Bay. He seems to have been born a bootleg explorer, hearty and enduring and cold. ("The delight of all gay fellows," said one of his contemporaries about Peter Ogden, who was fond of practical jokes and storytelling.) Ogden and his friend Samuel Black had been accused of murder in the frantic struggle for power between the North West and the Hudson's Bay, and both were at first shunned by the British. But they were considered "a pair of redoubtable characters, impressive traders of herculean proportions, rigorous and uncompromising to rivals and to Indians alike." In the end, Hudson's Bay hired them more for that reputation than in spite of it.

Ogden made his reputation in the West by a series of wintry journeys into Snake River country, along what is now the border of Oregon and Idaho. The Shoshonis (then called the Snakes) were one of the most dangerous and unrelenting tribes, and the landscape was daunting, especially so in winter when the trapping was done. A respected man named Finan McDonald had done the Snake trapping before, returning with more than four thousand skins in a single season. But he refused to go again; in his resignation he wrote, "When that Cuntre will see me agane the Beaver will have Gould Skin." When his colleague Alexander Ross proved unable to control the roving, criminal band of trappers working there—composed of freelancing Iroquois and Canadian French—Ogden, Ross' superior, went in his place.

He traveled the Snake in the winter of 1824–25, and again in 1825–26, and again in 1826–27, when he went even farther south, and then again to the Snake in the winter and spring of 1827 and 1828. In 1828–29, he went to the Great Basin as far as Great Salt Lake, and once more to the Snake country, in 1829–30. He came to believe that the Indians couldn't be made to understand the magnitude of his undertaking. An Indian, he wrote, "can form no Idea of a Country abounding in Beaver[.] a small stream with six Lodges appears to them inexhaustable, and it is not with an intention of deceiving that they represent their Country rich." On every trip he met Indians of many tribes—Shoshoni, Nez Percé, Klamath, Modoc, Shasta, Umpqua, Iroquois—and all claimed there were countless beaver just over the next pass. In mid-March of 1827, he wrote, "well do I know what an Indian calls a River of Beaver and probably we may be disappointed."

Ogden had a bon vivant's ability to complain; he began one trip with the comment "I am not over sanguine." His sometimes petty, sometimes immense problems all seem filtered through the same sieve to the size of an unpleasant dinner companion. He complained of badly made traps that often broke, and the scarcity of beaver in his own effort to eliminate the beaver altogether; he complained about freezing and murder and starvation as well as a lack of good conversation. (He could at times wax positively fierce. After one of his journeys, in which he led a company far into Mexican holdings by Salt Lake and had many confrontations with both American trappers and his own, irascible men, he wrote of the region, "Unfortunate, Cursed Country, I wish to God all these Villians were burning in Hell if there be such a place." His trips involved more than a few men and horses. In 1824, he set out with fifty-eight men, thirty women, thirty-five children, 268 horses, and supplies for all, including steel traps. On his second trip, he was reduced to eating horses and his employees stole each other's beaver meat: "I have no doubt our hunts are damned." After the third trip, Ogden described his men: "A convict at Botany Bay is a Gent living at his ease compared to them," and a short while later he left for the Snake country again. After that, Ogden spent nearly a year on a trip south, almost to the Gulf of California; on his way home, he lost five hundred animal skins and nine of his men in a boat wreck on The Dalles rapids in the Columbia.

They pressed on through the country, hiring Indian guides, kidnapping them if none could be hired, stealing boats for river crossings, and killing every beaver and otter they found. In mid-February of 1827, one of the party's horses was killed in the night. (It wasn't an uncommon event. "With Indians in general Horse stealing is not considered a crime but viewed more as a profession," wrote Ogden.) With characteristic fervor, he wrote of his shock at the natives' general lack of cooperation: "Natives most numerous bold and Insolant . . . they appear determined to oblige us to leave their Country and we are equally so not to leave it." A week later, his men brought in fifteen more beaver skins, "which completes our first thousand and leaves eight to commence our second with."

Ogden generally disliked Indians, though he was married to one, and in some cases—notably the aggressive Shoshonis—despised them.

One winter, his party camped in almost total deprivation along the Snake River near what is now Pocatello, Idaho. His patience was stretched very thin by the trip: "Acting for myself, I will not hesitate to say I would willingly sacrifice a year or two to exterminate the whole Snake tribe, women and children excepted." He felt he had suffered trials at their hands and his endurance was "carried beyond bounds ordained by Scripture and surely this is the only guide a Christian sh'd follow."

But his trips produced thousands of good-quality beaver and otter—and some not so good; the men took every animal they could find. Ogden knew, he knew all along what kind of world he had entered, and what kind of changes he and his hunters had made. He was in a kind of heaven, a cold and raw kingdom where the beavers and otters were the luckiest creatures alive. Now and then his peevish mood subsided. In the early spring of 1827, near Rogue River, Ogden wrote of his surroundings: "In a word it is a bold Stream containing a few scattered Beaver a fine Country rich in Timber and Animals good Pasture for Horses Climate rather *too moist* and natives so far as we can judge from appearances at least at this season not very numerous and the few there are very wild."

At the beginning of his fifth trip, on September 30, 1828, he wrote, "Almost every part of the country is now more or less in a ruined State," the beaver gone. Finally, the only beaver he could find were pregnant females, dead in his trap jaws. The fur desert had become a reality, and it extended south of the Snake River all the way to the Rockies. In 1826, the Hudson's Bay Company recorded the trapping of 2,099 large beaver. In 1827, they brought in 788 beaver. A group of trappers in 1835 found only 220. At last Ogden transferred north, to New Caledonia (now British Columbia), to struggle with the Russians for the remaining furs of the North.

For all the effort, for all the misery, the Hudson's Bay Company made a mistake in eliminating the beaver. They had thought it would keep the Americans out. But the Americans just gave up on fur, followed the maps and pathways made by the Hudson's Bay trappers, and settled in to log and farm. They even hired the unemployed fur men as guides.

The British should have won the territory; British Columbia should today contain Oregon and Washington and Idaho. They had the men, the momentum, the capital, and the advantage. But they didn't have the will—the British brought a single interest to the Northwest, and it wasn't enough. There was something in the differences of character, in the brutish determination and stubborn resistance of the Americans. The Americans never bothered with the linen tablecloths and pewter dishes famous in the genteel interior of the Hudson's Bay forts. They just dug in, and stayed.

In 1969 and 1970, a small group of otters was transplanted to the northern Washington coast from Alaska, a group that now occupies one distinct portion of shore and has grown to a total of 211.

At the Seattle Aquarium, visitors can watch a few sea otters from three heights: below, staring through glass up into the heart of their watery cage; at eye level, where the surface of the water laps against the sill of the glass; above, down into the cold blue where the otters burst from the opaque water without warning, and then disappear. They are busy, slick, steady-eyed: the rolling, back-paddling otter, propping its white fish treats on its fat chest and slipping backward, unerringly, through the water while it eats.

The otters here are lazy beasts, but to some extent every otter is; in the cold waters of the North Coast, one doesn't waste energy. But life in the kelp beds floating off the Aleutians, or in the rollers of the southern Oregon coast, or wherever an otter finds itself in these parts, is an easy life for an otter. At the aquarium, people watch unmoving for long spells, as the otters dive, and somersault, and shoot to the surface, and dive, and roll. It only takes an otter's halfhearted push to hit the bottom of the tall tank, and another to glide to the top of the water, and even less of one to slide backward around the perimeter of the tank during a meal. The tank is open to the air and the weather, to the scent of Seattle and the scent of the Sound that reaches all the way underneath, all the way to the pier on which the aquarium is built. Octopuses and abalone and salmon swim below the aquarium, free— for the moment—but no otters. The otters are gone.

NINE

Access to space is wealth. Light is wealth. The way the country here rolls out and opens is wealth—a kind of luxury, almost decadent. So much work, but so much room. Two counties in Oregon—Harney and Malheur—are each bigger than eight different states; Harney County alone could hold Rhode Island eight and a half times. One of the first miners into the Klamath Mountains called them "the best poor man's country I was ever in." You could starve and freeze in magnificence here, not in a small room in a small house on a crowded street. And as much as anywhere, the land might provide. This place is an estate, a mansion. And we are alone in the wilderness, unperceived: The solitude and privacy are themselves immense, and we are in a place that has no human bounds but our own. The horizon, seen so vaguely and dreamily far away, a layer beyond a layer of hills and valleys we've never walked, is the reach of our private world. Our sense of ourselves in these big places gets bigger, because it doesn't bump up against anyone else's sense of space. There are no intrusions.

At every pass up and down the length of the Cascades, on every ridge where the pines stand up like the bristles of a toothbrush, is a border: The soil changes, the trees and rocks change, the sky and the temperature and the light change. The transition is both reliable and abrupt. Sagebrush and scattered ponderosa replace hemlock and vine maple; tules and cattails replace ferns. Most of Oregon and Washington lies east of the Cascade spine, where the fall color arrives first. In the space of a half-mile, you can go from summer green to autumn gold.

Leaving the Douglas fir below Mount Hood for the open land of the Warm Springs Reservation, the desert appears so suddenly it is as though a glass wall stopped the trees. Tall ponderosa pines with orange and black bark mingle with green grass like the colors of a kilt, like plaid. The canyons and talus buttes are filled with quail, rabbits, coyote, deer, desert grasses, and of course, rabbitbrush and sagebrush; the low shrubs are everywhere, covering the land like stubble on a pale man's face.

I first saw the high-desert country at the age of ten, dropping out of the mountains, into the horizon with a thrill. I was leaving the embrace of the hills, seeing for the first time the flat plate of the world. The particular occasion was a church trip to the Mount Lassen Lava Beds in northeastern California, and since then I've made many trips out there—into the marshlands of Tule Lake, where migrating birds winter by the thousands, and to the toothy trail called Captain Jack's Stronghold. In that spine of black lava and in nearby, equally desolate, hideouts, the Modoc leader Keintpoos (called "Jack") and a shrinking band of men, women, and children, held out against hundreds of army regulars for six months. I could always imagine blood on the rocks out there, where little grows and the hard ground is sharp even through the thick soles of boots. When Keintpoos finally submitted because his people were starving—only to be hung for treachery—he submitted with these words: "I have said yes, and thrown away my country."

In the upper middle of the emptiness of eastern Oregon is a place known as the Painted Hills. The Painted Hills are weird mounds leaking the colors of mineral layers like paint—orange and yellow, black and dark green and rust. The soil here is a crumbly mix that looks from a distance like the texture of a sponge, and up close as though it had been milled to a uniform shape. In the spring, yellow bee plants grow in bundles along the indentations of the hills, outlining their shapes in crayon color. After a snowfall, the snow lies silver and as smooth as porcelain in clear air, unmarked, as though someone had draped a cloth of white silk over the land. All summer long, tourists by the twos and threes pant up the short trails to gaze down on the unbroken land, where fossils have been found, are still found, as though the ground grew them. There are signs posted telling people not to drive on the hills—on the hills as soft as the interior of an angel food cake.

East of the hills, the landscape becomes more varied. The Painted Hills are only part of an enormous fossil bed of the Cenozoic, an era when an inch of rain fell every three days in this now-arid plain. North are grey rock spires growing out of the flat ground like the towers of sand castles. The road through is shadowed and dark when the sun falls behind the cliffs; the fossiled land stretches for many, many miles. There are hills, and cliffs, and canyons, lonely ranches and small towns in the curving shadows of the cliffs, and far to the south, dark mountains rising above.

My great-grandmother, from whom I took the name Tisdale, lived her girlhood in Fort Rock, a town in southeastern Oregon near its geological namesake. Fort Rock is a very old, well-worn volcanic remnant, a tall near-circle of toothed rock, set down softly on the flat plain like a black crown. My great-grandmother used to go for picnics to a volcanic depression called Hole in the Ground. From here, the southern edge of the Blue Mountains is vaguely visible, and the land is penciled with narrow roads and hopefully fenced fields. North is Paulina Lake, a navy lake in the middle of Newberry Crater, a frozen lava flow around the tentacles of which trees have sprung and springs bubble.

Driving through the desert late at night, in midsummer, I passed one animal after another gambling with the road. I came around a curve and nearly flattened a peacock, a disappointed male dragging his long plume across the pavement behind him. One doe leaned back from my headlights, then forward, and suddenly darted across my path; I swerved right, then left, making a wild snake trail of rubber and missed her by inches, remembering the solid thunk of a deer on the fender of our car when I was a child: remembering her dazed, drugged freeze and then the leap, far too late, directly into steel. One feels a constant, fatalistic caution on these back roads at night, readiness for wild animals in the pool of light. A short while after I missed the doe, in a section of desert lit by a three-quarter moon, I passed two fawns, side by side in the other lane of the highway, standing still, waiting their fate.

Finally I reached Condon, leaving behind the desert for a little Oregon wheat town in open land. The whole place was strangely empty, wide, still in smoky yellow streetlights. I passed an intersection on the deserted main street and happened to glance to my left; the side street was filled with a dancing crowd, lit by the ochre light, still silent in my quick passing. Past the dance, all the streets were empty again, as though all of Condon danced. A few miles north of town, I passed a dark silo and was back in the flat, black land falling away from my white path on both sides of a sagging wire fence. All at once I could see a line of flame far away, radiant and orange under the black sky. It was nothing more than a straight line of flame, burning across the field like the signature of God in a dream.

Southeastern Washington and northeastern Oregon form a country called the Palouse, part of the immense Columbia River drainage. The Palouse is named after its natives, the Palouse Indians, who in turn named the Appaloosa horse, their favorite gift from the Spaniards. Vast numbers of people were expected in this country, which is outrageously lovely and fecund. The soil is a special kind, so fine and fertile you'd think it came through a sieve: loess soil, silt blown on the winds in the interglacial age, deposited hundreds of feet thick in places and full of growth. The Palouse is chiaroscuro, shaded draws and beams of light, stubbled fields of mezzotint and miles of wavering wheat. The county roads out here are sometimes no more than two dirt tracks cutting through a field of oats. The planted hills above the Touchet River ripple down the valley like a cloth rumpled into folds, as though someone had run his finger down the groove of the valley and gathered the grass into pleats. There is a native optimism here, and one hopeful year after the other it inspired grand platting schemes, big schools, tall silos, even opera houses to spring from the fertile ground.

The land has texture, like corduroy. You can see it best when the fields are in cultivation, dark and light and dark and light in an undulant variation; from above it looks like a striped sweater tight across a bosom. The land is sexual and abandoned in the sunlight, frosted in the cold. A kind of wanton heat drifts off the soil here, all the slow curves above and beyond the winding road, all the mounds of barley and rye and wheat, like a feast of hip and breast.

The sides of the canyons through which the roads of eastern Washington are laid are stacked, and the top layer is usually talus here, a basalt formation of hexagonal columns lined up side by side. Talus forms military rows for miles, and then suddenly a colossal chunk is twisted as though a strongman had bent it in a show of strength. Talus has the texture of a heavily worked oil painting—paint layered on paint and scraped up to form ridges like frozen water, pulling the painting out and up from the flat dimension of the canvas. One's finger strays thoughtlessly to touch it. Tiny dots of green hide in the draws, tugging groundwater from soil tawny and ochre. The coulee country is a strange and pretty place, with alkaline lakes rising into dry, rusty cliffs topped by miles of unbroken pillars, and now and then a dewy field speckled with yellow bales of hay and round spoke-wheel sprinklers. Puffs of tall ivory cloud hang in the sky and drop black, cool shadows on the land. Distant flocks of birds stand still in the light sky, iron filings dropped on a tile floor.

The *Wenatchee World*, the daily newspaper of central Washington, is published in what it calls "the apple capital of the world and the buckle of the power belt of the great Northwest." Every part of its region is outsize, even its own image. What seem like rolling hills from the ground—unusually rolling, particularly curvaceous hills—are called the scablands. Scablands form from violent action of various kinds. They run like busy water across the land, and in fact came from water, the cataclysmic floods that so marked this basin. Some farms are marked with a smaller kind of scablands, separate mounds called biscuits, which look from the air to have the artificial pattern of a planned community; they may be the result, depending on the particular history of the area in which they occur, of glacial or water action, wind erosion, or even earthquakes. Ripple ridges rise fifty feet in the air and stand five hundred feet apart. These are the unbelievably large lines sculpted in the ground by the flowing water of floods, like the little wiggles of sand left by a retreating tide on a giant scale.

The canyons through which the roads wind are actually coulees, old water channels left dry by historical water, braided channels of a flood system so big it would have drowned Texas. The ancient high-water mark is a thousand feet above the road, its walls striped with rhythmites, piled layers of silt and mud from flood on flood. Boulders were washed from Montana and Idaho to western Oregon in these floods. These rocks are called erratics, for obvious reasons: They're the hoboes of geology. A ten-inch round stone of granite erratic is pocketed neatly in a wall of the Columbia Gorge, with a little room on every side to spare; it sits in its hole like a ball in a socket joint. The coulees and channels can't be seen for themselves except from above, because the meandering trails they make run not for miles but for hundreds of miles. The lost, dry waterfalls are miles wide.

Washington state has nearly eight thousand lakes and reservoirs; more than eighty percent of its energy comes from hydroelectricity. There are so many reservoirs here and they are so incongruous at times as to be embarrassing; they seem dropped in the lap of tall timber or dry brush like moist dreams. Sometimes I come around a curve and see a bowl of water hanging in midair over a dry chasm, its dam jammed against the canyon walls like a shim. We destroy the land in order to inhabit it, destroy those parts that held the most light and hope: the streams, bright moisture in the midst of dryness, the surprise of a river bubbling up from the ground and shaded by riparian trees, drowned under the still water of an irrigation dam.

Just north of Yakima, in southeastern Washington, the big hills go dead into sagebrush and the opportunistic rabbitbrush that colonizes overgrazed lands. The view is all sere brown and grey with crumbling basalt ridges breaking through the powdery soil. This is the Yakima Firing Center and Military Reservation and not much else, rumpled coulees and silky hills and the tatting of sage. East of here, not even sagebrush grows, and the fields produce rocks instead. But at the top of the ridge, you can see the distant, smoky smudge of the North Cascades, and below a valley of green and yellow fields. The fields themselves are filled with precise rows, fresh, prosperous, abundant. This is irrigation land, silos and barns and roving sprinkler heads for corn, fruit, wheat. Orchards lie in a cleft, an oasis of apples and peaches like a wet heart held in a dry hand. The unfettered sagebrush, with its tender perfume, holds down the soil with its tangled roots. It crawls right up to the edge of orchards marked off as though with rulers. Here the wild land, the natural shape and colors of the land come to a halt, and an inch away, grass grows amid the order of hybrid apple trees and the mist from spray hanging in the air. The radio stations play Mexican songs.

In Miocene times, cypress, gingko, and hickory grew and outsize mammals prowled, lakes moistened the humid basin. In the Miocene, lava poured out of fissures in the eastern Washington ground, making one of the largest, deepest sets of basalt flows on the planet. Faults lifted and shifted and buckled the land, leaving the enormous lava plateau leaning slightly to the north, off balance. A million years ago, a brief blink, the Ice Age: The glaciers moved down into Washington, Idaho, and Montana five to ten thousand feet thick, digging out channels and damming enormous lakes with the waters of the Columbia. Lake Missoula covered western Montana before it broke through and flooded the plateau again and again.

The Grand Coulee (the granddaddy of coulees) is a huge trench marked here and there by lakes. It is fifty miles long, ranging from one to six miles wide, with steep walls of columnar and vesicular basalt almost a thousand feet deep. The Grand Coulee begins north of where the Grand Coulee Dam now stands and descends far south of it, with Dry Falls near its center.

Dry Falls is not a falls, but a series of sheer, dry, slowly eroding walls—three and a half miles of walls curved and layered one upon the other and standing more than four hundred feet high. The land comes flying from the invisible horizon through the haze of summer air, splitting and twisting on its arid course, opening here and there with fissures and cracks large enough to swallow whole towns. It flies up to the edge of the cliffs in shades of brown and tan, and drops into space, drops hundreds of feet down to distant ground wet with small lakes. Then the ground climbs in a vertical wall and races on again.

The main road passes Dry Falls on the other side of its burst into air, slightly higher than the height of the walls, so that one looks slightly down and across the wide, empty space. It is too much to see in one sweep of the eye; frame by frame, you must turn your head from one side to the other, straining to find the farthest reach of cliff in the hazy distance, to encompass the width of the falls.

The small lakes at the base of the cliffs are called "pothole" lakes, or "kolk" lakes. They are round hollows dug during the Ice Age floods of the Pleistocene epoch by the force of falling water, by the grinding of boulders in the spinning stream. (All the lakes of the Grand Coulee are really kolk lakes, puddles left behind of what used to run fresh by the cubic mile.) The floods that carved out the coulees and the gorge were so enormous that what we call Dry Falls—this series of overlapping cliffs—was under water when they ran, like rocks and troughs on the bottom of a stream. The sheer drop of Dry Falls—more than twice the height of Niagara Falls, higher than Victoria Falls—was nothing more than a bump in the river bottom.

A five-hundred-foot wall of glacial water poured through Wallula Gap when the earthen dam broke, draining "in a few hours," says the geologist John Eliot Allen, with a force ten times the combined flow of all the rivers in the world. Such a flood didn't happen once, or twice, but at least forty times, and smaller floods ran through by the hundreds. I can see it coursing over the four-mile width of Dry Falls Butte and down, down, too much water to get through the gap, climbing the walls to twelve hundred feet loaded with debris, chunks of ice and boulders, dead bodies, backed up and eddying in its rush. The river was a constantly widening and narrowing channel, powdered with the ash from various volcanoes. The huge quantity of flood water, sometimes a mile or two wide and steady and forceful, would be funneled through a gap only a few hundred yards wide, suddenly extreme in its power and mad rush to get through.

The Columbia River is older than the Cascade Mountains. What we consider the Columbia Gorge—seventy-five miles of great, ridged walls of stone beside its lower banks—are the piles of stacked basalt flows through which the ancient Columbia ran. The floods cleaned soil off the slopes of the gorge, tore off the ends of streambeds, leaving behind the abrupt hanging valleys and rivers turning to the veils of waterfalls.

Inside the pump house of the Grand Coulee Dam, every inch of floor and wall and air is vibrating at a high frequency; the air wiggles inside my ears. This is the old-fashioned space age—the space age of the new American technocracy, circa 1940. It's that white man's optimism again. The pump house is a long, long hall several stories high, with twelve giant green pumps spinning electricity out to Washington's power belt. There are catwalks and dials and arcane emergency equipment, rotary phones and not a soul in sight. I'm reminded of the cheerful movies we saw in elementary school, narrated by a middle-aged man with horn-rimmed glasses and a knee-length lab coat, carrying a clipboard. He points at esoteric machinery and chalked equations and discusses the magic of electricity, the momentous victories of the West. Even the toilets in the bathroom down the hall are like the short, round toilets I sat on in third grade, trying to get away from the movie.

Rows of huge, white ringed tubes pumping water from the reservoir are plopped on raw ground and rise over the steep cliff behind the dam. The cliff, the scrub, the dry grass beside the road, the camel-colored land rising away into the distance on every side is arid and dusty. But the visitors' center is surrounded by a neat square of lush green grass. The dam, which rises from frothy water, is so wide and tall it seems to be a stage set. (The dam is almost a mile wide.) Cars glide by across its top like little toy cars on an elevated track, stopping now and then so little toy people can stand by the edge and look down to the swirling pool and little Coulee City below. The school, the motels, grocery stores, houses, the little Colville Reservation museum are all below, in the path of the towering, artificial lake above and behind the dam. A constantly changing digital display by the edge of the water gives an up-to-the-second record of how much wattage has been produced here. The Grand Coulee generates more electricity than any other plant in the world. There will be none bigger around here: so many large hydroelectric plants exist in Washington now that there are no large-scale sites left. I have vertigo from the height above, from the drop below, and the vision of bursting dikes; I have vertigo from the millions of horsepower and kilowatts, millions of cubic yards of excavation, truckloads of cement to make a feet/second pumping capacity. The dam is a statistical menace; it leaks numbers.

Two guides in the visitors' center glance around quickly before quietly answering my question about suicides off the dam. Only one, they say: an Air Force major named Joseph Benner who leaped from the new section of dam in the winter of 1987. He didn't jump from the length of the dam spanning the water, the enormous, seductive tilt of concrete disappearing below the distant water of the river. Instead, for reasons that might have been more masochistic than strategic, Benner jumped off the railing of the section built over cliff, a sculpted angle of concrete dropping into boulders. "He hit and skinned himself all the way to the bottom," the young man says, and they shake their heads at his idiocy.

There are bleachers beside the circular visitors' center, by the hotel near the lower pool, and in the sandy parking lots over the water, in front of the dam. By nine-thirty on a summer night, when the light is finally gone beneath the towering edge of the cliff, the bleachers are full of cheerful people. Cars line up along the crescent edge of the parking lot, facing the dam with a sort of reverent attention. A bright half-moon drops behind the spooky pump pipelines crawling into darkness over the hills. The woman beside me leans over to say she and her husband had driven over from Spokane for the night, just to see the show.

A laser light show is projected onto the flat, grey expanse of dam on summer nights. Just before it begins, the spillway gates at the top are opened one by one, and lines of foamy white water pour down the dry front. A pulsing music begins (repeated on a local radio station) and precise neon lines dance across the screen of water. Gargantuan horsemen gallop and fish leap, waves roll and fields of wheat grow, in garish purples and daffodil yellows. Over the electronic mood music, the booming voice of Mr. Columbia River narrates his story.

It is the prettiest piece of propaganda I have ever seen. Mr. Columbia River exults in the achievement of the dam, explaining with a patient wisdom the necessity: the need to destroy the salmon runs, drown the towns, inundate the ancient Indian lands, to flatten his own wild roar. It was necessary, says the deep, comforting voice, so that man— White Man—could raise crops and live where no agricultural people had even considered living before. He admitted the sin of the deed and invited with his admission compassion and clear-eyed hindsight. We are watching history written not for the reeducation of history's victims but for the new generation of conquerors; it is history for the children of the winners: an apologia, a vague rationale, an expectation of more. It is like selling hamburger with Mr. Cow.

A few days after I watched the Columbia River dance across its own crypt in neon light, I crossed into the North Cascades. I had turned west again, and slightly north, leaving the flat coulee land. On the way through Colville, Washington, I passed a large sign with an arrow pointing to the left:

DEPT NAT RES

MENTAL HEALTH

ALCOHOLISM

GOLF

I was walking up a switchback trail beside Cutthroat Creek, and came into a chaos of fallen trees. One swatch of mature trees had been knocked aside, by some freak of weather or avalanche, the season before; the trail passed under and over the trunks of noble firs and hemlock lying tangled together. I happened to glance down and saw the ground moving right at my feet—moving as though the soil itself had somehow come to nightmarish life.

When I looked more closely, I could see the ants. They were engaged in a phenomenon of antdom called slave-making. Large red ants with big pincers battled much smaller black ants for possession of the black ant larvae. They swarmed across the trail. I followed the action back to a decaying log ten feet long next to the trail, and then down the trail and across the path to another dead log. Each of the red ants was carrying a white oblong egg as big as itself in its mouth, and racing from one log to the other. In slave-making raids, masses of invaders surround a nest, and the besieged ants attempt first to seal off their nest and then to defend or escape with individual larvae. Thousands of red ants overwhelmed relatively few pitiful, panicked black ants, only a few of them with eggs. A few black ants scurried wildly around as though in panic. I saw two red ants fighting a black ant for possession of an egg, and as I watched, the egg was torn apart and shredded, a defeat that seemed so pathetic to me that all at once my eyes blurred with tears. All the pearly larvae would be carried back to the red victors' nest, hatched, and imprinted with the scents of that nest, to work for life in nurturing their conquerers. The red ants formed a determined, implacable battleline over my shoe. I picked up a red ant with an egg on the end of a stick, and it raced to the middle, stopped, turned around and raced back to the end, stopped, and returned, back and forth until I gave up and laid the stick back down.

The North Cascades spread east and west of the long north-south line, a far more haphazard and convoluted set of pinnacles, ridges, and peaks. (Washington's topography is so rough that even now, large parts of the state are unsurveyed.) There are no single white mountain cones in the North Cascades, no wide plains paying homage to a mountain queen. In the North Cascades, the average visitor confronts a convolution of trails, sheer walls, and ragged rocks separated by thick evergreen and a multitude of waterways. On the east side are many little jewels of cold lakes, bordered with tules or covered in lilies. The winding, narrow road passes through birches and larch, spruce, hemlock, and pines. Little one-lane roads beckon to each side, to a campground here, a Bible camp or fishing resort there. The Forest Service proposed something called "star-fish conservation" in the North Cascades, a clumsy attempt to weld development with preservation. "Star-fish" refers to the appearance of such a plan: It would preserve the rock ridges and snowy draws that range out from a central spine like the arms of a star, while developing the valleys.

In the foothills of the piny Cascades are great groves of birch, each a foot in diameter, and cottonwoods. A small storm of cottonwood blossoms floats across the sky, like torn pieces of cloud. And then these give way to moist, green meadows with grass and wildflowers, and someone's dream house on a distant hill.

I stop for ice cream in Tonasket, where a thermometer in the shade reads one hundred degrees. The woman in the little store is playing old 45-rpm records and humming to herself. My daughter and I contemplate the array of candied flavors, and my husband orders vanilla.

The proprietor, who has been almost silent, suddenly begins to speak.

"I have a philosophy about ice cream," she says. "It takes a really strong person to order vanilla. Everyone always tries to talk them out of it. You know, 'Why order plain old vanilla when there's all these other flavors?' So you have to be strong to resist that. Young or old."

She hands my daughter a giant cone of something called Goo-Goo Cluster—chocolate, peanut butter, caramel, and marshmallow—and gives her a bright smile.

I think there are really two idylls here, two dreams of Eden. One is the lush idyll lived west of the mountains, in the wet valleys where everything grows easily, without effort. The second idyll is this one: growth and comfort born from luck and hard work. It is vanilla, plain and pure, a luxury doubly sweet.

The North Cascades Highway winds through scooped valleys and hanging cliffs. This road is a marvel, carved over decades through a granite tumble and still closed part of the year, drowned under drifts of snow. We had climbed up from Early Winters Valley and stopped a while at Kangaroo Ridge, turning to look back at the ribbon we'd traveled. I crawled down a boulder and perched behind a low log fence on a flat dish of rock hung high over the valley. It is a long, soft, green tongue tucked in between painfully sharp, bare peaks. Trees slid off the slopes in waves. I felt a sudden vertigo, the slap of height, and mass.

We stopped again at Diablo Lake, a glacier-fed lake opaque with the mountains' detritus. We came around a curve and saw a rest stop, and then a REST STOP CLOSED sign, and a crescent lot filled with trucks, vans, cars, lines of backpacks, milling people, and a small helicopter. All that day, helicopters had passed us every which way, disappearing over the cliffs. It was fire time, and not a whiff of smoke seen and the trees green beside us.

We followed the highway down, skirting a ledge on the cliff above the lake, finally dropping almost to its surface. There we found a parking lot, a dark pine grove, and a rocky spit jutting out. Diablo is filled with suspended particles of rock, which makes rivers grey and lakes jade. This powder is called rock flour; it is sanded off boulders and crushed to clay by the icy foot of a glacier, and then dribbled down from the peaks in melting snow. Diablo Lake is a milky aqua lacking any of the glassy quality of water, filling the valley like a puddle of spilled paint. Hill on hill of firs leaned up and back from the lake, turning to run into a narrow valley at lake's end, and out of sight. The highway came down, crossed, and turned away past our place. Cars slowed at the bridge, the people pointing at the strange water, and then drove on. We settled on the pebbly bank and darted at the waves. Nearby, a man leaned over a flock of floating Canada geese, tossing bits of bread at them. I tried to imagine swimming in water so impossible to see through, so spooky and seductive at once.

Then the air split with a boom, a pounding noise that quickly broke into a steady, panting *whapeta-whapeta,* the sound of long, flat blades slicing sky. From the far end of the lake, where the water trickled away, a huge helicopter came down, dropping in an arc from the end of the valley. The double rotors splattered the water into foam and the copter came down to hover right in front of us.

"Small fire," the parking lot volunteer had told me when I asked about the people at the rest stop. He was a retired mobile-home owner monitoring parking and picnic sites for the busy rangers. He was glad to talk. "A hundred acres or so, six miles south," he added, pointing into the tip of the valley. "It's nasty. Problem is, it's on a cliff. The jumpers are hanging on ropes and the fire's falling down on top of them. So they're dropping water."

We weren't alone on the narrow tongue of land; a half-dozen people shared the corner: children, a young couple, several older people I associated with the RVs along one side of the parking lot. We watched the helicopter coming in and saw the enormous red pail hanging from its underside. The pail hit the water with a bang and then slowly sank while the engine hummed. It lifted with a sudden, hungry whine and turned on an axis, without haste, and lumbered back away, mist flying off the top of the bucket like steam. Six minutes later, by my watch, it was back, swinging the empty red cup, sliding in close so we felt spray in our face. The noise bounced off the trees and back.

"Wow, this is a lucky chance," one man said to his wife, and I knew what he meant—this random combination of drama with beauty almost narcotic in its depth. Another man had a video camera and an Albertan accent, and he carefully filmed the sequence, lowering his lens to catch the disappearance of the bucket, raising it to follow the pilot's perfect spin. The Pacific Northwest is a gallery of land, a maze in which one room holds one view—another room, another view. Event and place blend with a twist like the twist of a Möbius strip, turning so it has only one side. Adolescent flocks of flowers run right over the random drapery of snow in springtime, bordered by larch and dark dashes of pine dripping like dye down the mountainsides; we live right in and through such things. The meadows are wet with light; the summer sun is as sharp as a knock to the head.

Every six minutes the copter returned, and we waited, timing the pilot, glad for another view. The conversation drifted into speculation—fuel capacity, flying speeds, death by burning. The bucket took three thousand gallons of Lake Diablo every trip, a great vat swinging back on its cable as though reluctant to follow. We stayed, cheered by the friendly, holiday feeling among the strangers on the spit. We stayed until the helicopter veered off the valley and up, instead of back to the lake. The crowd broke apart. And finally we left, too, down and out of the mountains, through hidden flame.

TEN

I feel toward the fourteen trees around our house as a steward toward a preserve; they stand rooted and I patrol their borders. I feel that I live with them the way I live with my dogs and cats: as animate things, looking out at the world from a different window than I. There are five forty-foot cedars with soft, sweeping fronds, an unidentified pine, the old cherry, and seven mature maples, with thick knobby trunks that branch out broad and high to form generous upturned cups. How one feels toward trees, both singly and in forest, is a large measure of how one lives here—literally *how* one's life is spent. I think it is possible here, where so much of our history is in our trees, to feel more strongly toward them than seems quite proper elsewhere. (And that improper depth of emotion is true for the logger as well as for me.) Those feelings, that relationship, are metaphorical, literary in the sense of story, of what stories we tell and how we use those stories to explain ourselves. As the forests disappear, those stories change, and who we are changes, too. The forests disappear; they have become towns, meadows, and tree farms. A forest, a single tree can be broken down into more manageable, less daunting parts. But so can I—reduced to a hand, a head, a grimace, with a single word or blow.

In Yreka, in Oakridge, Oregon, in McCleary, Washington, in a thousand small towns of the Northwest, what young men did was work in the mills. They started straight from high school, the back pockets of their jeans already marked with a circle from the tin of chewing tobacco. They put a down payment on a pickup truck with the first check from that first job, pulling the green chain. That meant grabbing newly cut planks as they fell off the big raw logs, dodging the evil teeth of the noisy saw. Men who worked very long on the green chain lost fingers, or more.

Other men worked in the yards, moving lumber, feeding waste into the hot wigwam burners, giant rusted cones of sheet metal. Sawdust was a problem for the early mills; it was dumped on muddy roads and used as fill in swamps until someone invented the wigwam burners. No matter that every mill with a wigwam was vulnerable to fire; they saved hauling the tons of pulp and bark to someone else's backyard. There was something comforting about the wigwams, something domestic about their curving, badminton-birdie shape and the smoky fragrance in the air day and night. On summer evenings, the sky darkened from white to black and the hills sank backward, as though turning invisible, and from the wire screen on top of the wigwams came a night-light's glow. Every few minutes, a soft shower of live red sparks, lightning bugs rising and drifting on the breeze, would float up through the mesh. During World War II, when the West Coast was considered at special risk for an invasion from Japan, blackouts were a regular drill. But the wigwams radiated hot light when everyone else sat in the dark; they could be seen by planes for miles, scattered all over the Northwest: little bright cups of fire.

Some years ago, when I was living on my own in a city far north of where I was raised, I had a friend whose home was heated by an archaic sawdust furnace. On frozen winter nights, when the whole house creaked and seemed to shake with the cold, he would go down to the dark basement and shovel sawdust. I liked to sit a few feet back of him, against the wall hot from the quaking furnace flames, and watch: a man's silhouette black against the red glow. The big scoops of pale-yellow flakes swung into the fire, back and forth, with the arc of his steady arms. We were all alone under the world, the world wet with sleet and wind, a wild, empty world with the moon quivering behind the mobbing clouds. Alone in a small, dark room lit only by the gasp of burning fuel, its gouty flame. It was like having my own wigwam in which to sit, a tipi of wood and fire with which to play, to curl up beside; it was like falling safely asleep within the flickering light of the mills of childhood.

I spent a lot of time as a child on logging roads; they were the most logical, and in many cases, the only way into the forest. We cut firewood up in the forests, bundled up in coats and hats and mittens while wet snow fell slowly around. My dad had a winch on his big Chevy pickup, an object I greatly admired. It was a machine I could understand, a big, noisy engine of power. It was deadly and strong and satisfactory. We children dragged small branches one by one to the pickup, and meanwhile my father wrapped the winch chain around the trees he'd dropped with the fast whine of a chain saw. A flip of a switch and the cable inexorably wound, pulled in the tree and the attendant brush without hesitation, pulling like a giant's arm and singing high and sharp in the crisp quiet.

My dad made a hydraulic log splitter from scratch. It was the perfect regional invention. In one end he stuffed a big round section of tree that would require both axe and wedge to become firewood. Then, BOOM! and a lethal axehead flew so fast it blurred in the eye, smack in the center of the log, which almost always fell graciously apart for the pile. He kept his shed full of enough seasoned firewood to last for years; our fireplace never smoked, never burned anything but the most fragrant, paper-dry oak and pine.

Several years ago, after I'd left home, children playing in the alley behind the shed set it on fire in the middle of the night. My father, a volunteer fireman, woke to the alarm and ran outside for his truck, only to find it was his own garage burning down. It was as though one of the dreaded sawmill fires had landed in his backyard; the log splitter and the firewood, his table saw and the balsa-wood models of his youth consumed in a single breath of flame.

Every year our Christmas tree came from these forests, and it was always a seven-foot baby noble fir. The noble fir grows quite tall and thin. The branches are parallel to the ground and at right angles to the trunk, unbunched and uncrowded. The twig bundles grow in the same way, parallel to the branches. The whole effect of a noble fir, whether seen from far or near, is of precision, geometry, and neatness.

My cousin worked for the Forest Service as a "cruiser," measuring trees at random in various units to determine the stumpage—one of the more telling logging terms. *Stumpage* refers not to stumps but to healthy standing trees; it is a complicated measure of the potential and real value of a particular timber sale. One of the advantages (although an illicit one) of knowing a cruiser was the ease of getting one's Christmas tree. The tree showed up on our doorstep about a week before Christmas, a tree so perfect and fresh it could have been painted. The tip of every branch was new, velvety, a slightly paler green, the branches perfectly flat and horizontal growing in parallel planes along the straight, sticky trunk. The branches stretched into the room, the calming scent of evergreen evaporated into the air. The strong branches barely bent under the load of lights and red globes and white china birds in golden nests we laid across them in reckless glee.

Here it is, late December again. We cut our tree last week. The green fields held a cold sheen, and the road itself glittered in winter's lemon light. The Christmas-tree farms are uniform blocks of thimbles, cornets of pine and fir between the fallow fields and grey orchards waiting for spring. We found a noble tree farm—NOTHING BUT NOBLES, said the sign—and tromped up and down the rolling bottomland for an hour, framing trees, comparing the prices on the colored ribbons. Behind the noble farm was a very old filbert farm, the nut trees grown tall and rambling with age. Nut farms are neat places, the ground beneath raked clear of debris, and in the cold, dry air of a snowless December, only the fall's filbert leaves lay around the trees in uneven circles. Behind the filberts rose a lane of Douglas firs two hundred feet high and not shaped at all like Christmas trees, and behind them—behind them, explained the farmer, a highway was being built.

The farmer is an electrical engineer working on microprocessors, and on the land where he was raised, he keeps five hundred noble fir trees. They grow at different rates, depending on genetics, moisture, sunshine; they grow slowly, quickly, straight, and uneven. From each stump he cultivates new trees; like a lot of other serious Christmas-tree farmers here, he's interested in cloning. Cloning produces identical trees—"close to perfect," said another farmer, a man settling for the more obvious Douglas fir. Other couples, other families, wandered between the nobles, which were planted in clumps and clusters instead of rows. Now and then I could see a car drive up, far away up the rise by the house, and a person would get out and point to a nearby tree without venturing a step into the soil. Down among them, passing between the dense knitting of needles and the horizontal sphere of branches, I was laughing out loud. Here's one! Oh, look at this one! It was narcotic, wet, aromatic, textured. We found ourselves in the farthest corner, near the filberts, looking up and away toward the road and the barn, and there we found the tree we'd been looking for. The children waved their silly yellow flags, wild scarves of color in the dull light, until the farmer in his Gore-Tex and Wellingtons wandered down with his chain saw.

When the French-Canadian Paul Bunyan moved to the United States, he and his blue ox Babe became "Real Americans." Real Americans, Paul knew, were hard workers, looking for opportunity. In the midst of his joy at his newfound citizenship, he sought direction.

"A whisper stirred in his heart: 'To work! Take advantage of your opportunity!' The whisper got louder and more insistent every moment; and at last the idea it spoke possessed Paul Bunyan, and he sat down to ponder it, letting Babe graze and roll on the clover-covered hills.

"Now the whisper became an insistent cry: 'Work! Work! Work!' Paul Bunyan looked up, and he seemed to see the word shining among the clouds; he looked down then into the vast valley, and he seemed to see—by the holy old mackinaw! he did see—the forest of his second dream! And now he knew it: his Life Work was to begin here.

"Real America was covered with forests. A forest was composed of trees. A felled and trimmed tree was a log. Paul Bunyan threw aside his pine tree beard brush and jumped to his feet with a great shout.

" 'What greater work could be done in Real America than to make logs from trees?' he cried. 'Logging! I shall invent this industry and make it the greatest one of all time! I shall become a figure as admired in history as any of the great ones I have read about.' "

Loggers, who were lumberjacks on the East Coast, began the press westward. First there was the long, slow cutdown in Maine and the rest of New England, with the most primitive of tools, and then, when the trees were down, the loggers crossed to the Great Lakes States, to Michigan and Wisconsin and Minnesota. The forests there were mostly white pine, which fell shockingly easy and fast, and the loggers ran south, to the southern pine and cypress, and then that was gone, too. They began to talk of "the Big Clearing."

Rumors about the far Northwest, where the trees were so big— bigger, taller, tougher, thicker, and harder than anywhere else—were at first discounted as simple loggers' lies. But itinerant lumberjacks found their way west, and found the rumors to be true. These woods, these trees, could never be cut down. "Hell, man, there was plenty of timber, timber without end, just over the Hump, and by the Holy Old Mackinaw, they'd cut her, cut her close, wide, and handsome!" So said Stewart Holbrook.

Grays Harbor, named for Robert Gray, was the best stand of all perhaps, best in the world: three to four million board feet in every forty acres, twenty million to a quarter section. The trees beat any bet any logger had made, and they were all lined up on the convenient hillsides for their chance to slide into the deep, cool water. Lindbergh's "Spirit of St. Louis" was made from Sitka spruce cut down here, and somehow that suited everyone: Grays Harbor flew, man, it was the place to be. It was so grand, they said, "you can't lie fast enough to keep up with the honest facts." Grays Harbor was a game, a boys' wrestling match, down and sweaty in the dirt. Heaven would be Grays Harbor, a large bay on the coast of Washington: endless hills of Douglas fir so tall it made the sky look wooded, and the swearing of the bullwhackers at their oxen so obscene the bark on the younger trees curled up in shock.

It was the towns and mills of Grays Harbor that complained most particularly about the loss of timber when the Olympic National Park was created. In the late 1800s, complaints first were voiced that the amount of timber was in danger of disappearing. Decade by decade, in a kind of ritual, the timber and mill owners warned that massive unemployment was right around the corner. By 1937, the biggest trees were gone and the mills that had once tooled up to accommodate the huge logs of the Olympic Peninsula had to tool down again for the smaller ones that remained. Men who had managed to stay working through the Depression would be out of work. (Some men kept themselves working in the Depression by setting forest fires, and then getting hired to put them out.) More warnings: Men would be thrown out of work, their families forced into poverty, and Grays Harbor would become nothing but ghost towns.

The towns of Grays Harbor, such as Hoquiam and Aberdeen, are sprawling and untidy. They are commonplace towns. There's something masculine about them, like apartments inhabited by young men who haven't got a feel for the extra touch. They are dull, mediocre, undecorative. Almost every watery view is marred by piles of logs and steaming mills. The standing trees are little oaks and maples now, and fuzzy shrubs, and seeing them, I find myself missing a forest I have never seen, knowing it was here. I never pass through without a sense of how small dreams can be.

There are different ways to talk about the impact of modern logging; one book mentions without elaborating that hundreds of thousands of acres in the Pacific Northwest "were converted to non-forest land" in the sixties. The state maps of Oregon and Washington and Idaho persist in outlining national and state forests in green, a cheering bit of art. And when I compare those state maps to the maps of other states— New York, Michigan, Maine—I am cheered twice, seeing how large are the irregular green ovals and squares out West, how few and small the forests in the East. But the green is only ink, and the reason Michigan and Maine and New York haven't got big state and national forests filled with trees is because they cut them down.

Complaints of lowered cuts and increasing wilderness set-asides—which reduce the amount of timber cut by as much as one-fourth—fail to acknowledge that even after the reduction, the cuts are higher than ever before. Billions of board feet of timber still come out of the Northwest's national forests every year; the harvest from federal land in Oregon was actually higher in 1989 than in 1979. But the complaints are ever of reductions, reduced yields, set-asides, too much wilderness, too much saved. In his book celebrating the ecology of old growth, the writer David Kelly asks if it is possible to say, "We can harvest what we didn't plant and don't plan to let grow back." The buffer strips are so thin you can see the clear-cuts through the branches at fifty-five miles an hour. No flier can suspend the disbelief required.

Not long after loggers got established in the region, signs showed up in store windows: NO CALKED BOOTS ALLOWED HERE. There are different signs in the stores of Forks, Washington, now. Forks, the most western incorporated town in the contiguous United States, is almost wholly dependent on logging. It rides the border of the Olympic National Forest and is only a few miles from the Olympic National Park, and in the winter drinks in almost ten feet of rain. The hills around Forks are completely nude, and slash covers the draws and valleys on either side of Highway 101. The older clear-cuts are softened with pink foxglove and little vine maples and soft green shrubs, and now and then the velvety short cones of newly planted trees. The ragged stumps are gradually turning grey and disappearing into the new grass.

The *Jobs Rated Almanac* of 1988 lists 250 careers. Reading the list makes me think of Forks up against what's left of its woods. The *Almanac* lists professions in order of desirability, dropping rapidly from Lawyer and Architect to Teacher and Nurse. You have to read almost to the bottom before you feel you're in the Northwest: Lumberjack is number

214, followed farther down by Farmer, then Dairy Farmer, Cowboy (way down at number 245), Fisherman, and, bringing up the rear, that staple of the Northwest agricultural industry, number 250, Migrant Worker. The timber industry—which is not the same as the timber worker—is happy to let the arguments over the future of our remaining forests turn into an argument over jobs. Save trees or save jobs? This way, the industry is represented by the average man, the millworker and logger with a high school education, a wife and small children, scared to death of unemployment. But the comparison—trees versus jobs—is fallacious. It is even wicked. It is undeniable that the current rate of logging in the Northwest is eliminating the forests. There is nothing sustained or sustainable about the level of logging that the Northwest has suffered in the last century, and that translates directly into unemployment. If not now, then in three, or ten, or fifteen years, many of the loggers and millworkers will be out of work because they will be out of trees. (There are people in the industry who hear that statement and point accusingly at the Olympic National Park, at the slopes of Mount Rainier, at the small bits of wilderness clustered around the region, and ask why that, too, can't be cut.) Reducing the yields, practicing less "efficient" methods, setting aside large areas to be preserved forever—these are such small things. So little to do in light of what has already been done.

Forks calls itself the timber capital of the world. It has a little tourist business, mostly fishermen coming to the nearby wild coast, or retired couples touring the Hoh Valley, coming through Forks because you can't get around the Olympic wilderness any other way. The stores now have posters that say, TIE A YELLOW RIBBON FOR THE WORKING MAN, and there are yellow ribbons on lamp poles and trees and doorknobs. All around the Northwest there have been Yellow Ribbon rallies since the issue began to heat up in 1989. That was the year it became clear that the northern spotted owl was endangered by logging, and that the species could not be saved without sweeping changes in the amount and kind of logging being done. Since then, almost no issue stirs such anger and passion here. Spotted owls have been shot, crucified, hung, and their corpses mailed to various people perceived as environmentalists. Some of the latter have chained themselves to trees, camped in the crowns of trees slated for cutting, laid down in front of trucks and been arrested by the hundreds. In the Yellow Ribbon rallies, three hundred, six hundred, sometimes twelve hundred log trucks in a line rumble through small towns and through the main thoroughfares of cities for an afternoon, their drivers and passengers hungry, angry, impotent.

Every business, every office and restaurant in Forks has a sign in the window. Some say WE SUPPORT THE TIMBER INDUSTRY, others, WE ARE SUPPORTED BY THE TIMBER INDUSTRY. In the empty windows of one of the many empty storefronts, a line of children's posters—SAVE A LOGGER—EAT A OWL. One in neat black crayon, with a childish picture of a tree and a man: A SPOTTED OWL NEEDS HUNDREDS OF ACRES TO LIVE—WHY CAN'T I HAVE SOME OF THAT LAND TO LIVE ON? AM I IMPORTANT?

At the end of a fifteen-mile gravel road a little farther south in the Olympics, I recently found more slogans. The road entered the park and had no houses, no buildings at all, and at its end I found only a closed ranger station, the doors locked and the curtains pulled, the grass overgrown and weedy. The road gave way to several narrow, muddy trails, one crossing a wide, deceptively quiet river to the section of forest where the world's largest-known Douglas fir stands. At the trailhead was a latrine, and on the inside of the door a mass of graffiti, hostile and sharp: STUMPS SUCK. IF YOU HATE LOGGERS USE DIRT FOR YOUR TOILET PAPER. LOGGERS GET OUT.

The loggers in Forks—which celebrated James Watts Appreciation Day in 1983—like loggers all around the Northwest, would like to blame the restrictions of wilderness advocates for their troubles, though some are aware of the problem of log exports. About eighty-four million board feet of timber comes out of this district every year, along with as much as two hundred million board feet more from state and private lands nearby. Logs cut from federal lands west of the 100th meridian cannot be exported. (There are exceptions to the ban, notably those which allow Port Orford cedar, a rare species, to be exported, and the small exception exempting Alaska from the ban completely.) Loggers still cut on private lands long after the millworkers are out of work; the logs roll down to the water and straight to Japan, which pays a higher price for the older straightest trees than any other market.

They've done so for a very long time; log exports began around the time the first tree was cut here, and people have alternately praised and blamed the countries of the Far East for our problems ever since. But exports are just part of the problem. Overcutting—cutting trees faster than they could be replaced—and overproduction—milling more timber or cutting more logs than the market could absorb—have been problems from the first time the little mill in Camas closed down for want of customers. It is a regular, almost ritual complaint, this complaint of lost jobs, closed mills, towns disappearing into history because of government restrictions and environmental fanaticism. (Somewhat newer, but heard before, is blaming child abuse, wife battering, and suicide on restricted access to trees.) Meanwhile, the timber companies near Forks are predicting a shortfall by the year 2000—a period when the old trees will all be gone and the second growth not yet big enough to cut. The amount of private timber was already falling off before the current rage over the northern spotted owl and other concerns about saving old growth began.

The loggers and millworkers are only pawns—we are all pawns here, where timber mined like gold is sold by distant conglomerates. We are marks in the game. The beaver trade has turned into a timber trade. We sell the Japanese our best, most irreplaceable trees, and they sell us electronic equipment and cars. The Northwest Passage is now realized, and the Northwest has become the Third World country instead of the other way around.

In the center of the main street of Forks, which is Highway 101 and crossed every minute or two by roaring, loaded logging trucks, is a section of a Sitka spruce tree. It is a log cut from a tree thirty-seven feet in circumference and 256 feet tall. That's quite a bit taller than the standing champion Sitka spruce.

After a few days in Forks, I found myself slipping into the Missouri accent of my mother and grandmother, a product of their own grandmothers. It's soft and vowel-heavy and slow, and my mother fell into it only when she was most at ease. Those long-forgotten relatives east of the Mississippi go ghosting by when I'm in a place like Forks, which is, after all, so much like Yreka and the places of memory. The streets are wide, the sidewalks run out after a few blocks and turn to dust, commerce is social and slow, and the minimarts sell hunting magazines and chewing tobacco along with corn chips and beer. Little towns, with big yards; in the yards are dogs, and sometimes goats, horses, and geese, and always television antennas and woodpiles covered with tarps flapping in the wind. The driveways are gravel and people drive trucks. Little gift shops, pizza parlors, grocery stores and gas stations, coffee shops and vacant lots like the vacant lots in every other little town in the country. Here there are also mills and chain-saw repair shops. Sweetness without irony—steadiness and nothing unknown. Even the wavering recession in Forks seems familiar, just another of the small recognitions that pop open for me here. If I feel like a voyeur here, then I'm a voyeur to my own history. If I'm an interloper in Forks, I'm an interloper in Yreka, in my own childhood, in my own memory.

I wandered into a little gift shop in Forks and fell into conversation with a man while we looked over salt shakers and oven mitts. He was wearing wide red suspenders with the words SPOTTED OWL HUNTER, a flannel shirt, jeans and leather boots. He was about my age, a good-looking, long-haired, lanky blond man. We chatted about Forks, and I made up little lies to explain my presence and told him of my own past, the little shivers of remembrance his town evoked. He nodded, smiled, turned over a ceramic bowl to see the price. It was the middle of the morning on a weekday, and I could only imagine his leisurely, pointless wandering to be that of the unemployed.

He is suspicious, I think; he is skeptical of my motives in being in Forks, in talking with him. I wanted to tell him that I'd known him all my life, that we were peers. I dated him, he's my brother, my neighbor all grown up. I smoked pot with him in high school and rode in the back of his old Buick to go swimming in the creek. He is as familiar to me as the streets of Forks. And our friendly, flirtatious talk is ringed with tension.

Rarely have I felt such a sense of being stuck on one side of an idea, whether I wanted to be or not. I am what he might call a "tree hugger," one of the less derisive terms coined lately by cornered people determined to go down with pride. We lack a common aesthetic, this man and I. I am inclined toward the raw and disused; I have faith in chaos. I imagine—without asking, reading the message on his red suspenders—that he has a separate faith, a trust in mechanism, an inclination toward control. He sees the miles of clear-cuts north of town, and sees work done, a project finished—and a field of slash to burn and Douglas-fir seedlings to plant. I see a scene of devastation and loss; I see Soleduck cut down, the Hoh Valley turned bare. I see something that cannot be made lovely by any cast of light or change of season. I see a kind of physical and psychological violence. It is I who am tense here, who am sad, and I who end the conversation and find my way back to the Forks Motel.

The logs were too big for horses to pull, so they used oxen, sometimes ten yokes at a time. The oxen were called bulls. The ground was too soft to use wheeled carts, so they invented the skid road: trees dropped in parallel like railroad ties, running from the deep woods to the mill, or the harbor. The skids were coated with whale oil or grease and the oxen handler, universally known as a bullwhacker, sometimes walked the length of the animals' backs in his hob-nailed boots, daring an ox to stumble so he could butcher it for Sunday supper. Sometimes the greasy cobble of skid road led into the muddy tumble of shacks constituting towns, and around it were built the bars and whorehouses serving the loggers. Skid road became skid row, today's term for the down and out, the lost and left behind. (Stewart Holbrook started the Society for the Preservation of the Old American Term "Skid Road" in All Its Purity. Walter McCulloch was on Holbrook's side. He called "skid row" a "miserable, phoney term," and added, "There's no such damn thing as skidrow and there never was.")

The trees sailed around the world. The trick was transporting these damnably big trees. Way back in 1791 some visionary had tried taking logs from Maine to England in a raft—a great mob of logs floating in the ocean and held together by a fence. The logs were abandoned off Labrador. Another raft, so big it was named, like a ship, *The Baron of Renfrew*, made it all the way to the English Channel before it broke apart.

Simon Benson, one of the millionaire mill owners of the Northwest, tried again in 1906. He got three million feet of logs down the coast to San Diego, 1,100 miles in twenty days, and then did it again and again for almost forty years. The method became known as the Benson raft—oblong cradles of chains up to a thousand feet long and holding enough logs to rise a dozen feet above the surface and sink two dozen below. ("They were like nothing God nor man had ever before, or since, turned loose on the Columbia River," wrote Sam Churchill.) An entire raft of trees was supposed to have been stolen off the Fraser River in British Columbia. All that was needed was a pint of whiskey and an inattentive watchman; when he woke, he found nothing but water and all the trees purloined away.

In 1905, the city of Portland held the Lewis and Clark Exposition, for which the city built a "forestry center," an immense building called "the biggest log cabin in the world." More than a million board feet of wood went into the Forestry Building, which centered on a corridor of trees: two parallel rows of evenly spaced, upright, perfectly proportioned Douglas-fir trunks, each fifty-four feet high. Each of the fifty-two firs was big enough to furnish the lumber for a small house; each had been searched for diligently, cut and handled with grave care, the way sacrificial lambs are fed and groomed with the best of food and the kindest of hopes. People were dwarfed inside the hall of virgin trees, dwarfed and given to staring around themselves with curious, sometimes dubious looks. The building stood a long time, held up as it was by the shoulders of the world's tallest trees. When it burned in 1964, it burned the way a forest fire burns in a droughty August wind: hot, explosive, spreading like tallow, shooting its flames and burning to ashes.

Loggers wanted only to work in the woods. They might or might not have families, but they were alive only in the woods. *Woods* "means more to a logger than any other word," wrote Walter McCulloch. "It is job and home both." They wanted to be woodsmen, to meet the myth and become it. Did men of particular endurance and power come naturally to the labor of the big trees, or did the trees make men durable and strong? (Or were the men *like* the trees?) Every story mentions the dialect, the drinking, the toil and the humor and the defiance. Listen to the reminiscence of a man raised in a turn-of-the-century logging camp, speaking of his father: "A man so tall you had to tilt your head way back to look up at his face.... A man who carried with him the rich, clean smell of freshly cut fir and hemlock timber and the heady, perfume-like odor of pitch.... Hot-tempered, rough-talking, and capable of blowing a month's pay on whiskey and women in a matter of hours during a Saturday night in town, they were always careful of their language around wives and young people."

Everything had a name in logging, a special slang to distinguish the timbermen from everybody else. They called a nice large log "a big blue butt," and canned milk "the tin tit." They cut trees to make flumes down which to send the logs, and to make bridges and trestles for the trains and carts, and to make the skid roads to slide the logs along. The trees were brought down in surrender to the destiny of trees.

"Daylight in the swamp," it was called. Letting daylight into the swamp. The loggers preferred the shade. The forest was a perpetual thing and couldn't be diminished. Where is the world of perfect sustained yield? "I'd rather cut big trees, you know," an Oregon logger said on a television show. "They're fun.... And if you leave them standing they're just gonna go to waste, rot and fall down and they're worth nothing." The loggers want a forest in which you can cut as hard and as fast as possible, cut the biggest, most daunting trees, and come out the next day and do it all over again, without end. An old saw, the long, thick-toothed kind pulled by two and known as a misery whip, was burned with engraving: I LOVE YOU TREE.

Loggers cleared a space and took off, no longer interested in the land. Then the stump ranchers and farmers took over, if they were desperate enough or had bought the idea from a distance. In the first few decades of the twentieth century, a new back-to-the-land effort began in the urban centers of Washington, designed to serve two purposes. First was to get the poorest people out of the city, thereby reducing congestion and removing their attendant problems to a distance. Second was the land itself, left by the loggers as a clearing covered in stumps and brush and tangles of roots. People believed—or claimed, depending on their motive—that any land that could grow such big trees could surely grow crops. The only drawback was getting it clear. Logging was "extractive," like mining; it was a matter of reducing the unmanageable woods into something worth having.

In photographs of logging and stump ranches taken around the turn of the century and before, trees grow straight to the sky. They are random, upright pillars stretching out of sight, disappearing into a woven canopy, with wedge-shaped slices called undercuts hacked out at the base. It is only when I look closely that I see the men in the picture, tiny and weak, dwarfed even by the underbrush in this gargantuan wood. They stand beside the trees, wearing short pants and high boots, suspenders and dirty long underwear and felt hats. They look stolid and worn, and they point their axes with weary pride at the undercut they've made after hours of pain. In many pictures, one of the men lies like an odalisque inside the undercut, his head propped rakishly on his hand, cupped in the wound under the great weight of the tree. Sometimes they all sit together in the undercut, brothers of the woods all in a row, leaning against the bark—the bark with ridges deep enough to hide an arm. These men, sticky with the blood of the woods, stand beside the tree with the weary triumph of the hunter standing beside his buck. They are proud to live in a land capable of such production, and proud to bend it to their use. The hillsides when they were finished looked as though a tornado had escaped over the Continental Divide and struck the Northwest forests in surprise. And all the great trees obediently lay down.

No idea of the West was more persuasive than that of the open, fertile land. The farm, and a new kind of farmer: not a tenant plowing another man's—a richer man's—land, but a freeman. A man who owned his land, given to him by a benevolent democracy, a man who worked free of constraint and unfair tax, free of eternal rent and the controls of the company store. Land for the taking, and people to farm it, and from that the philosophy of the land idyll. It was economically radical and socially profound, this experiment in land. The farms are mechanical now, the soil eroded, the vast wheat fields tilled by enormous combines. Even the famous fertility depends on chemicals now, so eaten up is the dirt. In the fall, the fields of the Palouse and the Willamette Valley are burned to sterilize the ground, and the air is filled with a sharp and ugly smell. Columns of dirty smoke curl up from the ground like pillars. For every town named by hope—for every New Era and Spangle and Rome—there were two named for disillusionment: Follyfarm and Needy, Lonerock and Remote, Mold, Dusty, Stinking Water, Deadhorse Lake, Coffin Mountain, Poison Creek, Starvout, and a pass called Freezeout Ridge.

Stump land was very cheap, but it cost hundreds of dollars and hundreds of hours of hard labor to clear. The stump farmers used fire, dynamite, muscle, and animals to break up and pull out the stumps so big they could be used for houses. The slash burning ruined what little fertility the land held, by burning out the organic humus with the slash. A farmer could plant and harvest a crop one year and begin clearing his land all over again the next, pulling up blackberry and vine maple and bracken. Vine maple is everywhere in this forest, a plant so tenuous and flexible it was called "wood of the devil." The Douglas-fir seedlings, the slide alder and red huckleberry and the rest of the understory would rise where it could, crowding out grass and wheat and corn until it was torn and burned. Each successive burning lowered the productivity of the next crop.

What was meant to be a bucolic land of new farms seeding produce for the future was a kind of hell instead. Each stump ranch was nothing more than a small, ragged clearing inside a canyon of trees, a choking circlet of trunks so close to each other it doesn't seem possible they could have grown—so close the branches wove together, tree to tree. John Muir compared these weary souls to the beaver whose land they inhabited: They "keep a few cows and industriously seek to enlarge their small meadow patches by chopping, girdling, and burning the edge of the encircling forest."

In an old photograph of a stump ranch, the small shake cabin is almost windowless. A stovepipe smokes endlessly. A haphazard fence winds between scattered stumps as big as small stages—bigger than the house. Laundry hangs limply in the background, already stinking of the perpetual wood smoke, and in between the stumps are piles of rough-hewn shingles and unkempt slash. An aproned woman, a man holding a horse, four children as ragged as the edges of the cut stand tiredly for the photographer under a sky that seems eternally grey. The stump farms were eventually abandoned, the poor farmers-to-be returned to the Hoovervilles and tenements from which they'd come. The land they left behind was so ill-used and sterilized that even the Douglas fir couldn't grow on it anymore.

Logging was and remains a desperately dangerous job, and dangerous not only in the risk of sudden, unwarned death, but also the danger of mutilation, the amputation of limbs and spine, the loss of fingers, eyes, livelihood. Still, nostalgia prevails; little is said about the way logging used to be without slipping into a wistful melancholy. It is nostalgia for men not only bigger, but better than life, and for life that is better remembered than it ever was lived: the "old days," the days of steam engines and donkey hauling. This is also nostalgia for the big forest that the steam engines and donkeys helped destroy. ("Put the forest back on its rotting and weather-stained stumps. Push everything back twenty-five years in time and start over.") It is as though logging weren't a profession, a deed, but a need, an *instinct*—a drive as primitive and uncontrollable as the drive to eat and sleep.

Public Law 273, the cooperative sustained-yield bill, was passed in 1944, partly due to the efforts of Oregon Senator Charles McNary, who had already made history by helping to get the Bonneville Dam built. It legislated the combining of private and federal forest lands when "such action would be in the public interest. . . . " The Forest Service would manage the land and the private operators would log it. The point of cooperative sustained yield was supposedly twofold: to keep mills operating and men employed, and to encourage private timber owners to practice sustained-yield management, a form of logging in which cutting and replanting are combined to provide both a continual source of mature trees for lumber and wild forestland. (True sustained-yield logging is the opposite of what the nineteenth-century loggers called "cut out and get out.") Mills all over the Olympic Peninsula and throughout Grays Harbor closed during the Depression, and kept closing into the 1940s, and that meant the closing down of whole logging camps, small towns, and subsidiary companies. The cries for more wood, for higher cuts, for stopping exports of logs out of the region had begun many decades before. The economic dismay expressed then and now has occurred regularly, in the same places, like a mysterious, intermittent fever. In 1937, eleven billion board feet of old-growth forest was transferred out of the Olympic National Forest—where it would have been cut—into the Olympic National Park, where no logging of any kind was allowed, largely because of stubborn presidential support. "The effect was precisely the same as the death of old Douglas firs amounting to eleven billion board feet in Oregon's Tillamook Fire of 1933. However, the 'wilderness values' of the Olympic Peninsula's eleven billion board feet were officially judged to be of more vital importance to the people than the 'economic values.' "

When World War II came, logging revived. ("Overcutting on private timberland was a patriotic duty," wrote James Stevens of the era.) It just so happened that the first—and only—cooperative unit established under the bill was the Shelton Cooperative Sustained Yield Unit, in the southeastern corner of the Olympic Peninsula near Hood Canal.

The Simpson Timber Company had been a major force in the Shelton area since the 1880s. In the 1940s, when so many companies were bailing out, Simpson bought up the entire McCleary lumber operation a few miles south. The McCleary buy-out included not only acreage and mills but also a number of other businesses, considerable commercial land, and, as a feudal touch, all of the private homes: in short, the entire livelihood and lives of almost thirty thousand people. The Shelton Unit was, to all intents and purposes, the Simpson Unit. In a history of the Forest Service, Harold Steen writes, "By shifting emphasis from the forest to the forest industry, sustained yield came to mean the continuous production of lumber rather than forests. Conservation meant conserving the industry. . . ."

Part of the sustained-yield legislation required the private operator to log with mixed use in mind: in other words, to protect wildlife habitats and streambeds, prevent erosion, replant according to the newest standards, and so on, in order to provide for recreation and future forestation. In exchange for the economic burden of careful management for the future—a new idea for West Coast loggers—the private operator got federal timber without bidding.

The Shelton Unit was a combination of two concerns. The Simpson Company contributed first 173,000 acres, and later another 53,000 acres, of lowland forest—not coincidentally, most of it already cut over, and either unplanted or planted with small trees less than sixty years old. The federal government contributed 111,000 acres of upland, centuries-old timber in the Olympic National Forest—not coincidentally, mature, virgin forest. No one at the time commented on the obvious fact. Simpson was a patrimonial company threatening to close its mills because its own rapacious practices had left it without trees to cut. And Simpson was invited to test a radically new conservation-oriented method of harvesting trees. What seems obvious in hindsight was considered a wonderful example of benevolence at the time—on the part of both the United States Forest Service and Simpson. The region was "the perfect proving ground for programs on which government and business might pool interests and plan and work together for the common good, in 'wise use' of the commercial forest resource," wrote James Stevens, he of the Paul Bunyan tales. "Surely Shelton was the place."

The Shelton agreement was written to last a hundred years: from January 1, 1947, until January 1, 2047. The allowed annual cut was that required to supply all the local mills and factories plus a new fiberboard plant being built, enough to maintain the local employment of 1,350 people. All the federal timber taken off the unit lands had to be processed within a few miles of the towns of Shelton and McCleary. New logging roads would be built with federal tax support. The yield was guaranteed:

one hundred million board feet of timber a year. As I write this today, in 1991, the Simpson Company still employs about fifteen hundred people. The annual allowable cut is now 223 million board feet of timber, but this past year only about 180 million was taken, and that number is dropping. Simpson hasn't bought any Forest Service timber for five years now, preferring to log only its own second-growth trees and leave the old growth on federal land alone. The reason is not one of environmental largess or concern for diminishing forests. It is, of course, economics: The remaining old growth is so remote and inaccessible that the cost of cutting it down and hauling it to market is prohibitive. Simpson has dismantled two logging camps and a mill designed to handle the larger, old-growth logs. In fact, the Forest Service would like to sell that old growth somewhere else, but the unit agreement prohibits anyone but Simpson from buying the timber. So the trees stand.

"There will never be another agreement like this one," a Simpson spokesman told me. What he calls "a change in society," a shift in what people want from their forest lands, has made logging under the restrictions of the Unit Law more trouble than it's worth. "We've seen a move from timber production to practically no production at all," he added.

It's all perspective. I see flayed squares of bare ground, broken only by thin buffer lines and timber already marked for a coming cut. Others see only that some trees still stand, and they call that sustained yield. James Stevens, like Stewart Holbrook, worked in logging camps as a young boy and grew up in the woods, where the loggers "started at one end of the valley and cut until they reached the other end." Of one photograph near Shelton, the hillsides skinned in jagged, muddy squares and the tiny town sitting under the shadow of the mill, Stevens writes, "...clean and comfortable living with efficient forest methods." It's all a matter of what we consider in the best interests of the community: whether conservation has intrinsic value, whether a community is healthier if all its eggs are not in one corporate basket. It's also a matter of who the community is, and how large: Shelton? the Olympic Peninsula? the globe?

The White Mountain fire of 1988 was started by lightning. It eventually burned about twenty thousand acres near Sherman Pass, Washington, east of the North Cascades. The burned-over land can be seen for a long way, strangely pretty, dancing over the hills. The trees burned in different ways, to different degrees. Thousands of black spars with bark peeling to reveal the orange heartwood stand beside grey trees like revenants. Some trees are orange and still hold dead needles. Scattered about are a few healthy green trees. It is a rainbow, a palette, of soft color in harmony. It is at once open and crowded, spacious and full of detail; the light pours through the many trunks uninterrupted onto a bright, soft, green grassy floor, and you look through the slats of black trees at a vista of black, orange, and green. It is lovely and healthy, too; fire cleans, and is essential to the eons-long generation of new forests. It is far healthier than a clear-cut.

The roadside parking area has educational signs describing the economic loss and the number of board feet of timber salvaged. There's a paragraph or two about "natural reforestation"—that is, what would happen if we did nothing to the burn but let it be. "The fact that natural reforestation proceeds rapidly after a fire does not necessarily mean that economically desirable kinds of trees will always appear or that they will do so at the convenience of a forester."

Near Taylorsville, on the Oregon side of the Columbia River, is a steep, denuded mountain on one side of the highway, shaved clean; on the other side, a giant pile of yellow sawdust growing taller in the perfume of a nearby pulp mill.

The signs describing the planting dates on clear-cuts often add the motto "America's Renewable Resource." True enough, if all you want is wood, and you have a few generations to wait, and the willingness to live among the dull monocultures of second-growth farms the rest of eternity. But old-growth, old virgin forests are as irreplaceable as oil reserves and extinct species: Gone is gone for good. They don't—can't—grow back in a dozen dozen generations.

Last spring, I wandered up a two-lane road north of Willamina in Oregon. No signs, no shoulder, only private fences to hug each time a logging truck rumbled by. I was climbing into the Coast Range, a long spine parallel and west of the Cascades, the first wall for the ocean rains. In April the road was still speckled with banks of snow, and a complicated tapestry of sunlight falling down the canyons filled with groves of birch and pine; the delicate, rose-red lace of the young birch buds hung in halo. I would get lost in the dappling of light sliding down into haze to the floor of thin, glaring snow, and then, around a corner, feel the slap of clear-cut: all the trees gone and the spring sunshine pouring down on an empty plain; sticky trunks, torn red clay in piles with tangled slash and ragged stumps. Then another curve, another corridor of trees, as though the desolation had never been.

Another day, driving from Astoria to Portland along the Columbia River, I told my son we were passing through the Clatsop State Forest. "Why do they call it a forest?" he asked, bewildered. "There aren't any trees."

Clear-cuts can be pretty, too, from a certain distance. On a clear day, the whole of the Pacific Northwest is freckled with them; the forest is like a quilt stitched together with the patches of clearing. (You have to be quite high to achieve this view; the trick lies in not getting too close.) If a clear-cut has been planted, it might look like an incongruous, strangely isolated Christmas-tree farm; if not, like leather or mud. Cuts come in every size and shape: here is a diamond, there a field like the outline of Idaho, here a shaved star, its arms sliding down from the cone of a hill. Wormy dirt roads are stenciled through the green like snail trails, and in some places, like the stretch of northwestern Oregon from Portland to Astoria on the coast, there is more cut than growth. But over there is a perfect egg, and there a wobbly rectangle, and beside it, two squares point to point like argyle. One peak has been peeled off in a circle, a tonsure of logging, and to the right, a spiraling road climbs a soft mountain round and round and round to the point at the top. These most unnatural shapes are plopped down in the soft curves of geological time the same way we insert bridges and buildings and a ribbon of paving, and it's possible to squint and see the art: a bridge in certain light, a glassed skyscraper catching sun have a kind of organic virtue. And clear-cuts on a clear day, from the heights, are warm and brown and brushed to the tender, bare uniformity of suede.

But we can't always keep that distance. For more than a century, timber companies and the Forest Service have practiced the preservation of something called a buffer zone, a row of trees between clear-cuts and busy roads. It's called "preserving the visuals," but the general term for a buffer zone is "fool-'em strip."

"Helping lay new railroad spurs as well as tearing up and maintaining old ones brought me in direct contact with the various logging areas," wrote Sam Churchill in his memoir of his lumberjack father and his own youth in a logging camp. As a child in the second decade of the 1900s, Churchill had longed for nothing more than to be a logger like his father. But as a young man, he saw what was left of the forest where he'd been raised: "The land was left a vast, silent waste of snags and stumps marching in melancholy dreariness across ridge and canyon for as far as the eye could reach. It left one with a feeling of shame and sadness. It reminded me of pictures I had seen of the tired white crosses in the Meuse-Argonne in France and Flanders Field in Belgium."

Old growth, so seductive to the logger because of the quality and quantity of wood, is as healthy as a forest can be. But these are the forests consistently dismissed as "decadent" and "overripe," dismissed as selfish systems hogging the most nutrients, the largest plots of ground for their own use. A pamphlet put out by the Caterpillar company— so anxious to sell bulldozers and cranes to ease the removal of these difficult trees—says this as a counter to the argument that old growth is a healthy system:

> THE FACTS SAY: Forests do not necessarily improve with age. Decaying stands lack the food resources animals require. Density of old stands blocks sunlight, discouraging new growth. Wood lost "nature's way" exceeds new growth, resulting in a net loss of wood volume, without revenue.

It's one thing to argue against that—to counter by explaining the use of decaying logs as food and shelter by various species, pointing out how much more life there is on the floor of an old-growth forest than in a tree farm. Such arguments are actually easy to make; biology is clearly, undeniably, on the side of old growth. What's telling, I think, is the existence of the argument in the first place. Rather than stating baldly their desire to treat wild forests as a crop, the timbermen insult the nature of the forests themselves. They grant enough sentience to an acre of silent trees to call them selfish; they allow the woods enough aesthetic to call them decadent. The forests can be easily transformed by metaphor into veins of gold to be mined, or wild berries to be plucked. But they can also be deconstructed entirely with a kind of revisionist biology. They can be changed into something almost wicked.

There are many loggers, and a few foresters, who will claim that large clear-cuts are healthy for a forest; it seems to be the flip side of the argument that mature trees are somehow "decayed" or "overripe." Clear-cuts allow sunshine to penetrate to the ground, encouraging the growth of sun-dependent trees such as Douglas fir—economically valuable trees. The openings provide forage for deer and elk (and deer and elk for hunters). Certain other species like the rough undergrowth and new vegetation. But beyond a very small size, clear-cuts are biological failures.

First of all, large clear-cuts cause fragmentation, leaving behind islands of old growth cut off from each other, preventing the migration of animals that won't cross the open land, and forcing crowding in the remaining forest. The new growth is usually a monoculture, a single species of a single age dominating all the other plants, susceptible to disease. The forage is actually poor, and the deer and elk crowd into the nearest old growth as soon as snow falls, to escape the open weather. There is little of the complex understory of a forest in a second-growth clear-cut, because the canopy closes very quickly, shutting out sun more in new growth than in the enormous virgin stands. This state of perpetual shade can last as long as 150 years, during which the ground beneath is almost empty of the tiny plants and flowers that flourish in natural woods. And last, the clear-cut destroys the snags that dozens of species completely depend upon for shelter, and usually destroys the cooling, camouflaging stream cover vital to virtually *all* animal species.

There is no view now without a cut. The eye follows the unbroken horizon of trees along the mountains and hits the shorn section of a clear-cut as though hitting a wall. The forest is broken as a promise is broken. The Pacific yew tree grows under the old growth canopy on moist ground. Its bark contains a cure for several cancers, a chemical called taxol. The yew loves the cool shade of the old forest. It will not grow in clear-cuts. The twisty, crowded stands of birch and alder, which make the roads a tunnel of filigree dripping with moss, are opportunists infiltrating old clear-cuts, the gradual overtaking of emptied land by new and lesser species. There are clear-cuts on hills so steep you'd have to belay down by rope in order to plant new trees. The soil runs off by the ton and leaves the hills barren and brown; the soil runs all the way down to the streams in the valleys, and kills the fish. One logger can fell a six-hundred-year-old Douglas fir in fifteen minutes now, and he does.

The American Forestry Association (AFA) has kept records since 1940 on the largest known specimen for each particular species of tree. (Some less-common species don't have official records yet.) It's called the Big Tree Program, and the trees on record are called champions. The AFA has a careful set of qualifications to determine what makes a specimen the largest, involving points based on height, circumference at chest height, or four and a half feet above ground, and the average diameter of the crown. A fair number of hobbyists spend their weekends orienteering across hills and valleys in search of a rumored big tree—perhaps one whose wide crown was spied from a distant road, or a tree mentioned in passing by a store clerk or gas-station attendant. Big Tree hunters are a tenacious bunch; just in the small region of the Pacific Northwest, there are twenty-one champions found by a single, undaunted seeker named Frank Callahan. Big Tree hunters can get into esoteric arguments—one still raging is whether the spruce, which has a very wide spread at the base, should not have its circumference measured higher than four and a half feet. A casual reading of the list is instructive—and surprising. A black cherry tree in Michigan with a crown spread of 128 feet? A Pacific madrone almost a hundred feet tall? The list challenges our beliefs not only about the reality of trees but the *possibility* of trees, what trees are. (And it shakes our belief in what we see: The largest Douglas fir on record, hidden up the Queets Rain Forest in the Olympic National Park, is not even three hundred feet high. It would have stood in the shadows of the trees already cut for timber.)

Up a long road off Highway 101 is the Hoh Rain Forest. The Hoh is like the Disneyland of Big Trees. It's safe and well marked and the trails are short, but the trees are some of the biggest around. The road passes one of the largest of the Sitka spruce in a little cul-de-sac off the road, and ends in an enormous parking lot packed with RVs, trailers, vans, and station wagons. I watched a ruddy man with silver hair unload a pile of packs and begin sorting crampons and ropes. The visitors' center at the Hoh is also the trailhead for one of the more popular backwoods trails into the wilderness. A large crowd of people wandered around; 150,000 people a year come here, 1,500 in a single day on a sunny weekend.

The trails, all but the long, hardy one up to the peak, are marked by plaques for a self-guiding tour. (And warning signs, the basic rules of civilization: DON'T THROW COINS IN THE CREEK, DON'T PICK FLOWERS, DON'T DISTURB WILDLIFE.)

Nearly twelve feet of rain falls on the Hoh every year. But on a hot summer afternoon, the sheets of moss crackle to the touch. The trail is hard and the small plants beside it dusty with the dirt of many passing feet. Many of the hanging curtains of vegetation are epiphytes, air-loving plants that hang off the branches of the trees. They, too, are light and cottony with summer. I walked on, around the gentle curve of trail leading each visitor back to where he began, as I followed fathers videotaping their stumbling toddlers and groups of Japanese photographing each other in front of exaggerated trunks of trees. I noticed the dead trees by the trail, the fallen mature logs that become nurse logs if untouched. New trees would feed on them and grow into the kind of formal colonnades barely visible in the hidden distance. But these logs are cut in pieces to keep the trail clear, and along their sides visitors dazed by their breadth and length have carved their names and dates by the hundreds.

South of Forks, south of the Hoh, is the largest known western red cedar. I would never have found it but for a small paragraph hidden in a weekly newspaper. The tree grows off the highway up a series of logging roads. Washington's Department of Natural Resources (DNR), which handles logging on public lands (and is variously described as the Department of Nothing Remaining, or Do Nothing Right), used to have signs on Highway 101 directing tourists to the tree. A lot of people detoured in search of it, and their RVs and trailers slipped on the slick gravel or blocked a truck from its appointed rounds. People got lost; the site was vandalized. The signs were removed.

I turned off 101 at the apparent place, the only left turn for miles, and around the first curve knew I'd been correct: An enormous stump taller than my van stood by the road, with the words BIG TREE and an arrow carved into it. Behind the buffer of tall firs near the highway was a maze of old clear-cuts, with second plantings at various heights. It was a hot summer afternoon, and the strange landscape was deserted. I saw no cars, no trucks, no people, heard no sound but the buzz of a cricket. White gravel roads forked right, left, doubled back, turned at sudden angles marked only by obscure signs listing specific cuts and contracts. In this flat land, I couldn't see past the edge of the road, where the fluffy, spring-green firs stood six, ten, twelve feet tall, utterly alike and tightly spaced. The sky was big and light and dusty, the sun very hot in the open, and now and then when the road rose a few feet, I could see across the rug of Douglas fir into other, newer clear-cuts, with shorter trees, and far away the line of tall, old firs bordering the road, almost black. Two birds darted past my windshield and were gone. Finally I turned a corner and could see, far away, a grey spar reaching out of the green carpet like the hand of a drowning man. I wondered for a few minutes why the spar still stood, bleached and almost branchless in the unnatural sun, and then I understood: This was the tree, the western red cedar I had come to see.

A neat sign beside it listed measurements: 197 feet tall, 762 inches in circumference—63.5 feet. An uneven plank walkway of weathered cedar circled its bulbous base; around the rear, I could see where the big, spreading roots that rise out of the soil had been cut off to make room for the path. The bark had gone almost white, like weathered driftwood, and the ragged crown sported only a few green branches, very tiny against the width of the trunk. It is a beautiful tree, beautiful like bones, gnarled and twisted and cleaned of flesh. But the red cedar is a shade-loving tree, and this one had nothing but sun.

I called the Department of Natural Resources a few days later, trying to find a tactful way to talk about this tree, which seemed so wounded, so caged by space. This particular cut was a land trust, I was told. The bidder gave up the timber income possible from the tree in order to save it. I asked the DNR man why the DNR didn't advertise the site better, and he explained the problem with the roads. "Folks who are unhappy with managing forest lands for wood fiber were vandalizing the sign," he added. "Without someone up there to explain intensive forest management, they just didn't understand." He wanted me to know it was a logger on the site who realized the red cedar was unusual and took the measurements necessary for the AFA record. "He said, 'Gosh, this is a big tree. This one might be worth saving.' There were a lot of shakes, a lot of shingles in that tree. Not all the fellows who make their living in the woods are heartless and thinking just about themselves and their family. I like to say that those of us who work in the woods are environmentalists."

ELEVEN

The Teton Dam was built forty miles northeast of Idaho Falls in the early 1970s; it was built, as have been all the newer dams around here, against lawsuits and a variety of protests. Environmental activists complained that the Teton Dam would ruin the Teton River habitat; geologists warned about inherent weakness in the site, the soil, the dam structure itself. The dam was begun, but it was never finished; when the reservoir behind the dam was almost full, on June 5, 1976, the earthen dam split and collapsed and dropped a wave of eighty billion gallons of river water on four hundred thousand acres of the valley below—killing nine, injuring more than a thousand, and leaving another three thousand people homeless.

What is it about dams? The great Klamath River, its upper reach still wild, is the proposed site of the Salt Caves Dam, a project destined to destroy fishing runs and white-water rafting. The Round Butte Dam, at the junction of the Deschutes, Metolius, and Crooked rivers in Oregon, inundated a popular state park and all the state-owned facilities built over the years. Tacoma City Light built two dams, Mossy Rock in the 1950s and Mayfield in the 1960s, on the Cowlitz River in Washington. The engineers didn't include the fish ladders necessary to allow spawning fish to cross over the dam for their home beds, in spite of considerable opposition. Instead they built a hatchery, which failed, and tried trucking the salmon around the dam at spawning season, which also failed. The Bonneville Dam on the Columbia was finished at the same time as the Grand Coulee. Bonneville was a project of Senator Charles McNary, a Republican from Oregon, and President Franklin Roosevelt. Nothing has changed the Columbia as drastically as the Bonneville, not even the later dams at The Dalles and John Day, which drowned the fishing grounds of Celilo Falls.

Drift gill nets were used on the Columbia River from 1853 on, hulking draperies of woven net catching fish when their gills became entangled in the net's weave. The nets got bigger and bigger, until they ran twenty feet deep and almost a half-mile long. When the number of big chinook salmon started to drop—after hundreds of millions of pounds had been caught—the fishermen just made the weave of the nets smaller and caught steelhead and silver salmon and chum. Such nets were so successful that the fishermen organized themselves into "snag unions," parceling out exclusive rights to particular portions of the river, or "drifts." It was a strict, carefully enforced system, and it made a few people rich. For a few years before such practices were regulated, tired little Chinook, Washington, had one of the highest per capita incomes of any town its size in the nation.

The fishermen of the Columbia invented fish wheels in the late 1800s. Fish wheels spin in the current and scoop out the fish like a waterwheel scooping up water to turn a millstone. (A maritime historian called the fish wheel "unquestionably one of the most ingenious labor-saving pieces of apparatus ever invented for the purpose of capturing fish.") Fish wheels could each pull out a hundred thousand pounds a year. One wheel near the Cascades caught sixty-four hundred large salmon in a single day; another single fish wheel brought in seventy thousand pounds of salmon in one day.

The sturgeon were so big and common—the white sturgeon of the Columbia River grew to a thousand pounds, half a ton of a single, barbaric, whiskered fish—that they fouled all the gill nets and tore up the webbing. So the cannery people started catching sturgeon and mutilating them with axes before they tossed them back. Dead sturgeon coated the beaches until someone figured out you could can and eat sturgeon, too. By 1894, the fledgling sturgeon industry was a failure—there weren't enough sturgeon left to make it worth fishing for them. And in 1990, on the castrated Snake, one single sockeye salmon beat his way up the dams and the fish ladders and came home.

Not so long ago, people were cheered by, and longed for, the changing of the landscape from wildness to civilization—for "the handiwork of intelligence and industry," wrote one settler in a homesick letter east. The land was like a patchwork of rumor: Any person passing through would see either his Eden or his hell. I've only recently come to realize that my ancestors stayed here in spite of all that keeps me here—in spite of the mountains, and the storms, the high plains and the wild coast. It was a land that seemed meant for solitude and isolation, for the singular existence of the single man, and it had to be turned into a world of commerce and families.

Now, so soon, we've grown sick of industry and civilization and long for the signs of wildness, so diminished and narrow and rare. We failed to stop, once the momentum got rolling, our energies devoted to development until all around us were houses and bridges and stores and logging roads, fences and factories and walls. The hunger of a century and more ago, to see the wilderness tamed, is so like today's hunger to see wilderness unchanged. Oregon has more officially designated "wild and scenic" rivers than any other state in the country. Portions of more than forty rivers have been set aside from most development and industry. But there is no river in the state wholly wild, no place to follow from head to mouth without coming up against a wall.

Both hungers, the one for the human-made, the other for the untouched, are part of the search for balance, for a little of each, for the knowledge that humans, superior or no, are a species among species on a shared planet.

We are still reeling from the force of one belief above all others: that European man was in charge, that he had been given a mandate by God to expand, control, and tame the world. The forests, no matter how big, would fall; the deserts would bloom and the rivers be dammed and the cities grow. And the Red Man and his environs would, however sadly, fall in the natural course of things. Such a force is a force beyond reckoning and the wounds are inevitable, like Christ's wounds; the blood is God's blood, and can be excused.

My recent ancestors, my grandfathers—and yours—had a vision of astonishing breadth, and an astonishing reach with which to grasp what they saw. And the work is so new. The first settlers didn't arrive here until it was nearly time for the Civil War, until the other regions of the country were settled to the point of decadence. The fact that they destroyed what they found in the taking of it is an act without irony, and therein lies the surprise. There seems almost to be a kind of artistry in the subjugation of the land and the savage. Stories that are both sad and shocking today were wedged into the pioneer newspapers between civilized discussions of "mammoth radishes" raised by a farm wife, praise for "the sweetest pound cake we've had in some time," and reports of concerts, merchant discounts, advertisements for patent medicine, stoves, shoes, and mining equipment, marriage announcements, proverbs, admonishments to temperance, reports of new laws and real estate transactions. Those poor savages had no idea what momentum was moving them, how big, determined, and powerful the breaking wave had grown by the time it hit.

In 1888, Albert Bierstadt painted *The Last of the Buffalo*, a large, melodramatic vision of a dying land. The perspective is grand, and near: a distant, soft, white peak rises from a vast plain, and up close, at the edge of the frame, a small crowd of bison steps hesitantly among the white bones of their fellows. A shirtless Indian on a gleaming white pony rears over a charging, dying buffalo. Bierstadt painted *The Last of the Buffalo* twenty-five years after he'd watched white men, not Indians, slaughter buffalo in numbers alarming to him even then. The painting was the stimulus for the first serious census of buffalo in decades; an animal that had crossed the Plains in a population greater than twenty million not forty years earlier had been reduced to 551 single animals.

Still, Bierstadt was criticized for sentiment and melodrama, for geographical inaccuracy, for an overly large scope. (He had a habit of moving mountains and rivers around to improve composition.) His canvases have physical sweep, and the vistas grew larger as he worked through his memories of the West—Yosemite, the Sierras, Mount Hood, the Columbia. One critic chided him for mistaking quantity of vision for quality, as though his choice of subject was pretentious in itself. The fashion was changing late in the 1800s, when the West was no longer a dream and big was no longer grand. The buffalo were finished. The art world sought detail, irony, and smallness. Ecstasy had gone out of fashion.

The history of white expansion is so embedded in what I have been taught all my life that it has the flavor of the inevitable. I grew up considering the history of this place as a fact tantamount to gravity or photosynthesis. It was an undisputed condition, an absolute. It was logical, too, compellingly so when placed in the context of all that passed before. Could anything else have happened? How could anything else be possible?

I hate to admit how susceptible I am, even now. It's like a fever: The power of the myth is invisible and vigorous and the blood runs warm. Our summers are filled with theatrical reinventions of an imagined past: "The Story of Oregon," "The Oregon Trail Pageant"— amateur family productions set in the original sites with great earnestness and self-congratulatory pleasure. There are Lewis and Clark Days, and Hudson's Bay Days, when you can learn to skin a beaver or load a flintlock. But there are the movies, too: John Wayne and Jimmy Stewart and Barbara Stanwyck; they gaze out over the land, the chorus swells, and so does my throat, though I feel shamed by the unconscious response. Gary Cooper stands in the dusty street all alone, watched by the virginal Grace Kelly, for whom he fights. How potent this story is, how simple and clear. And I know how it ends; it always ends happily—at least, it does for *my* ancestors.

The town of Leavenworth lies in the Icicle Valley of central Washington, near the source of the Wenatchee River. It sits among hills so steep and peaked they look man-made, layers of sun-glazed pyramids hovering against the sky, and pear and apple orchards carefully groomed beside the pyramids' shadows. The breath of wind off the river is cool with coming deep, light snow. The Wenatchee River along the back porch of my hotel room runs clear and green past a cobbled beach. I sit under tall ponderosas frosted with the brown-tipped needles of autumn, in dry grass and thistles, above a patio of shale. The sky is empty and hot, the sun dropping in late afternoon to lie along the river like a resting man.

Leavenworth is a designed town, a wildly successful experiment in tourism. The Icicle Valley was fading into nothing thirty years ago. The Great Northern Railway closed its switching yard, the main mill went out of business, and one by one the stores closed and buildings stood empty for years. A number of people, some of whom had grown up in Leavenworth, formed a committee in the early 1960s to figure out a way to make Leavenworth work. They worked while gazing up at almost pruriently beautiful mountains, mountains no one wanted to leave. One subcommittee, composed of people concerned with industry, suggested establishing a vodka factory. Another subcommittee suggested a Gay Nineties theme. But one by one, businesspeople began remodeling their storefronts in the style suggested by the surroundings: In a country of fjords and natural ski jumps, Bavarian seemed like the right idea.

So began Project Alpine, and a boom business in shutters and gingerbread overhangs and leaded windows. Even the ranger station looks Bavarian, as are fences, gas stations, the liquor store, the banks. I stroll through the small center of town listening to accordions and watching couples dance the polka on a small park stage. People struggle to read the ornate Old European script in store windows in an atmosphere of clinking beer steins, robust German singing, and music boxes. Great pots of gorgeous pansies hang from below the shuttered windows. People eat ice cream at outdoor tables, wander in and out of crowded shops, wait in line for a seat in the Beer Garden. The atmosphere is unrelenting.

The Chickamin Hotel became the Edelweiss, an empty electrician's shop became the Alpen Haus. Now a million visitors a year come to Leavenworth, which has a year-round population of 1,585 prosperous people, and shop at the Nussknacker Haus and Der Sportsmann, the Schatzkammer and the Hansel and Gretel Deli, Katzenjammers, or Der Kitterhof, Das Meisterstück, Rumpelstilzchens, and the Tannenbaum Shoppe. At various times of the year, for festivals and holidays, there are gangs of bell ringers, and men playing alpenhorns longer than an elephant's trunk. A local newspaper says only that the Project Alpine members "relied on community pride to influence the owners' decisions to 'go with the flow.'" But no one seems to have resisted. Even the building codes were changed to allow the necessary architectural modifications. I walked from one end to the other, from my pretty hotel with its European name and American hot tub, all the way to the supermarket tucked up beneath the cross-country ski trail. And all at once it makes sense. The architecture, the guttural European language, the crowds of visitors: Here is the pioneer hope brought full circle. The New World is tamed and conquered, and then, at last, reconstructed— as an exact imitation of the long-lost Old World. European decorum and geniality at long last win the raw, rough land of the West.

Taken in a certain framework, the history of the West is, like the native people used to tell each other in reference to white men, crazy. All the calm presumption of right and destiny smacks of a deranged way of thinking, with its interior logic and deadly inflexibility. It is narcissistic.

One's choice of words literally shapes one's world view. At the turn of the century, Indians of the Pacific Northwest were counted in a census conducted by the Smithsonian Institution. The results are long, dry, and speckled with telling words: Tribal members are "stock," and some of the tribes are considered "extinct," while others dwindle to numbers so small the authors wonder if they should any longer be "enumerated separately." Only decades earlier, Indians were "assisted" to "the proper lands," where they were to "settle." The Indians seemed unable to make "proper use" of their resources; those who resisted such obvious charity were "traitors" and "malcontents." One rationale commonly employed was that the Indians had to be moved to distant reservations for their own good, because contact with white settlers had a degenerative effect. The Nez Percé people were ordered to leave their ancestral lands in the Wallowa Mountains because that land was "too cold" for Indians to live in.

A pungent pine smell drifts in my window and it grows into an abrupt bubble of sorrow: longing and hunger, loneliness for something lost a long time ago, lost when I was too young to know what I was losing. The disappointments of the West—the West, we write, with self-conscious solemnity—are more than the disappointments of rough land, dead otters, and lost trees, though such disappointments are great. Our disappointments are of the heart, of spirit. I wake up to being a child inside such a world as this, a world current, continuing, immediate. I am a child inside a beautiful land scraped of its life. The world! The whole world bent to our will. And yet I wake up glad to be here.

Like almost every American family, mine kept a collection of photographs: faded pictures of clear-skinned, sad-eyed men and women and children staring into the nearby camera with a suspended weariness. The faces are bare, exposed, and a trifle embarrassed at the profligate waste of the moment, and somewhere in them I can trace a line of cheekbone or the set of a nose and see my brother, my father, myself. There are so few photographs of that pioneer time, and they are repetitive and emblematic: haggard, craggy Indian faces; muddy streets caught in grey light; raw, lean men in hats and short black pants leaning on a plow.

The pictures are staged and frozen, the one fine piece of furniture artlessly dragged onto the porch for background, the father's hand laid across the boy's starched shoulder. I have only the picture of my laughing grandfather as a young man, leaning back in a chair against a rough wood wall with his dirty calk boot crossed gaily on his knee. I have one of my great-great-grandmother, dumpy and white-haired in a long gingham dress, standing with her several sons outside a flat cabin so sunken and windowless it looks like a dungeon. I have these and a million fictitious images I've conjured for myself: the few true moments before and after the recorded events. My grandfather brings the chair down with a resounding crash and picks up his saw; my great-grandmother leaves the sunlight and goes back to her stove in the dark and smoky house.

The Columbia River is not, and never was, the Great River of the West. But it *is* the greatest river in the West. It is the Passage—not the broad, deep, straight, God-given canal expected, but a passage that can be fashioned from its parts, from the combination of water, road, and rail. I am only just aware of how I see this land: carnal and sacred at once. We came here and found not a finished paradise, but the parts of one. The dream shifts, as dreams do: Here are the raw materials, to be turned into the Paradise of industrial, imperial man. He won't be going to the Far East for ivory and china. He will be going to the Far East to sell his furs and timber, until the fur is gone and the timber is cut. And then? Well, something will come up. The West will provide.

So this is my heritage. The dapper, bemused white man stands at the rail of a steamship, a bowler on his head and a cigar in his hand. His wife in her high-necked dress and his children in their linen blouses are still home, back east, waiting for the final settling up of accounts. The ship chugs up the river and passes banks on which a few Indians still live among the stumps, scarred by smallpox. He looks at them with pity, and a certain distant kindness. The ship will reach a rapids soon, and the man will have to disembark and enter a train, but even the days of trains are numbered. Even the rapids will fill and disappear, like the trees. For now, content with his labor, he gazes upon his new world with the eye of a father gazing on his young, ill-mannered child, knowing that only time can finish a work as great and holy as this one.

On a clear October day, I flew from Los Angeles to Portland, the late autumn sun tilted low and golden-pale in the chalky sky. We skimmed with a steady roar up the gentle curve of the Willamette Valley, the broad drainage of the river that runs a hundred miles north and south in Oregon between the Coast Range and the Cascades, up the valley's center, soft as the line between two breasts. I looked down on softened, domestic bounty, on fertility almost unseemly in its profusion. There were pockets of trees scattered between the fields and the winding, dark-blue waterways—islands of trees tall and stately, with houses nearby like tents near an oasis, fields of every shade of green and tan and gold with perfect rows, a scatter of rusty pumpkins, a single tree left standing and circled with plow lines, and hayricks, and long, silver barns. I could see the stubbly corduroy of a Christmas-tree field, and the gentle rise of hills to the distant white peak of Mount Hood.

I had come over the giant, arid fields north of Los Angeles. They were brown, hard, scrabbled with tractor cuts; the lonely houses were separated by treeless miles. I had pressed against the window, against that high, light southern sky, and tried to find my way into that life below. And that life had looked like hard labor; it tasted like dust in the back of my throat. And this one looked like peace. I had flown up the corridor of the Pacific coast, the way the Spanish sailing ships flew a long, long time ago to find their cities of gold, and here it was. A city glided slowly underneath, braced on all sides by groves of trees and green hills, by neighborly houses and moist lawns. I thought that the easiest of lives could be lived there below me, a life of slow exaltation. I suddenly wanted that life very much. Here was the land, the grand, longed-for land where the beavers were as big as bears, where the trees stood as tall as the Temple of Apollo. And the mountains, when they opened like the wings of a bird, reached five miles into the sky.

I wanted nothing more than to live in that most charmed of places, that Paradise, Buonaventura, that Great River, that Oregon. All those hungry souls combing the seas, paddling across the Plains on that long search for home, and I was falling into it as easily as taking a breath. I'd lived here and there in that particular valley for fifteen years, and watching it, I was afraid I would wake from this good dream, this best dream of all, with a shiver of grief at its passing.

NOTES AND REFERENCES

The plethora of Native American place names in the Northwest creates a problem for the visitor. It matters little whether these names are real or imagined, they remain mysteries of pronunciation. Regional chauvinism being what it is, the visitor is advised to take care in his speech. The most common mistake in pronunciation, in fact, is the word *Oregon* itself. It is not pronounced *ary-gawn*, but *ory-gun*; like all Oregonians, I take a certain pleasure in correcting this particular lapse. The second most common mispronunciation I hear is *Willamette*—said correctly with the emphasis on the second, not the first, syllable. But what is one to do with Yachats? (Say it *yah-hots*.) And Sequim? (That's *skwim*.) I will leave you to decipher Tuality, Mukliteo, and Bogachiel on your own.

Regarding both the pronunciation and the spelling of Native American tribal and personal names, it is important to note that there is really no such thing. (Few of the "names" are names at all, and fewer still are pronounced now as they were when whites first arrived.) Each ethnologist, historian, and anthropologist differs in both large and small ways. The arrival of the white man to this area was sudden and overwhelming, and the depopulation of the Native Americans of the Northwest abrupt. Efforts to record the languages, especially the phonics and appropriate Roman spellings, were inadequate at best. A lot of what we consider "Indian" place names are not the names applied to a particular place by the local tribes (who often as not came up with more prosaic monikers) but names of individual Indians who lived near those places. In a lot of those cases, these are names given to the Indians by whites, or misheard or misspelled or misunderstood to be names. This appears to be true of Seattle, Ilwaco, Whatcom, and Steilacoom, all of whom were chiefs, and all of whom had real names not quite like the names they've been given in history.

Who knows how a native son of the Duwamish tribe would have pronounced his own tribe's name? Such things are lost to time. But there is a small, slightly silly joy in the sound of such words, in their felicitous roll off the lips and tongues. Washington, especially, is blessed with such names—better than Duwamps, better than Seattle: Moclips, Nooksack, and Puyallup; try Washtucna and Humptulips, Muckleshoot and Duckabush, Quilcene, and Hamma Hamma, Pysht, and Lilliwaup. Washington had "the most barbarous names imaginable," to the nineteenth-century traveler Charles Nordhoff. "On your way to Olympia by rail you cross a river called the SkookumChuck; your train stops at places named Newaukum, Tumwater, and Toutle; and if you seek further, you will hear of whole counties labeled Wahkiakum, or Snohomish, or Kitsap, or Klikatat; and Cowlitz, Hookium, and Nenolelops greet and offend you. They complain in Olympia that Washington Territory gets but little immigration; but what wonder? What man, having the whole American continent to chose [sic] from, would willingly date his letters from the county of Snohomish, or bring up his children in the city of Nenolelops?"

Place names in general are found in various state-specific reference books. None beats *Oregon Geographic Names*, 5th ed., by Lewis A. McArthur (Oregon Historical Society Press, Portland, 1982).

Lewis McArthur took on the task of cataloguing the origin of place names—a task surely doomed to a deadly aridity in many hands—with panache and humor. (Lewis A. was the author of editions one, two, and three; his son, Lewis L., is author of editions four and five.) Every page has entries with appended notes bringing a new mood to the discipline. Of the town of Joy, he wrote, "J. H. Horner told the compiler in 1931 that the office was named because of the joy settlers expressed at the possibility of mail service. These people did not then know about circular letters and advertising by mail." McArthur was especially angered by efforts to change historical names to fit the fashion of the times, a kind of cosmetic surgery he seemed to consider tantamount to painting over the nudes in a Renaissance mural. Of Nigger Ben Mountain, changed to Negro Ben in the 1960s, he wrote, "If every name that might now or in the future offend some ethnic group must be altered to suit the changing times, the authorities might just as well resort to a simple numerical designation." When Whorehouse Meadows was changed by the Bureau of Land Management to Naughty Girl Meadows in the 1960s (it has since been changed back to the original), McArthur called the new moniker "a namby-pamby name," and added, "O tempora! O mores!"

PROLOGUE

Early voyages and exploration can be studied in a variety of ways: through general histories, journals, annotations of journals, and in works focusing on specific aspects of the period, such as the early fur trade or relations with North Coast tribes. The amount of literature available is huge. I am indebted for my own small understanding to the following works, which together provide a foundation in an enormously complex and somewhat daunting field: S. W. Jackman, ed., *The Journal of William Sturgis* (Sono Nis Press, British Columbia, 1978); Derek Pethick, *First Approaches to the Northwest Coast* (J. J. Douglas Ltd., Vancouver, B.C., 1976); John A. Hussey, *Champoeg: Place of Transition; or a Disputed History* (Oregon Historical Society Press, Portland, 1967); Warren L. Cook, *Flood Tide of Empire: Spain and the Pacific Northwest, 1543–1819* (Yale University Press, New Haven, Conn., 1973); Gordon B. Dodds, *The American Northwest: A History of Oregon and Washington* (Forum Press, Arlington Heights, Ill., 1986); Malcolm Clark, Jr., *Eden Seekers: The Settlement of Oregon, 1818–1862* (Houghton-Mifflin, Boston, 1981); David B. Quinn, ed., *New American World: A Documentary History of*

North America to 1612, vols. 1–5 (Arno Press, New York, 1979); and Oscar Osburn Winther, *The Old Oregon Country: A History of Frontier Trade, Transportation, and Travel* (University of Nebraska Press, Lincoln, 1950). A collection of essays on various aspects of Pacific Northwest history can be found in G. Thomas Edwards and Carlos A. Schwantes, eds., *Experiences in a Promised Land* (University of Washington Press, Seattle, 1986). Joseph Schafer, *A History of the Pacific Northwest* (Macmillan, New York, 1922), provides an example of past treatments of the region. H. K. Hines, *An Illustrated History of the State of Oregon* (Lewis Publishing, Chicago, 1893), is a useful record of the way in which the Native American is treated in history written even very closely on the heels of conquest. Every student of the West should read Frederick Jackson Turner's essays in *The Frontier in American History, 1893* (Holt, Rinehart & Winston, New York, 1962).

For specific regional anecdotes, I've used a number of local histories and historical sources, plus Samuel N. Dicken, *Pioneer Trails of the Oregon Coast*, 2nd ed. (Oregon Historical Society Press, Portland, 1978); Samuel N. and Emily F. Dicken, *The Making of Oregon: A Study in Historical Geography* (Oregon Historical Society Press, Portland, 1979); and Carl Abbott's work on Portland history, especially *Portland: Gateway to the Northwest* (Windsor Publications, Northridge, Calif., 1985).

For details of the fur trade and its influences on the lands and the native people, as well as on settlement, I have relied on the following: Lewis O. Saum, *The Fur Trader and the Indian* (University of Washington Press, Seattle, 1965); Frederick Merk, ed., *Fur Trade and Empire: George Simpson's Journal, 1824–1825*, rev. ed. (Harvard University Press, Cambridge, Mass., 1968); Jennifer S. H. Brown, *Strangers in Blood: Fur Trade Company Families in Indian Country* (University of British Columbia Press, Vancouver, 1980); Alexander Ross, *The Fur Hunters of the Far West*, ed. by Kenneth A. Spaulding (University of Oklahoma Press, Norman, 1956); Peter C. Newman, *Company of Adventurers: The Story of the Hudson's Bay Company*, vols. 1 and 2 (Penguin, New York, 1985–1987); and William H. Ashley, *British Establishments on the Columbia and the State of the Fur Trade, 1831* (Ye Galleon Press, Fairfield, Wash., 1981).

Three excellent works telling the story of exploration and settlement in the Pacific Northwest from the point of view of Native Americans are Alvin M. Josephy, Jr., *The Nez Perce Indians and the Opening of the Northwest* (Yale University Press, New Haven, Conn., 1965); Clifford E. Trafzer and Richard D. Scheuerman, *Renegade Tribe: The Palouse Indians and the Invasion of the Inland Pacific Northwest* (Washington State University Press, Pullman, 1986); and Christopher L. Miller, *Prophetic Worlds: Indians and Whites on the Columbia Plateau* (Rutgers University Press, New Brunswick, N. J., 1985). For more on the trials of the Nez Percé tribe as well as neighboring tribes, and another perspective on the man who called himself Lawyer, see A. J. Splawn's work of conscience, *Ka-Mi-Akin: Last Hero of the Yakimas (1917)* (Binford and Mort, Portland, Ore., 1944), and *Noon nee-me-poo (We, the Nez Perces): Culture and History of the Nez Perces*, by Allen P. Slickpoo (Nez Perce Tribe, Lapwai, Idaho, 1973).

An examination of the changing beliefs about the shape of the Western Hemisphere can be found in *A Book of Old Maps*, ed. by Emerson D. Fite and Archibald Freeman (Harvard University Press, Cambridge, Mass., 1926). A more detailed analysis of the history of cartography and the effect of maps on popular belief is contained in *The Mapmakers* by John Noble Wilford (Knopf, New York, 1981).

The journey of Meriwether Lewis and William Clark has been dissected, annotated, analyzed, and even reenacted a number of times. Their journals are available in several editions, some of which include the less polished but equally enlightening diaries of other members of the party. Entire books have been devoted to Sacajawea, a Shoshoni woman who accompanied the party on its latter leg. I am indebted for journal quotes and details of the expedition to the following works: Reuben Gold Thwaites, ed., *Original Journals of the Lewis and Clark Expedition* (Arno Press, New York, 1969); Bernard DeVoto, ed., *The Journals of Lewis and Clark* (Houghton-Mifflin, Boston, 1953); Robert G. Farris, *Lewis and Clark: Historic Places Associated with Their Transcontinental Exploration (1804–1806)* (U. S. Department of the Interior, Washington, D. C., 1975); and Gerald S. Snyder, *In the Footsteps of Lewis and Clark* (National Geographic Society, 1970).

Finally, there are works on the philosophy of westward movement.

William Appleman Williams was a philosophical historian—or, perhaps, a historian's philosopher. Few academic historians are fond of his work, and his position in the canon of western history is controversial. Nevertheless, his work is unique, thought-provoking, and well written, which is more than one can say for many standard works of history. For a look at issues of imperialism and western expansion, there is no better place to start than with Williams' book *Empire as a Way of Life* (Oxford University Press, New York, 1980), a persuasive revision of westward movements. *Empire* challenges the view Americans hold of themselves, a view central to our education. We fail even to question it until someone like Williams comes along and puts each of us squarely in the role of the inheritor of imperialism. For an earlier work on the same subject, but with a more literary bent, see Henry Nash Smith, *Virgin Land: The American West as Symbol and Myth* (Harvard University Press, Cambridge, Mass., 1950). Another way of approaching the same subject, through visual arts, can be found in Chris Bruce, Brian W. Dippie, Paul Fees, Mark Klett, and Kathleen Murphy, *Myth of the West* (University of Washington Press, Seattle, 1990).

Page 6
The "Pacific Powerland" radio program lasted seventeen years, from 1961 to 1978. "Pacific Powerland" began as a way to frame the commercials of the power company but gradually took on a life of its own. There were more than thirteen hundred separate programs. Each was a true story, and each began with the firm, comforting words, "Hello there . . . this is Nelson Olmsted."

ONE

The number of exotic travel guides written about the Pacific Northwest is seemingly endless. The nature of travel in the 1800s led to a number of books encompassing Hawaii (then called the Sandwich Islands) and the Pacific coast, and a few describing the rigors of overland travel. The granddaddy of western travel guides, of course, is Francis Parkman,

Jr.'s memoir, *The Oregon Trail* (Caxton House, New York, 1945); Parkman is lyrical and exciting, and in the end it doesn't matter much that he never got to Oregon after all. Then there is Gustavas Hines and *Wild Life in Oregon* (Hurst & Co., New York, 1881). Among the most readable and detailed of the many commercial books are Albert D. Richardson, *Beyond the Mississippi* (American Publishing, Hartford, Conn., 1867); Lansford W. Hastings, *The Emigrant's Guide to Oregon and California, 1845* (Da Capo Press, New York, 1969); Samuel Bowles, *Across the Continent: A Summer's Journey to the Rocky Mountains, the Mormons, and the Pacific States* (Samuel Bowles & Co., New York, 1866); C. Aubrey Angelo, *Sketches of Travel in Oregon and Idaho, 1866* (Ye Galleon Press, Fairfield, Wash., 1988); Ceylon S. Kingston, *The Inland Empire in the Pacific Northwest* (Ye Galleon Press, Fairfield, Wash., 1981); Charles Nordhoff, *Northern California, Oregon and the Sandwich Islands, 1874*, centennial edition (Ten Speed Press, Berkeley, Calif., 1974); and Robert Greenhow, *The Geography of Oregon and California and the Other Territories on the Northwest Coast of North America* (Mark H. Newman, New York, 1845). The work of Frances Fuller Victor, generally considered one of the most accurate reporters of the details of Northwest settlement, is discussed below.

For that matter, consider Hall J. Kelley—a man, wrote Robert Cantwell, whose "capacity for wonder was unlimited." Kelley was a Bostonian of the early nineteenth century, a quiet, unprepossessing man unfortunately infected by a vision. It was a real vision, too, a religious experience of certainty for which he changed the course of his entire life. Rather suddenly and for no apparent reason, Hall Kelley came to see himself as the appointed missionary of God for the Oregon Country, a servant whose job was to bring civilization and religion to the heathen Northwest. He became, to that end, a kind of divine civic booster.

In 1824, some long time after the publication of Lewis and Clark's diaries, Kelley started the American Society for Encouraging the Settlement of the Oregon Territory, without having visited said place. All who spoke against him, derided him, or ignored him Kelley saw, with a paranoiac's lucidity, as the enemies of his vision; every small misfortune that befell him—from debt to a lack of social standing—he considered the deliberate work of the demons who opposed his mission to Oregon.

In fact, when he finally managed to arrange a trip in 1832, it took him more than two years to reach Oregon Territory. He left behind a number of lawsuits and bills, an unhappy wife, and several children. Kelley made it to New Orleans with little trouble, but once there, he was promptly robbed by his traveling companions. On the boat to Mexico, the customs people took what he had left. He stumbled through Mexico and made it to southern California, where he found himself with malaria, alone, but determined to get north. A few more thieves and brigands accompanied him north, stopping on the way to rape, rob, and kill Indians and threaten Kelley's life when he protested. He arrived at last at Fort Vancouver, where he was greeted by the Hudson's Bay Society factor Dr. John McLoughlin with less than the hero's welcome he so urgently wanted. He was an unwelcome American in a British stronghold, and suspected of being a horse thief just like the men with whom he had traveled. He stayed only six months—through the rainy winter, in a cold, isolated hut once used for cleaning fish outside the fort, estranged from the fort society and treated as a pariah. Finally he sailed to Hawaii, never to return to this country that he thought, after all, to be ripe with "beauty of scenery, fertility of soil, and other natural advantages." Kelley never quit believing in his own dream. "Stupid, ignorant and crazy: I have often been spoken of in this way," he wrote in the latter part of his life. "Not to my face, but in whisper . . . when planning and effecting great and good things for the people of my country." For more of Kelley's writings on Oregon Country, see *Hall J. Kelley on Oregon*, ed. by Fred Wilbur Powell (Princeton University Press, Princeton, N. J., 1932).

The best guidebook I've found for the entire region west of the Cascades is Daniel Mathews, *Cascade-Olympic Natural History* (Raven Editions, Portland, Ore., 1988). I have all but discarded my specialty guides on rocks, wildflowers, and trees in favor of carrying this one all-around work, now covered with sap and dirt. I have been able to solve a number of aggravating mysteries with Mathews, most notably that of gopher cores. If I hadn't had Mathews in my backpack, my first sight of a meadow full of gopher cores would have driven me crazy for days.

Considering its mystery, there is very little written about the Klamath and Siskiyou region. One of the best introductions is the unassuming book (small enough for a back pocket) by John Hart, *Hiking the Bigfoot Country: The Wildlands of Northern California and Southern Oregon* (Sierra Club Press, San Francisco, 1974). Not your average hiking guide, *Bigfoot Country* has a great deal of information as well as informed opinion—just what is needed to put one's steps into a broad, deep context of history both human and natural. Writes the author, "In 1968, a Forest Service Report dismissed the bulk of the High Siskiyou as 'average mountain country' not worthy of special status. Others (including me) dispute that conclusion. But I am a biased source. After all, *I* have seen the place."

For Siskiyou County, Klamath region, and Yreka history, I used Harry L. Wells, *History of Siskiyou County* (D. J. Stewart Publishers, Oakland, Calif., 1881); *Siskiyou County: A Time of Change* (Siskiyou County Historical Society, Yreka, Calif., 1976); various issues of *The Siskiyou Pioneer* (Siskiyou County Historical Society, Yreka, Calif.); J. Roy Jones, *The Land of Remember* (self-published, Yreka, Calif., 1971); and Thomas K. Worcester, *The State of Jefferson and Other Yarns* (TMS Book Service, Beaverton, Ore., 1982). This last book is a collection of some of the stories told on the "Pacific Powerland" radio program.

I am also grateful for the help of the Siskiyou County Historical Museum, and of Bernice Meamber, an assiduous amateur historian of the area and one of my neighbors throughout my childhood in Yreka. Bernice and her husband, Fred, have published a social history of early Yreka called *Houses That Talk* (Nolan Litho and Printing, Yreka, Calif., 1986).

Much of Joaquin Miller's memoir, *My Own Story* (Saxon & Co., London, 1891), takes place in Yreka and around the Klamath Mountains and Mount Shasta. Joaquin Miller was a man known for self-aggrandizing tales and exaggeration perilously close to falsehood. His real name was Cincinnatus, not Joaquin. He was wildly popular while alive; schoolchildren were made to memorize and recite pages of his doggerel. Miller was called—by some—both the "Byron of Oregon" and the "Poet of the Sierras." (Literary critics had other names for him.) He was hopelessly sentimental, especially concerning himself, and relinquished actual facts only when and where they served his own image of himself. That image, consistent with his vision of the frontier and its effect on men, was that of a sensitive, liberal, yet powerfully masculine figure. Joaquin Miller was his own best advertisement for a mythic West.

Mary Arnold and Mabel Reed's memoir, *In the Land of the Grasshopper Song: Two Women in the Klamath River Indian Country in 1908–09* (University of Nebraska Press, Lincoln, 1957), is thoroughly delightful: well written, funny, poignant. It leaves the reader both sad and entertained: sad that the country of the Karuks changed so; sad that the two women are dead and cannot be met, cajoled by a cup of tea into telling more. Theirs is a selective memory, as all memories are, and it is often the unspoken words that linger longest: Why, I wonder most especially, did they never return to their beloved Rivers?

Joseph and Stephen Meek have both inspired numerous books, many somewhat less than sterling in their scholarship and style. Frances Fuller Victor, *The River of the West: The Adventures of Joe Meek* (Mountain Press Publishing, Missoula, Mont., 1983), is one of the most popular. Also see Peter H. Burnett, "Recollections and Opinions of an Old Pioneer," *Quarterly of the Oregon Historical Society*, vol. 5, ch. 4, March, 1904; Harvey Elmer Tobie, *No Man Like Joe: The Life and Times of Joseph L. Meek* (Metropolitan Press, Portland, Ore., 1949); the multivolume work edited by LeRoy R. Hafen, *The Mountain Men and the Fur Trade of the Far West* (Arthur H. Clark Co., Glendale, Calif., 1965); and Keith Clark and Lowell Tiller, *Terrible Trail: The Meek Cutoff, 1845* (Caxton Printers, Caldwell, Idaho, 1967).

page 9
Yi-fu Tuan, *Space and Place: The Perspective of Experience* (University of Minnesota Press, Minneapolis, 1977). Tuan is solemn, almost pedantic, but he covers certain themes better than many another philosopher of geography. If you are interested in his work, see also *Landscapes of Fear* (Pantheon, New York, 1979).

Eugene Victor Walter wrote *Placeways: Theory of the Human Environment* (University of North Carolina Press, Chapel Hill, 1988).

Page 13
William Kittredge, *Owning It All* (Graywolf Press, St. Paul, Minn., 1987).

Page 20
Phoebe Goodell Judson, *A Pioneer's Search for an Ideal Home* (University of Nebraska Press, Lincoln, 1984).

Page 26
Olympia Pioneer, March 10, 1855.

TWO

For general forest ecology, I relied on the following books: Elliott A. Norse, *Ancient Forests of the Pacific Northwest* (Island Press, Washington, D.C., 1990); two books by Chris Maser: *Forest Primeval* (Sierra Club Books, San Francisco, 1989 and *The Redesigned Forest* (R. and E. Miles, San Pedro, Calif.,1988); Stephen Spurr and Burton V. Barnes, *Forest Ecology*, 3rd ed. (John Wiley and Sons, New York, 1980); and Harold W. Hocker, Jr., *Introduction to Forest Biology* (John Wiley and Sons, New York, 1979). Especially good as an introduction, and for its telling photographs, is *Secrets of the Old Growth Forest*, written by David Kelly with photographs by Gary Braasch (Peregrine Smith Books, Salt Lake City, 1988). *"This Was Logging!": Selected Photographs of Darius Kinsey* with text by Ralph W. Andrews (Superior Publishing, Seattle, 1954), is a good collection of Kinsey's invaluable record of logging practices and life in the woods. Information on historical attitudes toward the forests can be found in: Harold K. Steen, *The Forest Service: History* (University of Washington Press, Seattle, 1976); Thomas R. Cox, *The Park Builders: A History of State Parks in the Pacific Northwest* (University of Washington Press, Seattle, 1988); and Michael Frome, *The Forest Service* (Praeger, New York, 1971).

Stewart H. Holbrook wrote several books about logging and loggers, among them *Holy Old Mackinaw: A Natural History of the American Lumberjack* (Macmillan, New York, 1938). Holbrook, who deserves at least a postage stamp in his honor, drives modern historians crazy. (At least his work has that effect on the historians I know.) Holbrook fancied himself a historian and wrote many books of so-called commercial history, including somewhat slipshod biographies and memoirs so easy to read and pleasant to recall that their errors of fact seem almost unimportant. (I can hear the gnashing of historians' teeth already.) Holbrook was wildly popular in his day. By most accounts a charming man, Holbrook was an insecure and somewhat ill-bred boy who matured in the logging woods but yearned to be accepted by what he considered good society. All his books are entertaining, riddled with poetic license, and quite well written. He even wrote a latter-day summing-up of his own career called *Far Corner* (Macmillan, New York, 1952). You can still read Stewart Holbrook, whatever the topic, and savor a phrasemaker of the finest kind. He describes at one point the now-defunct liquor barn in Portland called Erickson's. Erickson's had a "mile-long" bar (actually 684 feet in length) that traveled the length of a block on two sides with an extra turn down the middle of the room. There were a lot of "mile-long" bars on the frontier, but Erickson's was thought to be the longest; local loggers used to describe something big, like a tree, as being "as long as Erickson's bar." Holbrook adds, "It grew in size and magnificence until loggers, hard-rock miners, and other hearty men from all over the West, and sailors from the Seven Seas and beyond, vowed they had rather see Erickson's with its gaslights in full blow than to view Niagara Falls tumbling into the Grand Canyon of the Colorado, with Lillian Russell, nude, riding the rapids in a glass barrel, to music by John Phillip [sic] Sousa. Praise could reach no greater height."

Stewart Holbrook is also credited with inventing the still-active James G. Blaine Society in 1940, naming it for a long-forgotten nineteenth-century Maine politician. The James G. Blaine Society is an antidevelopment joke, determined to convince all outsiders that there is nothing to bring them to the Northwest. Holbrook used to get pictures of smog and industrial decay of East Coast cities such as Pittsburgh and make them into postcards to send to friends, claiming the pictures were of Portland.

SALLIE TISDALE

Page 41
A. J. Allen, ed., *Ten Years in Oregon: Travels and Adventures by Doctor E. White and Lady* (Mach, Andrus & Co., Ithaca, NY, 1848).

Page 43
Paul Schullery, *Island in the Sky: Pioneering Accounts of Mt. Rainier, 1933–1894* (The Mountaineers, Seattle, 1987).

Page 44
Sam Churchill, *Big Sam* (Ballantine, New York, 1965).

Page 46
Robert Greenhow, *The Geography of Oregon and California and the Other Territories on the Northwest Coast of North America* (Mark H. Newman, New York, 1845).

Page 48
The Oregon Caves is a spelunker's paradise many miles long almost completely hidden from view in the depth of a thick conifer forest. That is, the entrance to the caves is hidden behind a plate of rock, and was only discovered by a hunter whose dog chased a bear inside around the turn of the century. The tourist cannot miss the caves, which are now surrounded by buildings, tourist trails, guides with joking patter, a gift shop, and even asphalt trails inside. The road up to the caves from Cave Junction is extremely narrow and twisting, a slow and somewhat anxious several miles. The intrepid traveler makes it all the way to the caves as much from fear of turning around as from a desire to enter their narrow passages. (Halfway up this road and still a long way from the caves is a sign that reads, NARROW WINDING ROAD AHEAD.) The caves have spawned a unique phenomenon in the nearby towns of Cave Junction and Grants Pass. A fraternal society of sorts has sprung up over the decades— Cavemen, who used to perform "traditional caveman weddings" in the natural room deep inside the caves called Joaquin Miller's Chapel. In one picture of such a rite, the bride and groom are dressed in furs, with fur slippers, bare legs and shoulders and arms, their hair loose and

knotted and festooned with flowers and leaves. The "minister," called Chief Bighorn, is dressed the same way but wears an animal-head hat with horns. The Grants Pass Oregon Cavemen supposedly granted a "passport for life" to the caves to their favored friends. When I was little, the Cavemen never missed a county fair parade. They wore loincloths and carried clubs and pushed a cage on wheels through the streets, "kidnapping" young women and locking them up for display in the cage for the duration of the parade, an act I found wildly exciting.

THREE

Books about the Cascade Mountains range from personal memoirs to complex works of geology. An example of the former is that of Supreme Court Justice William O. Douglas, who grew up near Mount Adams, an experience described at length in *Of Men and Mountains* (Harper & Row, New York, 1950). Climbing stories can be found in the following, as well as in other works: Paul Schullery, *Island in the Sky: Pioneering Accounts of Mt. Rainier, 1933–1894* (The Mountaineers, Seattle, 1987); Aubrey L. Haines, *Mountain Fever: Historic Conquests of Rainier* (Oregon Historical Society Press, Portland, 1962); Nicholas A. Dodge, *A Climbing Guide to Oregon* (Touchstone Press, Beaverton, Ore., 1975); and Jack Grauer, *Mount Hood: A Complete History* (self-published, 1975). A basic geological approach to the Cascades can be found in Stephen L. Harris, *Fire and Ice: The Cascade Volcanoes* (The Mountaineers, Seattle, 1976).

An excessive number of tales and anecdotes are told about Mount Shasta. They involve colored, animate fogs and fluorescent snow; tall, bald humanoids; and eerie bells and caves full of unrecognizable jewels. Many of the legends center on the Lemurians, and the cult of St. Germain. A good beginning is the true believer's manual, *Lemuria: The Lost Continent of the Pacific* by Wishar S. Cervé (Supreme Grand Lodge of Amorc, San Jose, 1931).

An especially entertaining memoir of life on Mount Rainier can be found in Floyd Schmoe's memory of his honeymoon year, *A Year in Paradise* (Harper & Brothers, New York, 1959). It describes the honeymoon of a young forestry student and his nineteen-year-old, city-bred bride, taking place over the very long winter of 1919, when the couple lived alone in Paradise Inn, buried under more than thirty feet of snow, without electricity.

For geology of the Klamath Mountains, I used: M. C. Blake, Jr., D. C. Engebretson, A. S. Jayko, and D. L. Jones, "Tectonostratigraphic Terranes in Southwest Oregon," in William P. Irwin, *Tectonostratigraphic Terranes of the Circum-Pacific Region*, ed. by David C. Hwell (CircumPacific Council for Energy and Mineral Resources, Houston, 1985); Bates McKee, *Cascadia: The Geologic Evolution of the Pacific Northwest* (McGraw-Hill, New York, 1972); David D. Alt and Donald W. Hyndman, *Roadside Geology of Oregon* (Mountain Press Publishing, Missoula, Mont., 1978); William P. Irwin, "Geology of the Klamath Mountains Province," Bulletin 190, Division of Mines and Geology, California, 1966; R. H. Whittaker, "Vegetation of the Siskiyou Mountains, Oregon and California," by Ecological Monographs, vol. 30, no. 3, July 1960; and R. H. Whittaker, "The Ecology of Serpentine Soils," Part IV, *Ecology*, vol. 35, no. 2, April 1954. Most especially, I am indebted to David Rains Wallace, *The Klamath Knot: Explorations of Myth and Evolution* (Sierra Club Books, San Francisco, 1983), who accomplished the important task of writing a literate, scientifically precise book solely about the Klamath Mountains.

Page 76
Richard M. Strickland, *The Fertile Fjord: Plankton in Puget Sound* (Puget Sound Books, Seattle, 1983).

FOUR

Many of the histories of the gold rush neglect the northern states in favor of California. (This is not, however, news.) Try Ruby El Hult, *Lost Mines and Treasures of the Pacific Northwest* (Binford and Mort, Portland, Ore., 1957), and Vardis Fisher and Opal Laurel Holmes, *Gold Rushes and Mining Camps of the Early American West* (Caxton Printers,

Caldwell, Idaho, 1968). Michael Frome in *The Forest Service* (Praeger, New York, 1971) gives a good history of mining in national forests.

A good, contemporary discussion of the Rogue War can be found in Stephen Dow Beckham, *Requiem for a People: The Rogue Indians and the Frontiersman* (University of Oklahoma Press, Norman, 1971). The useful book by Robert H. Ruby and John A. Brown, *Indians of the Pacific Northwest* (University of Oklahoma Press, Norman, 1981), covers the Rogue War, as well as other conflicts, with considerable detail. An earlier and more opinionated history is that by J. P. Dunn, *Massacres of the Mountains: A History of the Indian Wars of the Far West* (Capricorn Books, New York, 1886). Sheila Whitesitt and Richard E. Moore, eds., *A Memoir of the Indian War: The Reminiscences of Ezra M. Hamilton* (Stump Press, Ashland, Ore. 1987), is a historical memoir by one of the so-called white volunteers. Many other histories about the Rogue War, some more balanced than others, are available.

The Karuk tribe, small and unprepossessing as it was, has been mentioned by a number of writers, most notably Alfred Kroeber. With E.W. Griffith, he wrote *Karok Myths* (University of California Press, Berkeley, 1980), a very extensive and rather esoteric discussion. Rosemary Holsinger collected tribal myths in *Shasta Indian Tales* (Naturegraph Press, Happy Camp, Calif., 1982).

A book by B. K. Swartz, Jr., *Klamath Basin Petroglyphs*, abridged (Ballena Press Anthropological Papers, #12, New Mexico, 1978), describes the many extant petroglyphs still visible in the Klamath Lake region. A general discussion of the Karuks and their neighbors can be found in R. F. Heizer and M. A. Whipple, eds., *The California Indians: A Source Book* (University of California Press, Berkeley, 1951).

Page 93
Joaquin Miller, *Unwritten History: Life Amongst the Modocs* (American Publishing Co., Hartford, Conn., 1874).

Page 95
Elizabeth McLagan, *A Peculiar Paradise: A History of Blacks in Oregon, 1788–1940* (Georgian Press, Portland, Ore., 1980).

The Whitman mission has been written about extensively. The many works by Clifford Drury, on individuals as well as historical aspects of the missions, are considered standard. For background, see *The Whitman Massacre (1916)* by Mary Saunders (pamphlet reissued by Ye Galleon Press, Fairfield, Wash., 1977). Erwin N. Thompson gives a detailed history in *Shallow Grave at Waiilatpu: The Sagers' West* (Oregon Historical Society Press, Portland, 1969). Christopher L. Miller, *Prophetic Worlds: Indians and Whites on the Columbia Plateau* (Rutgers University Press, New Brunswick, N. J., 1985), is a careful and literate analysis of the spiritual world into which the Whitmans unknowingly moved.

Frances Fuller Victor wrote two major popular works of history: *All Over Oregon and Washington* (John H. Carmany & Co., San Francisco, 1872) and *Atlantis Arisen, or, Talks of a Tourist About Oregon and Washington* (J. B. Lippincott, New York, 1891). There is considerable repetition between the two books.

I imagine Frances Fuller Victor as a stiff-breasted, daunting woman, with a wide skirt and a firm mouth, sweeping through the muddy streets of the frontier Northwest with her head held high. I think of her as a doughty and indomitable woman, a kind of pioneer Margaret Dumont.

She was born in New York and didn't arrive in Oregon until 1865, at the age of thirty-nine. Her husband died ten years later, and Frances found herself alone and without funds. She chose to support herself by writing. Frances Victor was, and is, highly respected as a historian, known for including the finest detail of place—the kind of detail often scorned by contemporary writers describing their own times, and loved by readers of the past. True to her times, she wrote without credit virtually all of the two-volume *History of Oregon* typically attributed to Hubert Howe Bancroft, not to mention the lion's share of Bancroft's *History of Washington, Idaho, and Montana*; his *History of Nevada, Colorado, and Wyoming*; and parts of his *History of California* and *History of the Northwest Coast*. Frances Victor also wrote the biography of Joseph Meek, *The River of the West*, from interviews with the man himself.

When she finished working for Bancroft, Frances ended up selling toiletries door to door in Salem, Oregon, making barely enough money to survive. Eventually she was rediscovered by her readers and became a lecturer. "She was poor and widowed and kinless and childless," another historian writes. "She was the perfect observer, living quietly and moving unobtrusively in a colorful and historic land, all of which she saw, and all of which she knew." (All of which, I must add, she saw with the jaundiced eye of the nineteenth-century white woman, praising the small steps of progress by which Western civilization is measured, abhorring the resistance of the native, describing with sometimes breathless and baroque prose the inexorable movement of the East, West.)

Page 105
Nancy Stringfellow, *Report From Grimes Creek After a Hard Winter* (Limberlost Press, Boise, Idaho, 1990).

Page 106
Theodore Roosevelt, *The Wilderness Hunter* (Literature House, New Jersey, reprint of 1900 ed., 1970).

Page 119
Jerry Gildemeister, ed., *A Letter Home* (Bear Wallow, Union, Ore., 1987).

Daniel Sylvester Tuttle, *Reminiscences of a Missionary Bishop* (Thomas Whittaker, New York, 1906).

Page 121
Lewis O. Saum, *The Fur Trader and the Indian* (University of Washington Press, Seattle, 1965).

Page 125
Lee quote: *Oregon Spectator*, July 13, 1848.

Page 127

Asa Bowen Smith, letter of September 3, 1840, in the Oregon Historical Society Collection; American Board of Commissioners for Foreign Missions Papers.

Page 128

Jarold Ramsey, ed., *Coyote Was Going There: Indian Literature of the Oregon Country* (University of Washington Press, Seattle, 1977).

Page 130

Versions of Seathl's speech can be found in many sources, including: Roger Sale, *Seattle: Past to Present* (University of Washington Press, Seattle, 1976), and W. C. Vanderwerth, ed., *Indian Oratory* (Ballantine, New York, 1971).

SIX

Puget Sound, the Strait of Juan de Fuca, Vancouver Island, Queen Charlotte Strait, the San Juan Islands—the region is so rich and textured that one could read about it for years. Floyd Schmoe, who also wrote about his experiences on Mount Rainier, wrote about research off a small, uninhabited island in Puget Sound in *For Love of Some Islands* (Harper & Row, New York, 1964). Schmoe was a Quaker-bred scientist who saw light and order in the world—or wanted to see it. He was a philosopher of the natural, and more than once in his writing, it is clear how puzzled he sometimes was at nature's violence, and what affection he had for the waters of the Sound. A good guide to air-breathers of the area is *Marine Birds and Mammals of Puget Sound* (Puget Sound Books, Seattle, 1982), by Tony Angell and Kenneth C. Balcomb III. One of a series of books for potential homeowners is Thomas A. Terich, *Living with the Shore of Puget Sound and the Georgia Strait* (Duke University Press, Durham, N. C., 1987), which describes the geological and climatic variations of specific sections of shoreline.

In her memoir, *When God Was an Atheist Sailor: Memories of a*

Childhood at Sea, 1902–1910 (W. W. Norton, New York, 1990), the author Burgess Cogill explains with charm the story of an unusual little girl's unusual life. Relatively little of it was spent in the proximity of Puget Sound, but those days and nights loom large in Cogill's memory.

One of the best books about the Olympic Peninsula seems to be fading into obscurity. Betty MacDonald was a well-bred girl from the city who went to live on a chicken farm deep in the Olympics as a young bride. After she left a few years later, she wrote *The Egg and I* (J. B. Lippincott, New York, 1945), about her experiences. It is a very funny and acerbic book that promptly sold two million copies. (There is now an Egg and I Road not far from Port Townsend.) The Ma and Pa Kettle films were based on the characters of MacDonald's nearest neighbors, who sued her—unsuccessfully—for slander. MacDonald divorced the chicken farmer.

It is several decades old, but *Between Pacific Tides*, 3rd ed. (Stanford University Press, Stanford, Calif., 1952), by Edward F. Ricketts and Jack Calvin, can't be touched for either charm or telling detail. Ricketts covers most of the American Pacific coast, concentrating—for largely biological reasons—on Monterey Bay and Puget Sound. Ed Ricketts was John Steinbeck's model for the character of Doc in *Cannery Row*, a dubious honor that followed him all his days. The preface to *Between Pacific Tides*, by Jack Calvin and Joel W. Hedgpeth, explains it like this: "In the things that were important to him—music, literature, automobiles, women, and, in the days when he wore one, his beard—Ed insisted gently and very firmly on having the finest quality available. He would drive the hundred and forty miles from Pacific Grove to San Francisco because he knew a posh barber there who was an artist at beard trimming. . . . Yes, *Cannery Row* is a true story, but it is not the whole truth. The laboratory, the phonograph records, the beer milkshake, and the establishment across the street—these details are true. . . . We mean no criticism of John in suggesting that the Doc of *Cannery Row* is half Ricketts the man and half Steinbeck the author."

My favorite book about Seattle (partly because one doesn't have to love Seattle to enjoy it) is Murray Morgan's *Skid Road* (Viking, New York, 1951). There is also Nard Jones, *Seattle* (Doubleday, New York, 1972), and Roger Sale, *Seattle: Past to Present* (University of Washington Press, Seattle, 1976), as well as many others. The anecdote about payment for the use of Chief Seathl's name occurs in Frederick Webb Hodge's *Handbook of American Indians North of Mexico* (Pageant Books, New York, 1959), as well as in common folk history about Seattle.

Page 158

M. J. Wells, *Octopus: Physiology and Behavior of an Advanced Invertebrate* (Chapman and Hall, London, 1978).

SEVEN

The life of David Douglas has attracted a number of scholars and writers, among them Athelstan George Harvey, *Douglas of the Fir* (Harvard University Press, Cambridge, Mass., 1947); John Davies, *Douglas of the Forests: The North American Journals of David Douglas* (University of Washington Press, Seattle, 1980); Vera Joyce Nelson, *David Douglas on the Columbia* (self-published, Portland, Ore., 1978); and William Morwood, *Traveler in a Vanished Landscape: The Life and Times of David Douglas* (Clarkson N. Potter, New York, 1973).

The Weyerhaeuser Company, Frederick Weyerhaeuser, and various other Weyerhaeuser relatives and projects are described in most of the histories of logging, and, to a lesser extent, in many of the general histories. See Thomas R. Cox, *Mills and Markets: A History of the Pacific Coast Lumber Industry to 1900* (University of Washington Press, Seattle, 1974). For work specifically on Weyerhaeuser, see: Ralph W. Hidy, *Timber and Men: The Weyerhaeuser Story* (Macmillan, New York, 1963), and Charles E. Twining, *Phil Weyerhaeuser: Lumberman* (University of Washington Press, Seattle, 1985), and official company literature. Information on the O & C lands is available in similar places, and in the following detailed works: Elmo Richardson, *BLM's Billion-Dollar Check-*

erboard: Managing the O & C Lands (Forest History Society, Santa Cruz, Calif., 1980), and the most entertaining and baroque work, S. A. D. Puter, *Looters of the Public Domain* (Portland Printing House, Portland, Ore., 1908). Puter, who went to prison for his role, calls himself "King of the Oregon Land Fraud Ring." The current official history of the O & C is in *O & C Sustained Yield Act: The Land, the Law, the Legacy, 1937–1987* (U.S. Department of the Interior, Bureau of Land Management).

The literature of Sasquatch and his Asian cousin, Yeti, is a thicket of acrimony, opinion, fabrication, and undeniably engaging anecdote. Books both trivial and solemn have been written on the topic, by writers both serious and silly. See, and contrast, these: John Green, *The Sasquatch File* (Cheam Publishing Ltd., Agassiz, B. C., 1973); Kenneth Wylie, *Bigfoot: A Personal Inquiry into a Phenomenon* (Viking, New York, 1980); John Napier, *Bigfoot: The Yeti and Sasquatch in Myth and Reality* (Jonathan Cape Ltd., London, 1972); and Roderick Sprague and Grover S. Krantz, *The Scientist Looks at Sasquatch* (University Press of Idaho, Moscow, 1979).

Page 170
There really is a life-size replica of Stonehenge on the Washington bank of the Columbia River. When I was little, my mother used to express disbelief by saying, "What in Sam Hill?" The Sam Hill of whom she spoke lived near here, and he built on the buttes above the Columbia a castle called Maryhill, which is now a strange, eclectic museum housing chess sets, clothes worn by Queen Marie of Romania, and sculptures by Rodin. After World War I, he built a replica of Stonehenge as a memorial to the local men who had died in the war; he was trying to make an ironic comment on sacrificial death. The replica represents Stonehenge as it is thought to have looked in its original form, and it is situated to take advantage of certain of the astronomical theories presented about Stonehenge's purpose. Hill used casts of reinforced cement lined with crumbled tin to make the "stones" look hand-carved. Tiny plaques dedicated to the dead soldiers compete with scribbles and

graffiti, gentle dates and names. For more information, see John E. Tuhy, *Sam Hill: The Prince of Castle Nowhere* (Timber Press, Portland, Ore., 1983).

EIGHT

An excellent history of the Hudson's Bay Company can be found in E. E. Rich, *Hudson's Bay Company: 1670–1870*, vols. I–III (Hudson's Bay Record Society, London, 1959). The Hudson's Bay Record Society continues to publish and revise an extravagant amount of literature about the Pacific Northwest as well as the Canadian Northwest and other regions touched by the traders and practices of the Hudson's Bay Society. A more "popular" work is Mari Sandoz, *The Beaver Men: Spearheads of Empire* (Hastings House, New York, 1964). See also all the fur-trade histories mentioned at the beginning of this section.

The lengthy travels of Peter Skene Ogden can be examined in several ways. For biography, see the various histories of the Hudson's Bay Company, and *Peter Skene Ogden and the Hudson's Bay Company*, by Gloria Griffin Cline (University of Oklahoma Press, Norman, 1974). Ogden's detailed (sometimes exceedingly so) diaries have been collected by the Hudson's Bay Record Society in several volumes: E. E. Rich, ed., *Ogden's Snake Country Journals, 1824–26* (Hudson's Bay Record Society, London, 1950); K. G. Davies, ed., *Peter Skene Ogden's Snake Country Journal, 1826–27* (Hudson's Bay Record Society, London, 1961); Glyndwr Williams, ed., *Peter Skene Ogden's Snake Country Journals, 1827–28 and 1828–29* (Hudson's Bay Record Society, London, 1971).

More recently, Jeff LaLande, a historian, published *First Over the Siskiyous: Peter Skene Ogden's 1826–1827 Journey Through the Oregon-California Borderlands* (Oregon Historical Society Press, Portland, 1987), a revisionist approach to one particular journey. It is LaLande's proposition that Ogden, when he entered the more southern reaches of Oregon Territory in the winter of 1826 and 1827, became the first Euro-American to see Mount Shasta and cross the Siskiyou Pass. Disgusted with the winter and the local tribes, as well as the lack of fur-bearing mammals to kill, Ogden turned north after passing Mount Shasta, ignoring the fertile valleys of the Shasta Basin. Several decades later, Stephen Meek, brother of Joseph and a renowned trapper, said that the Scott River nearby was a swamp from all the beaver dams, "the richest place for beaver I ever saw."

Page 181
Terence O'Donnell, *That Balance So Rare: The Story of Oregon* (Oregon Historical Society Press, Portland, 1988).

Page 182
Thomas Vaughan, ed., *Paul Kane: The Columbia Wanderer; Sketches, Paintings, and Comments, 1846–1847* (Oregon Historical Society Press, Portland, Ore., 1971).

Page 189
Edward C. Bowlby, Barry L. Troutman, and Steven J. Jeffries, *Sea Otters in Washington: Distribution, Abundance, and Activity Patterns* (Washington Department of Wildlife, 1988).

NINE

The geological mystery of the Columbia River has been one of shocked orthodoxy and daring flights of imagination, centered on the work of J. Harlen Bretz, the man who first proposed—and bet his reputation on—the flood theory. (The historical floods that Bretz called the Spokane Floods are now known as the Bretz Floods.) The principal bearer of the Bretz mantle, as well as a geologist in his own right, is John Eliot Allen, author of *The Magnificent Gateway* (Timber Press, Forest Grove, Ore., 1979), and, with Marjorie Burns and Sam C. Sargent, *Cataclysms on the Columbia* (Timber Press, Portland, Ore., 1986). For Harlen Bretz' own work, see *The Grand Coulee* (American Geographical Society, New York, 1932). A lengthy historical discussion of the region is D. W. Meinig,

The Great Columbia Plain: A Historical Geography, 1805–1910 (University of Washington Press, Seattle, 1968).

TEN

The Big Woods: Logging and Lumbering, from Bull Teams to Helicopters, in the Pacific Northwest by Ellis Lucia (Doubleday, New York, 1975) is a good general history of regional logging. See as well the books on forest ecology cited earlier, and the following: Walter Fraser McCulloch, *Woods Words: A Comprehensive Dictionary of Loggers' Terms* (Oregon Historical Society Press, Portland, Ore., 1958), and *Green Gold Harvest: A History of Logging and Its Products* (Whatcom Museum of History and Art, Bellingham, Wash., 1969). James Stevens, of Paul Bunyan fame, wrote a number of adulatory stories about company logging, as well as the accurate, if affectionate, *Green Power: The Story of Public Law 273* (Superior Publishing, Seattle, 1958).

And then there is *Paul Bunyan*. Paul Bunyan is a surprisingly current figure. James Stevens' version (Knopf, New York, 1925) is apparently the first print record of the tall tales invented by the Lake States loggers. It is clearly the best, and was written for the adult, not the juvenile, reader. Stevens writes that Paul Bunyan, "the supreme inventor, the noble historian, the master orator, the grand field marshal of industry," disappeared with the advent into the logging woods of two inexplicable things: the steam engine and women.

ELEVEN

Rivers and dams are central to the Pacific Northwest past and present. Tim McNulty explores the human impact of the waters of Washington in *Washington's Wild Rivers: The Unfinished Work* (The Mountaineers, Seattle, 1990). Works on the geology of the Columbia Basin, discussed earlier, also cover the Columbia River and its history. In regard to the Columbia River, see also Michael S. Spranger, ed., *The Columbia Gorge*

(Washington State University Press, Pullman, 1985). For a history of fishing in the area, see Joseph Allen Craig and Robert L. Hacker, "The History and Development of the Fisheries of the Columbia River" (*Bulletin of the Bureau of Fisheries*, vol. XLIX, U. S. Government Printing Office, Washington, D. C., 1940).

For records of the Indian census taken around the turn of the century, see the exhaustive work of John Reed Swanton, *Indian Tribes of Washington, Oregon and Idaho* (Ye Galleon Press, Fairfield, Wash., 1952).

INDEX

houses built in biggest, 43
individual's attitude toward, 207–8
in Klamath Mountains, 78–79, 80
largest, 43–44, 232–35
microclimates contained in, 42
Trevor, Frances Hornby, 4
Trinity River, 83
Trout, 83, 90
Tuan, Yi-fu, on place, 9, 10–11, 256
Tule Lake, 192
Turner, Frederick Jackson, 26, 28
Tututni tribe, 91, 97

Umatilla Reservation, 124
Umpqua Mountains, 172
Umpqua River, 167
Umpqua tribe, 96
United States, competition with Great Britain for Oregon Country, 25–26, 188–189
U.S. Congress, land grants made by, to railroad and timber industries, 170, 172
University of Washington, College of Forest Resources, 171–72

Valerianos, Apostolos (Juan de Fuca), 3
Vancouver, George, 4, 5
Vancouver Island, 145
Victor, Frances Fuller, 66, 82, 95, 253, 263–64
Volcanoes, 65–67, 193

Waiilatpu (Whitman Mission), 120–26, 263
Wailaki tribe, 96
Walla Walla Indians, 122
Wallula Gap, 198–99
Warm Springs Reservation, 192
Washington

blacks in, 96
coastline, 137–40
coulee region of, 195–99
Palouse region of, 194–95
prestatehood territory of, 27
Weather. See also Rainfall; Snowfall
fog, 62, 137
ice glaze, 143
in Klamath Mountains, 79
of Olympic Peninsula, 134–38
sudden changes in, 56–57, 71–73
West, Governor Oswald, 140
Westering, 4
Western hemlock, 48–49, 52, 79
Westward movement in American history
Native Americans and, 243–44
philosophy of, 14–16, 251–52
references on, 251–52
search for Great River, 4–8
search for Northwest Passage, 1–4
settlers' dreams and myths about, 16–18, 203–4, 239–41
Weyerhaeuser, Frederick, 170–72, 267–68
Weyerhaeuser Company, 170–74, 267–68
Weygandt, Mark, 71
Whidbey, Joseph, 4
Whidbey Island, 4
Whilkut tribe, 96
White, Dr. Elijah and Mrs., 41–42, 127, 138
White Bird Battle of 1877, 118
White Mountain forest fire of 1988, 228
Whitman, Marcus and Narcissa, 121–26
Whitman, Walt, 7–8, 13, 18
Whitman Mission, 120–26, 263
Willamette River, 25, 137
Willamette Valley, 26, 119
ice storms in, 143
Native American tribes of, 97–98, 121
Willapa Bay, 139
Williams, Lucia Lorain, 119
Wintun tribe, 96